Copyright © 2015 by Tim Kinsella

All rights reserved. No part of this book may be reproduced in any form or by any electronic or mechanical means, including information storage and retrieval systems, without permission in writing from the publisher, except for review.

Published by
***f*eatherproo*f* books**
Chicago, Illinois
www.featherproof.com

First edition
∞

Library of Congress Control Number: 2015912887
ISBN 13: 978-1-943888-01-6

Design by Zach Dodson
Cover Illustration by Tim Kinsella
Set in Georgia

Edited by Naomi Huffman
Proofread by Joseph Demes and Claire Gillespie

Printed on demand

ALL OVER AND OVER

Tim Kinsella

All Over and Over

Tour Diaries Fall 2006

Tim Kinsella

*fe*atherproof BOOKS

Reading this back to myself, just shy of a decade after living it, I hardly recognize the angry young man that wrote it. Some hazy affection keeps me rooting for him. But he is remote, deep within my shuffling networks of "self." The tricks of the light and circumstances necessary for this self to emerge never converge these days.

He is certainly not my best self, but I won't disown him. And this distancing is not to shirk any accountability. I mention it simply to point out how and why I might feel free to share this now. I do remember some of these things, and they are all true to the best of my recollection, biased and fried as it may be.

I fully acknowledge and 100% respect that Sam, Bobby, Nate, and Amy each have their own versions of events, all equally true. And I am endlessly grateful to all of them for our time together, so deeply invested in this strange shared dream.

With all my love, I dedicate this book to them, my true friends for life.

Tim — April, 2015

ALL OVER AND OVER

MAKE BELIEVE

2003

Nov 12 Chicago at our loft on Elston

Nov 14 Ames, IA at Iowa State University with Ted Leo and The Pharmacists

Nov 15 Urbana, IL at University of Illinois with Ted Leo and The Pharmacists

Dec 6 Chicago at The Fireside Bowl with Lungfish and Red Eyed Legends

2004

(Jan 6 Joan of Arc "Live in Muenster, 2003" CD released)

Jan 23 Chicago at The Empty Bottle with Califone

Feb 6 Milwaukee, WI at unknown with Chin Up Chin Up

Feb 27 Cleveland, OH at The Grog Shop with JOA and Love of Everything

Feb 28 Rochester, NY at The Bug Jar with JOA and Love of Everything

Feb 29 Cambridge, MA at The Middle East Upstairs with JOA and Love of Everything

March 2 Brooklyn, NY at North Six with JOA and Love of Everything

March 3 Philadelphia, PA at The Khyber with JOA and Love of Everything

March 4 Washington, DC at The Black Cat with JOA and Love of Everything

March 5 Montclair, NJ at The Bloomfield Ave Cafe with JOA and Love of Everything

March 6 Pittsburgh, PA at The Eye with JOA and Love of Everything

ALL OVER AND OVER

March 7 Detroit, MI at Shelter with JOA and Love of Everything

March 19 Minneapolis, MN at Triple Rock with JOA and Love of Everything

March 22 Seattle, WA at Graceland with JOA and Love of Everything

March 23 Portland, OR at Berbatis Pan with JOA and Love of Everything

March 24 Arcata, CA at The Placebo with JOA and Love of Everything

March 25 Sacramento, CA at Capitol Garage with JOA and Love of Everything

March 26 San Francisco, CA at Bottom of the Hill with JOA and Love of Everything

March 27 Los Angeles, CA at Spaceland with JOA and Love of Everything

March 28 Las Vegas, NV at Balcony Lights with JOA, Love of Everything and Year Future

March 30 Salt Lake City, UT at Crimson Underground with JOA and Love of Everything

March 31 Denver, CO at The Larimer Lounge with JOA and Love of Everything

April 1 Lawrence, KS at Replay Lounge with JOA and Love of Everything

April 2 Ames, IA at Maintenance Shop with JOA and Love of Everything

April 3 Champaign, IL at Nargile with JOA and Love of Everything

April 4 Chicago at The Fireside Bowl with JOA and Love of Everything

April 15 Akron, OH at Square Records

April 16 Pittsburgh, PA at The University of Pittsburgh with Pinback & Enon

April 17 Chicago at Logan Square Auditorium with Pinback & Enon

April 19 Lawrence, KS at The Bottleneck with Pinback & Enon

April 30 Chicago at Open End Gallery

ALL OVER AND OVER

May 11 MAKE BELIEVE SELF-TITLED EP RELEASED

May 18 Austin, TX at Emo's with Hella and Need New Body

May 19 Houston, TX at Proletariat with Hella and Need New Body

May 20 Denton, TX at Hailey's with Hella and Need New Body

May 21 Texarkana, AR at Living Room with Hella and Need New Body

May 22 Lafeyette, LA really in someone's living room with Hella and Need New Body

May 23 New Orleans, LA at Banks St. Warehouse with Hella and Need New Body

May 25 Gainesville, FL at Common Grounds with Hella and Need New Body

May 26 Tampa, FL at Orpheum with Hella and Need New Body

May 27 Sarasota, FL at Brownstone Cafe

May 28 Orlando, FL at The Social with Hella and Need New Body

May 29 Atlanta, GA at Drunken Unicorn with Hella and Need New Body

May 30 Carrboro, NC at Go! Rehearsal with Hella and Need New Body

May 31 Washington, DC at Warehouse Next Door with Hella and Need New Body

June 1 Baltimore, MD at Talking Head with Hella and Need New Body

June 2 Philadelphia, PA at First Unitarian Church with Hella and Need New Body

June 3 New York, NY at Knitting Factory with Hella and Need New Body

June 4 Brooklyn, NY at Northsix with Hella and Need New Body

June 5 Providence, RI at The Green Room with Hella and Need New Body

June 6 Cambridge, MA at TT The Bears with Hella and Need New Body

June 7 Syracuse, NY at Jared Larson's mom's house

June 8 Akron, OH at Lime Spider

ALL OVER AND OVER

June 9 Detroit, MI at Detroit Art Space with Hella and Need New Body

June 10 Chicago at Bottom Lounge with Hella and Need New Body

June 17 Chicago at Open End Gallery with Battles and Lichens

July 23 Bloomington, IN at Second Story

July 24 Chicago at Abbey Pub with Cex and Dream Weapon

July 25 Detroit, MI at Detroit Art Space with Cex and The Billy Nayer Show

July 26 Pittsburgh, PA at Garfield Art Works with Cex

July 27 Philadelphia, PA at First Unitarian Church with Cex and Automato

July 28 New York, NY at Sin-e with Cex

July 29 Hamden, CT at The Space with Cex and Short Pants Romance

July 30 East Hampton, MA at The Flywheel with Cex and Nadelle and Thom

July 31 Cambridge, MA at The Middle East with Cex and Certainly Sir

July 31 Providence, RI at Century Lounge with Cex and Ur Dog

Aug 1 Baltimore, MD at Ottobar with Cex

Aug 2 Charlottesville, VA at Tokyo Rose with Cex

Aug 3 Greensboro, NC at Gate City Noise

Aug 3 Carrboro, NC at Go! Rehearsal with Cex

Aug 4 Mount Pleasant, SC at Village Tavern with Cex

Aug 5 Atlanta, GA at Drunken Unicorn with Cex

Aug 6 Orlando, FL at Will's Pub with Cex

Aug 7 Miami, FL at Poplife with KRS-1 and Cex

Aug 9 Houston, TX at Mary Jane's Fat Cat with Cex

(Aug 10 Joan of Arc "Joan of Arc, Dick Cheney, Mark Twain" 2xLP/CD released)

Aug 10 Austin, TX at Emo's with Cex

ALL OVER AND OVER

Aug 11 Denton, TX at Hailey's with Cex

Aug 12 Oklahoma City, OK at Conservatory with Cex

Aug 14 Chicago at Jinx Cafe with Safety Pin

Sept 11 Chicago at The Empty Bottle with Red Krayola

(Oct 5 -- JOA -- Pittsburgh, PA at Garfield Artworks)

(Oct 6 -- JOA -- Cambridge, MA at Middle East)

(Oct 7 -- JOA -- Philadelphia, PA at First Unitarian Church)

(Oct 8 -- JOA -- Brooklyn, NY at North Six)

(Oct 9 -- JOA -- Wallingford, CT at American Legion Hall)

(Oct 10 -- JOA -- Wilkes Barre, PA at Café Metropolis)

(Oct 11 -- JOA -- Washington, DC at Black Cat)

(Oct 12 -- JOA -- Raleigh, NC at King's Lounge)

(Oct 13 -- JOA -- Atlanta, GA at The Earl)

(Oct 14 -- JOA -- Gainesville, FL at Common Grounds)

(Oct 15 -- JOA -- Tampa, FL at The Orpheum)

(Oct 16 -- JOA -- Orlando, FL at Will's Pub)

(Oct 17 -- JOA -- St. Augustine, FL at Café Eleven)

(Oct 18 -- JOA -- Houston, TX at Mary Jane's Fat Cat)

(Oct 19 -- JOA -- Austin, TX at Emo's)

(Oct 20 -- JOA -- Denton, TX at Hailey's)

(Oct 21 -- JOA -- Fayetteville, AR at Dickson Theater)

(Oct 22 -- JOA -- Urbana, IL at Café Paradiso)

(Oct 23 -- JOA -- Madison, WI at Club 770)

(Oct 29 -- JOA -- Chicago at Empty Bottle)

Nov 11 Chicago at Logan Square Auditorium with Mates of State and Bishop Allen

Nov 16 MAKE BELIEVE PINK 7" RELEASED

Nov 27 Lawrence, KS at Jackpot Saloon with Chin Up Chin Up

Nov 28 Denton, TX at Rubber Gloves with Paper Chase and Chin Up

ALL OVER AND OVER

Chin Up

Nov 29 Odessa, TX at The Roadhouse with Paper Chase and Chin Up Chin Up

Nov 30 El Paso, TX at Surges with Paper Chase and Chin Up Chin Up

Dec 1 Phoenix, AZ at Modified with Paper Chase and Chin Up Chin Up

Dec 2 Los Angeles, CA at Spaceland with Paper Chase and Chin Up Chin Up

Dec 3 Long Beach, CA at Koo's with Paper Chase and Chin Up Chin Up

Dec 4 San Luis Obispo, CA at The Dwelling with Paper Chase and Chin Up Chin Up

Dec 5 San Francisco, CA at Bottom of the Hill with Paper Chase and Chin Up Chin Up

Dec 6 Chico, CA at Moxie's Cafe with Paper Chase and Chin Up Chin Up

Dec 7 Portland, OR at Meow Meow with Paper Chase and Chin Up Chin Up

Dec 8 Olympia, WA at Eagles Hall with Paper Chase and Chin Up Chin Up

Dec 9 Seattle, WA at Graceland with Paper Chase and Chin Up Chin Up

Dec 11 Salt Lake City, UT at Kilby Court with Paper Chase and Chin Up Chin Up

Dec 12 Denver, CO at Hi Dive with Paper Chase and Chin Up Chin Up

Dec 13 Colorado Springs, CO at Navajo Hogan with Chin Up Chin Up

Dec 14 Omaha, NE at O'Leavers with Chin Up Chin Up

Dec 20 Chicago at The Empty Bottle with Narrator and Perfect Panther

2005

Feb 18 Champaign, IL at Cowboy Monkey

Feb 19 Grand Rapids, MI at Division Ave Arts Cooperative

ALL OVER AND OVER

Feb 20 Lansing, MI at Mac's Bar

Feb 26 Chicago at The Hideout with Pit Er Pat

March 12 Chicago at Bottom Lounge with Paper Chase and Saturday Looks Good to Me

April 28 Chicago at The Fireside Bowl with Chin Up Chin Up and Major Taylor

April 29 Springfield, MO at Nathan P. Murphy's

April 30 Norman, OK at The Opolis

May 1 Austin, TX at Emo's with The Good Life and Bella Lea

May 2 Denton, TX at Hailey's with The Good Life and Bella Lea

May 3 Houston, TX at Mary Jane Fat Cats with The Good Life and Bella Lea

May 5 Gainesville, FL at Common Grounds with The Good Life

May 6 Orlando, FL at The Social with The Good Life

May 7 St. Augustine, FL at Cafe Eleven with The Good Life

May 8 Atlanta, GA at Drunken Unicorn with The Good Life

May 9 Carrboro, NC at Cat's Cradle with The Good Life

May 11 Washington, DC at The Black Cat with The Good Life

May 12 Philadelphia, PA at First Unitarian Church with The Good Life

May 13 New York, NY at Knitting Factory with The Good Life

May 14 Cromwell, CT at The Cromwell Knights of Columbus with The Good Life

May 15 Boston, MA at The Paradise with The Good Life

May 16 Winooski, VT at Higher Ground with Ghosts of Pasha

May 17 Syracuse, NY at The Mezzanotte Cafe

May 19 Cleveland, OH at The Grog Shop with The Good Life

May 20 Grand Rapids, MI at The Intersection with The Good Life

May 21 Chicago at The Bottom Lounge with The Good Life

May 22 Minneapolis, MN at The Triple Rock with The Good Life

ALL OVER AND OVER

May 23 Des Moines, IA at Vaudeville Mews with The Good Life

May 24 Omaha, NE at Sokol Underground with The Good Life

June 7 "ASSOCIATION OF UTOPIAN HOLOGRAM SWALLOWERS" DOUBLE 7" RELEASED

June 11 Des Moines, IA at House of Bricks with MewithoutYou

June 12 Omaha, NE at Sokol Underground with MewithoutYou

June 13 Denver, CO at Rock Island with MewithoutYou

June 15 Salt Lake City, UT at Kilby Court with MewithoutYou

June 16 Boise, ID at The Venue with MewithoutYou

June 17 Seattle, WA at Studio 7 with MewithoutYou

June 18 Arcata, CA at The Placebo

June 19 Berkley, CA at Blake's on Telegraph with MewithoutYou

June 20 Anaheim, CA at Chain Reaction with MewithoutYou

June 21 Los Angeles, CA at Knitting Factory LA with MewithoutYou

June 22 Tempe, AZ at The Clubhouse with MewithoutYou

June 24 Austin, TX at Emo's with MewithoutYou

June 25 San Antonio, TX at Sanctuary with MewithoutYou

June 26 Houston, TX at Mary Jane's Fat Cat with MewithoutYou

June 27 Dallas, TX at The Galaxy Club with MewithoutYou

June 28 Bartlesville, OK at The Where-House with MewithoutYou

June 29 Springfield, MO at Outland Ballroom with MewithoutYou

Sept 13 Pittsburgh, PA at Garfield Art Works

Sept 14 New York, NY at 169 Bar with Euphone, End of the World, Narrator, Sybris, and Ume

Sept 15 Annandale-on-Hudson, NY at Bard College with Euphone

Sept 21 Chicago at The Bottom Lounge with XBXRX, Bobby Conn, and The Coughs

Sept 22 Urbana, IL at The Courtyard Cafe

Oct 3 Chicago at The Fireside Bowl—Katrina Benefit

Oct 4 MAKE BELIEVE "SHOCK OF BEING" LP/CD RELEASED

ALL OVER AND OVER

Oct 6 Lawrence, KS at The Jackpot Saloon with Bird Show

Oct 7 Denver, CO at The High Dive with Bird Show

Oct 8 Salt Lake City, UT at Kilby Court with Bird Show

Oct 10 Seattle, WA at The Paradox with Bird Show

Oct 11 Portland, OR at The Hawthorne Theatre with Bird Show

Oct 12 Redding, CA at The Dip with Bird Show

Oct 13 Roseville, CA at The Underground with Bird Show

Oct 14 Bakersfield, CA at Jerry's Pizza with Bird Show

Oct 15 Los Angeles, CA at The Echo with MaeShi and Bird Show

Oct 16 La Jolla, CA at The Che Cafe UCSD with Bird Show

Oct 17 Tucson, AZ at Solar Culture Gallery with Bird Show

Oct 19 Austin, TX at Emo's with Bird Show

Oct 20 Dallas, TX at The Cavern with Bird Show

Oct 28 Chicago at our loft on Elston, Halloween Party with Bird Show

Nov 4 Akron, OH at The Lime Spider

Nov 5 Philadelphia, PA at Space 1026

Nov 6 Brooklyn, NY at Northsix

Nov 7 Long Branch, NJ at Brighton Bar with Michael Columbia

Nov 8 Baltimore, MD at The Talking Head with Michael Columbia

Nov 9 Cambridge, MA at The Middle East Upstairs

Nov 10 Gambier, OH at Kenyon College

Nov 11 Kalamazoo, MI at Kraftbrau

Nov 12 Chicago at Metro with Promise Ring and Tristeza

Dec 2 Chicago at Beat Kitchen with Islands

Dec 9 Dayton, OH at The Night Owl with The Occasion

Dec 10 Nashville, TN at The End with The Occasion

Dec 11 St. Augustine, FL at Cafe Eleven with The Occasion

Dec 12 Gainesville, FL at Common Grounds with The Occasion

ALL OVER AND OVER

Dec 14 Orlando, FL at The Social with The Occasion

Dec 15 Tampa, FL at The Orpheum with The Occasion

Dec 16 Tallahassee, FL at Beta Bar with The Occasion

Dec 17 Atlanta, GA at Drunken Unicorn with The Occasion

Dec 18 Louisville, KY at Old Louisville Coffee House

2006

Jan 15 Tokyo, Japan at O-West with Nisennenmondai

Jan 16 Nagoya, Japan at Imaike Tokuzo

Jan 17 Osaka, Japan at Unagidani Sunsui

Jan 18 Kobe, Japan at Blueport

Jan 19 Kyoto, Japan at Takutaku

Jan 20 Tokyo, Japan at O-Nest

March 24 Lake Forest, IL at Lake Forest College with Piglet

March 25 Madison, WI at Club 770

March 26 Chicago at The Fireside Bowl

(April 18 Joan of Arc "Guitar Duets" CD released)

July 5 Champaign, IL at The Canopy Club with Cursive

July 6 Lansing, MI at Temple Club with Cursive and LaSalle

July 7 Cleveland, OH at Grog Shop with Cursive and LaSalle

July 8 Pittsburgh, PA at Mr. Smalls with Cursive and LaSalle

July 9 New York, NY at Mercury Lounge with Cursive and LaSalle

July 10 New York, NY at Bowery Ballroom with Cursive and LaSalle

July 11 Norfolk, VA at Norva with Cursive and LaSalle

July 12 Lancaster, PA at Chameleon Club with Cursive and LaSalle

July 13 Newport, KY at Southgate House with Cursive and LaSalle

July 14 Des Moines, IA at Vaudeville Mews with Cursive and LaSalle

July 15 Omaha, NE at Sokol Auditorium with Cursive and LaSalle

July 21 Chicago at Stop Smiling HQ with The Narrator

ALL OVER AND OVER

July 23 Chicago at Wicker Park Fest with Dead Meadow

(July 25 Joan of Arc "Eventually, All At Once" LP/CD released)

(July 25 Joan of Arc "The Intelligent Design Of . . ." CD released)

(Aug 31 -- JOA -- Chicago at Beat Kitchen)

(Sept 1 -- JOA -- Dayton, OH at the Night Owl)

(Sept 2 -- JOA -- Rochester, NY at Bug Jar)

(Sept 3 -- JOA -- Allston, MA at Great Scott)

(Sept 4 -- JOA -- Wallingford, CT at American Legion Hall)

(Sept 5 -- JOA -- Washington, DC at Black Cat)

(Sept 6 -- JOA -- New York, NY at Knitting Factory)

(Sept 7 -- JOA -- Philadelphia, PA at First Unitarian Church)

(Sept 8 -- JOA -- Cleveland, OH at Grog Shop)

(Sept 9 -- JOA -- Chicago at South Union Arts)

Sept 21 Chicago at Logan Square Auditorium with Man Man

Oct 3 MAKE BELIEVE "OF COURSE" LP/CD RELEASED

Oct 13 Chicago at The Empty Bottle with Chin Up Chin Up and Oxford Collapse

Oct 25 Wichita, KS at The Electric Snake with Ecstatic Sunshine

Oct 27 Salt Lake City at Slow Train Records with Ecstatic Sunshine

Oct 27 Salt Lake City at Urban Lounge with Ecstatic Sunshine

Oct 28 Boise, ID at Neurolux with Ecstatic Sunshine

Oct 29 Seattle, WA at Comet Tavern with Ecstatic Sunshine

Oct 30 Portland, OR at Holocene with Ecstatic Sunshine

Nov 1 San Francisco, CA at Hotel Utah Saloon with Ecstatic Sunshine

Nov 2 Fresno, CA at Fagan's Pub with Ecstatic Sunshine

Nov 3 Los Angeles, CA at Spaceland with Ecstatic Sunshine

ALL OVER AND OVER

Nov 4 La Jolla, CA at Che Café with Ecstatic Sunshine

Nov 5 Phoenix, AZ at Modified with Ecstatic Sunshine

Nov 6 Santa Fe, NM at Warehouse with Ecstatic Sunshine and Yellow Fever

Nov 7 Austin, TX at Emo's with Ecstatic Sunshine

Nov 8 Houston, TX at Walters with Ecstatic Sunshine

Nov 10 Atlanta, GA at Drunken Unicorn with Ecstatic Sunshine

Nov 11 Charlotte, NC at The Milestone with Ecstatic Sunshine

Nov 12 Baltimore, MD at Floristree Space with Ecstatic Sunshine and Thank You

Nov 13 New Brunswick, NJ at The Court Tavern with Ecstatic Sunshine

Nov 14 Philadelphia, PA at North Star Bar with Ecstatic Sunshine

Nov 15 Cambridge, MA at The Middle East with Ecstatic Sunshine

Nov 16 Brooklyn, NY at North Six with Ecstatic Sunshine

Nov 17 Buffalo, NY at Soundlab with Ecstatic Sunshine

Nov 18 Bowling Greene, OH at Howards Club with Ecstatic Sunshine

Nov 19 Lansing, MI at Mac's Bar with Ecstatic Sunshine

2007

Jan 8 Chicago at Schubas with Pit Er Pat

Jan 21 Tokyo, Japan at O-West with Owen

Jan 22 Nagoya, Japan at Apollo Theater with Owen

Jan 23 Osaka, Japan at Unagidani Sunsui with Owen

Jan 24 Kyoto, Japan at Negi-Posi with Owen

Jan 25 Matsumoto, Japan at Alex with Owen

ALL OVER AND OVER

Jan 27 Tokyo, Japan at O-Nest with Owen

Feb 22 Minneapolis, MN at 7th Street Entry with Rob Crow

Feb 23 Chicago at Empty Bottle with Rob Crow

March 6 Offenbach, Germany at Hafen 2

March 7 Hamburg, Germany at Fundbreau

March 8 Dortmund, Germany at FZW

March 9 Cologne, Germany at Mutze

March 10 Luxembourg at Votre Choix Schifflange

March 11 Brighton, UK at The Hope

March 12 Sunderland, UK at Independent

March 13 Chatham, UK at Tap N Tin

March 14 Liverpool, UK at Magnet

March 15 Birmingham, UK at Chapter 11

March 16 London, UK at The Windmill

March 17 Paris, France at Batofar with Pit Er Pat

March 20 Milan, Italy at unknown

March 21 Vienna, Austria at Arena

March 22 Esslingen, Germany at Komma

March 23 Saarlouis, Germany at Juz

March 24 Basel, Switzerland at Hirscheneck

March 25 Prague, Czech Republic at unknown with The Blow

March 26 Berlin, Germany at Knaack

March 27 Dresden, Germany at AZ Conni

March 28 Wurzburg, Germany at Cairo

March 31 Chicago at Empty Bottle with Azita and Sharks and Seals

April 14 Bloomington, IN at Bloomington Fest with Xiu Xiu and Nomo

June 30 Minneapolis, MN at Cedar Cultural Center with Tortoise

July 1 Chicago at Metro with Tortoise and David Daniell

ALL OVER AND OVER

(July 24 Joan of Arc "Many Times I've Mistaken" 7" released)

2008

Feb 22 Chicago at Subterranean with Singer and De Triomphe

March 8 Chicago at Hideout

March 9 Chicago at People's Project

March 14 Austin, TX at Skyscraper Magazine Party at Emo's IV

March 15 Austin, TX at Flameshovel Records Party at BD Riley's

March 17 Little Rock, AK at The Whitewater Tavern

May 25 Chicago at Permanent Records

May 25 Chicago at Double Door

(May 28 -- JOA -- Omaha, NE at Waiting Room)

(May 29 -- JOA -- Denver, CO at Hi Dive)

May 29 MAKE BELIEVE "GOIN' TO THE BONE CHURCH" LP RELEASED

(May 30 -- JOA -- Salt Lake City, UT at Urban Lounge)

(May 31 -- JOA -- Missoula, MT at The Badlander)

(June 1 -- JOA -- Seattle, WA at The Vera Project with 31 Knots)

(June 2 -- JOA -- Vancouver, BC at Media Club)

(June 3 -- JOA -- Portland, OR at Holocene with 31 Knots)

(June 5 -- JOA -- San Francisco, CA at Rickshaw Stop with 31 Knots)

(June 6 -- JOA -- Los Angeles, CA at Knitting Factory LA with 31 Knots)

(June 7 -- JOA -- Anaheim, CA at Chain Reaction with 31 Knots)

(June 8 -- JOA -- Los Angeles, CA at Pehrspace with 31 Knots)

(June 9 -- JOA -- La Jolla, CA at Che Café with 31 Knots)

(June 10 -- JOA -- Phoenix, AZ at Modified)

(June 12 -- JOA -- Austin, TX at Mohawk)

(June 13 -- JOA -- Fort Worth, TX at Lola's)

ALL OVER AND OVER

(June 14 -- JOA -- Tulsa, OK at Continental)

(June 29 -- JOA -- Sendai, Japan at Birdland)

(June 30 -- JOA -- Yamagata, Japan at Sandanista)

(July 2 -- JOA -- Nagoya, Japan at Tokuzo with Ichi)

(July 3 -- JOA -- Matsumoto, Japan at Alecx)

(July 4 -- JOA -- Tokyo, Japan at Daikanyama Unit with Nhhmbase)

(July 6 -- JOA -- Osaka, Japan at Unagidani Sunsui with Nhhmbase and Vampilla)

(July 7 -- JOA -- Kyoto, Japan at Metro with Nhhmbase and Bed)

(July 17 -- JOA -- Toronto, ON at Lee's Palace)

(July 18 -- JOA -- Montreal, QC at Club Lambi)

(July 19 -- JOA -- Cambridge, MA at Middle East)

(July 20 -- JOA -- New Brunswick at Junkyard Palace)

(July 21 -- JOA -- Brooklyn, NY at Market Hotel with Ponytail)

(July 22 -- JOA -- New York, NY at Knitting Factory with Ponytail)

(July 23 -- JOA -- Philadelphia, PA at First Unitarian Church with Ponytail)

(July 24 -- JOA -- Baltimore, MD at Floristree with Ponytail)

(July 25 -- JOA -- Cleveland, OH at Grog Shop)

(July 26 -- JOA -- Chicago at Wicker Park Fest)

(July 27 -- JOA -- Chicago at Beat Kitchen)

Aug 23 Chicago at AV Aerie

Oct 12 Chicago at Bottom Lounge with Pinback

Oct 13 Madison, WI at High Noon Saloon with Pinback

All Over and Over #1

CHICAGO—SAN FRANCISCO

ALL OVER AND OVER

OCTOBER 26, 2006

Got picked up by Bobby and Nate at 7:45 in the morning to head out for Wichita. Stayed up all night watching Amy sleep, happy to feel the time pass slowly, basking in my last night at home.

She and I piled my stuff in the doorway and sat together on the stairs to wait. I laid my head on her shoulder. She kissed my forehead and I half-dozed off, knowing I only had a moment. We didn't speak much. The hallway amplified our every sound, projected every tap or mumble upwards and sideways towards the neighbors all getting moving for the day in their own quiet rooms.

When the van pulled up, a school bus was waiting behind it. I had to load my shit quickly, had no time for a protracted goodbye.

As I stuffed my bags away in corners and beneath seats I already knew I'd packed too much. I regretted bringing my laptop by the time we turned the corner on Division.

When we pulled up to Sam's, he popped out the door and went back inside twice before running up to us.

Rush hour, still sitting in Chicago suburbs, I felt like puking and considered making a dash for it. The dread and sickness lasted all day. Leaving home had never been this bad before, I guess because I'd never had such a happy and together life at home before. It never mattered much to me if I was home or away. Until a little at a time over the last couple years I started to suspect that on tour I was wasting about 23 hours a day.

Fourteen hours across Iowa, down through Missouri and into Kansas, I couldn't even begin to understand what it would mean to be away from Amy for 25 days.

The zillions of times I've zigzagged back and forth across the states with my bands, with friends' bands, with friends and alone just to zigzag, attempting to recall specifics and distill one trip from another, I got hung up on the metaphysics of memories—distance and haze. Like that Bob Dylan song that he wrote with Sam Shepard about Gregory Peck, it may as well have all been some movie I'd seen; I can really recall only an image at a time from here and there, America. And what about this *Eternal Present* that the mystics speak of? If it were true, experientially real, wouldn't any *Right Now* be the same as every other?

Crossing barren Kansas in rain, I told myself over and over *There is no spoon*. I hoped the van would spin out and flip over, injuring me enough to send me home and keep me there while my friends could all get up and walk away, each without a scratch.

The people of Iraq, refugees everywhere, half the world's population with more immediate access to Coca-Cola than clean drinking water — I can *conceptualize* how lucky I am. My problem: in the coming months I have to go to Portland, Paris, Rome, Austin, Baltimore, Tokyo. My life must be right on track for where I hoped ten years ago to be right now. But ten years ago I never counted on Amy or marriage or being happy—*actually happy*—staying home and doing nothing, so happy that I might not want to go anywhere.

I ate my bi-annual Egg McMuffin breakfast around 9:00, last chance to eat before the expansive hunger flats of Iowa. I regretted eating it by 9:15, but didn't get to eat anything more than a handful of nuts from a gas station ten hours later.

Wichita was no surprise pulling into town: sister city to Lawton, Oklahoma, or Odessa, Texas, or wherever. The surprise was 100 kids waiting for us in the parking lot. The same *Cool Kids* as everywhere else. From the parking lot of The Electric Snake we were immediately transported from Wichita to Make Believe Show Anywhere—so strange how that happens.

The Electric Snake was next to a spooky bar complete with bumper stickers about all the guns that the patrons were all carrying: "I'd rather go hunting with Cheney than driving with Ted Kennedy."

ALL OVER AND OVER

A few kids lived upstairs in a small, soily college-dudes pad. There were the standard scene-guys that wanted to talk about a lot of bands that I don't know anything about. And their standard drunk pothead friends: guys whose ultimate ambitions seemed to be just to chill. After a 14-hour drive through silence except for the occasional sudden white-noise bursts of rain, reading the new issue of *Harper's* cover to cover in a single sitting, I felt unprepared to return to my life as—*what*? Certainly not *Rock Star*. I have no illusions of that. But these kids all know me wherever I go. And they all have questions for me—"What have you been listening to?" And in hushed tones, "Really you can tell *me* the Captain Jazz inside story. I know there's more to it and I swear I won't tell anyone."

And I just could not fucking stomach it. Not that socializing has ever come too easy to me. It's always awkward. But when I get some momentum with it, I re-learn little tricks to make things easier. Some kid will come up and I can tell by his mannerisms or approach if the situation will take some defusing. And when it works: great, we are two people talking, no big deal. We are obviously sort of both drawn to similar things, so no big deal. It can be nice even. Why not?

But when it doesn't work, when I can't defuse the situation, I still have no idea how to ever get out of these conversations without both of us feeling like jerks. So I had to get in and out of that kitchen quick: grab a PBR, nod hello, be as polite as possible and get the fuck out.

I was pleased to learn that The Electric Snake was named after a vivid Salvia trip one of the locals had and I couldn't help but gush about how treasured my own experiences with Salvia were. The Visionary himself wasn't present, but his recounted experience had become enough of a local lore to have the local show space named in its honor. Unfortunately, the second-hand accounts of his bliss couldn't sustain my attention. I was admittedly irritable. All this embarrassing talk about whoever it is these kids *think* I am, versions of me that have zero in common with any sense of the *Me* it feels like I am from my perspective — am I supposed to high-five these guys? Do they expect me to head bang or air guitar along to my own song from twelve years ago that they play on the kitchen stereo?

The upside of a fourteen-hour drive the first day is getting in and out of the show quick, less sitting around while still in vulnerable Home-Self mode before the defenses have had a chance to re-callous.

I ducked next door for a quick bourbon. Luckily I'd sold a record already so I had some dollars to do so. The bartender couldn't believe I wasn't the brother of some local guy, probably just the guy that comes around not dressed like a cowboy. All of us non-cowboy costumed-types must all look alike. A long, waist-high shuffleboard-type game took up a good amount of the room, leaving only a tight space to squeeze between the people surrounding this table and the bar. There were only about ten people hanging out: a couple old cowboys, a couple young cowboys and a bleached-blond woman with sweatpants that said *Bling Bling* wide across her ass.

They of course all knew each other, and the only open seat was at the far end of the bar. I survived the squeeze between all of them. Their silence was punched through by the bartender's repeated shouts upon seeing my ID, "She-Cah-GUH! She-CAH-GUH! SHE-CAH-GUH!" I ordered a Jim Beam on the rocks and she slowly, seemingly purposefully, with a smile, poured me a Jack Daniels on the rocks.

I lit a cigarette and made up my mind to not hurry out of there just because the whole bar was now silent, staring me down. *I will sit cool as long as it takes me to smoke this cigarette.* Everyone there was between me and the door. Mad violent anti-fantasies flashed through my mind. I made myself prolong my sit, fighting down the instincts kicking at me to run. Had to build up my fear-of-hillbillies tolerance. Needed to actively inoculate myself against the paranoia that those Rob Zombie movies have so generously visualized for me. Me and my active imagination will be traveling together for a while.

I returned to the show to see a kid on stage that I'd met

before in London and then Springfield, MO and then Lawrence. Turned out he's local to Wichita.

Half a dozen different kids claimed either to have set up the show, lived there or organized the space in some way. Maybe it really was a cool, functioning collective-type thing.

It was D_____, the young girl—nineteen years old? twenty-three?—who signed the contract and answered the phone when I called earlier to say we were running late. It was her that called me back later to tell us something else. Because her voice on the phone was such a smoldering coo, I expected her to be frumpy like a radio personality. But in compliance with the circular laws of inverted expectations, turns out that she was in fact distressingly cute: choppy blond hair and big eyes and full lips, a summer dress and knee-high socks.

She was very formal with us at first, and even seemed a little bummed out when I ran into her across the parking lot a little later. But it must've just been the sullen demeanor that being the hottest hip girl in any small town requires.

Ecstatic Sunshine played and it was packed and people were even dancing a little.

We loaded on to stage. Because this would be my first show in years without ephedrine, I chugged a Red Bull. The ephedrine opened my chest, and oxygen's a vital necessity for breathing at the rate that Make Believe requires of me. But I wouldn't survive one more paranoia-hangover. The anxiousness and nerves are too much. I needed to learn a new way.

Once set up on stage, Nate's Wurlitzer was sweating from being transported through the cold and then brought into such heat and humidity. It was shorting from the condensation, so he had to open it up and sort it out right there on stage. The audience crowded around him, half of them so engrossed in the guts and inner workings of his Wurlitzer and his surgical mastery of the situation that one wouldn't be blamed for mistaking this for our usual entrance.

Other people were just stuck in the press against the stage. After a good half hour of suspense, the Wurlitzer was back in its shell and ready for its pounding.

From the first note, the whole place was bananas. The whole audience collapsed against us, keeping me pinned back to Nate behind me. D_____ stayed on stage and occasionally pressed her breasts against me as I sang. Another young girl in the front row kept rubbing her hands up the insides of my thighs. I felt trapped in the middle of a sex mob. Thrown around this way and that way, getting creeped out by all the touching on this side of the stage, I would head over to the other side only to find D_____ with one of the other "promoters" making out slowly, their mouths opened wide. Pushed back that way, just trying to get through the song, a hand came up my shirt from behind, felt me up slowly and firmly. I turned around surprised to find D_____ standing behind me—completely statue-still in the middle of it all, staring into my eyes as the guy kissed her neck. The stage was hers now. I was pushed back towards Bobby, which pushed him back into a corner. Kids kept pulling me back up to the front and center of the stage by the waist of my jeans, their fingers gripping down the front. My hair was being pulled by I couldn't tell how many people at a time. When I opened my eyes to peek for a second at a time, everything was constant motion and mayhem—wide-smiling, sexually charged mania.

Wichita.

I'd written a strange set list, loaded with songs that we hadn't played in a year. As we closed with "A Band Room of One's Own," the crowd, which had been singing back every word to me through the whole show, reached a fever pitch with the line about "All the stupid Christians."

People yelled stuff at me the whole time. I acknowledged what I caught as best as I could at the moment. I ignored the particularly aggressive dudes grabbing me and shouting in my face. But one thing one kid said stuck with me. Very softly, slipped in perfectly within the beat, in between howls of the room, he whispered in my ear, "Why the fixation with time?" And I responded, "It's not my fixation. It's our culture's and I'm just trying to live with it."

But that assumed that he was referring to my lyrics. Honestly I'd never noticed if the words betray some fixation with time, but I wouldn't be surprised to find out that they did. Maybe instead he meant all the funny time signatures of our songs, which might function as attempts to divide time in unique ways opposed to what we all become socially accustomed to. So it could be understood as an implicit, demonstrative critique, entirely tautological in some regards with the riddles and wide parameters that the songs often evoke lyrically. Hmmm. It's funny to figure out what you've been doing years deep into doing it.

When the show ended, I stumbled out to the parking lot and along the fence that our van was parked next to. I climbed through tall weeds. The top of the van door got caught in barbed wire at the top of the fence. Sitting shotgun, catching my breath, I saw it coming from only a second away; I doubled-over in the weeds, puked up the cough drop gunk coating my throat. That was all I had in me. After five minutes of wretching and heaving I settled down. I wiped myself clean and leaned back against the van to find D_____ standing silently. She'd been watching me and now walked off without saying a word. The young man she'd been making out with on stage walked up and offered to suck me off. I told him no thank you.

Very nice downtown hotel. Drove around for 45 minutes looking for food this morning before finally finding a Subway.

Crossing Kansas west on 70 through dense white fog. There's a blizzard in Denver. Promoter already called to say don't worry about it if we can't make it. There's no getting off course, no escape route for another 200 miles through Kansas. Schools are closed in Colorado. The storm is moving east and we expect to meet it at right about the state line.

*

ALL OVER AND OVER

OCTOBER 27, 2006

Denver show cancelled last night. I-70 closed down between Burlington and Denver, we had no way to even get into town. The promoter called us to cancel, saying that last year a band on their way to play the Hi-Dive through snow spun out and a guy got killed.

Calling around to hotels in Goodman, Kansas and Burlington just across the state line, there was panic. *"We've got a lobby full of people! I can't guarantee anything!"*

We were able to get two rooms — one for us and one for Ecstatic Sunshine — twenty miles past where I-70 was shut down. I drove. We took a two-lane country road next to the highway. It too was closed, but we drove around a barrier and took it anyways. We still hadn't seen any snow, but the radio and the promoter and the road closings had us panicky. We stopped at a Safeway and got beer and peanut butter and bread.

We were relieved to get to the hotel around sundown and escape the threat of this supposed icy bluster. We were in what Bobby called a "half-light town": one blinking yellow light at the intersection of the hotel and a gas station. That was the town. Ecstatic Sunshine arrived shortly after us.

I sat in the van and did an interview for New City with Tom Lynch and it was generally unmemorable, except that I know that I like him. Returning to the room I found Sam on Myspace, where he would remain for the next ten hours. Bobby announced that besides our eleven-hour drive to Salt Lake City the next day, and our two shows to play there, we would also be doing a one-hour interview for MTV2. Not sure what that means, but we'll see.

After peanut butter sandwiches and an hour or two of generalized restlessness, the sky had cleared up. I called Andrea in Denver. She said the sun was out and the snow was melting. We found the storm online and it had blown south. It had already blown right past us as we sat cooped

ALL OVER AND OVER

up in our room. The highway was re-opened and we all got excited to try to make the show after all. It meant that we'd blown $100/band on the rooms, but at least we'd have the night back. We were all excited and beginning to pack when we finally reached the promoter. It was 6:00 or 6:30. We could be there by 9, but he said the show was too cancelled to resuscitate. We pleaded, but to no avail.

Bobby and Nate and Dustin sank into a poker game that would take the next four hours.

Gene Hackman stopped Tommy Lee Jones from executing some plan hatched by Chicago white power people in cooperation with Chicago Police, and US and Russian armed forces higher-ups to assassinate the president. Tommy Lee's finger was already squeezing the trigger when Gene got there and was like, "*NOOOOOOOOOOOOOOOOO!*"

Dennis Hopper kidnapped Asia Argento and kept her in a cage in his basement. He was able to get away with it for a year because he was the chief of police. Asia Argento, God, I hate to see her suffer. It makes me ache and pant a little just to write her name.

Tobe Hooper got the credit for some short scenario in which Robert Englund owned some sort of dystopian, futuristic, industrial-rock, S&M bar and there were zombies and people with some kind of virus. We watched it with the volume off to try to make it a little more interesting.

Falling asleep around 11:30, everyone else long since passed out, production values troubled me—*plagued* me even. How could these things be made *so* stupidly and with *so* little regard for the potential viewer as a cognizant being? There were three Showtimes to choose from and Tobe Hooper's stupid short was our best option. All of our choices were meant to provoke paranoia and fear. What budgets these people have to make people paranoid! *Conspiracies and threats are all around you all the time! The details of their workings and eventual thwartings are all kind of vague and uninteresting beyond some flashing strobes and jerky editing. Just know to be afraid.* God, what might me and my friends come up with and be able to do with Asia Argento and Dennis Hopper and that budget?

Bobby announced that we'd be waking up at 6:00 and we all groaned, but understood the necessity. I was confused why he was so inconsiderate and loud at 5:00, 5:15, then 5:30 while packing up his stuff with a light on. When he asked who wanted to go get the free breakfast with him and in my half sleep I told him it was still too early, only 5:30 and they hadn't opened yet, that's when he realized that he'd forgotten to set his clock back.

Half-hour later we walked across the parking lot under big bright stars in the full crisp chill of pre-dawn in The West.

Our shower had two dispensers with no names on them and as I became more and more itchy, I grew more and more certain that I must've put shampoo all over myself.

We each ate one of four breakfast combos. Grease-wet and cold eggs, gross. And we were off before sunrise, the outlines of the horizon ahead just beginning to swell in pink and orange. Bobby drove. I was out by the time we left the parking lot.

Around 8:00 I woke up as we were getting to Denver and Bobby told Sam, who was now driving, that he had just missed his exit. So instead we drove through Denver morning rush hour, the snow and the snow-peaked mountains in the distance. The houses all flat in a valley, it feels like The West and I love it. Standing around a gas station parking lot just north of Denver, it's a bright 60 degrees and there's snow on the ground.

Meeting Ashton and his lady at the Wild Oats in Fort Collins to carpool across Wyoming together. Some Ginsberg eulogy poem for Neal Cassady made Denver beautiful to me like it never was before. Heading up towards Colorado's top, I recall the poem vaguely.

Straight flat 80 across the bottom of Wyoming has always

given me the creeps—the radical totality of its barren land, cracking dry, its sparse population so dense as to champion Cheney. But driving straight west into the wind, a dusting of snow covering The Nothingness everywhere, all at once it's beautiful. Union Pacific trains roll. Long slopes are cut with fences the same mud-color as their shallow peaks. No sense of scale or distance in such wide open.

*

OCTOBER 28, 2006

Twelve-, thirteen-hour drive yesterday. An hour at a time sleeping, then reading, looking out the window at the beautiful open powdered moonscape—*cake-scape*. Half an hour at a time, nothing until the occasional burnt-out shack or a refinery bright with fire breaks the free and open patterns of the land.

I hadn't talked to Amy the night before. She was working for The Bens, then over to The Hideout for a going away party. She had a shoot early the next morning. With each infrequent blip of cell phone reception through Wyoming I'd call or text her more frantically. My mind was getting worked up into a shit-ton of possible troubles: *she's been kidnapped, she's left me, blah blah blah.* Crazy how finally just talking to her for a minute calmed my mind. Realized how ridiculous my worries were and felt more settled than I'd felt on tour in a good while. Skipping the ephedrine helps a lot. That shit builds up, worries compound.

Read the first 90 pages of *The Idiot*, got swept up in it really quickly. I haven't read any fiction in so long. I try sometimes but always fizzle out. But this is immediately engaging. Such a simple narrative style, ideas much larger than the language implies. And I love a self-conscious omnipotent narrator, getting ahead of himself a little and doubling back. Made me think of editing strategies that might be interesting if done well. Not Ferris Bueller-isms or *Alfie*, and not Godard's interviews or direct addresses. I don't know what, but I'm happy to see the ambiguous shape forming, happy to be half-aware of it developing in the back of my mind while I read.

Re-read the first 40 pages of Ram Dass' *Grist for the Mill*. Good to re-acquaint myself with these things that I take for granted as fully absorbed. I re-read them and realize how superficial my understanding is compared to the depth of the text: wonderful simplicity and immediacy, peace.

ALL OVER AND OVER

Pulled into Salt Lake and went straight to the in-store, the storefront in the pretty, old-fashioned downtown. Slow Train Records was opened three months ago by a nice young married couple living me and Amy's dream, sort of. We'd of course require books and movies and vinyl at our store and this is mostly new indie-rock CD's. But as a lifestyle it sure seemed cool. They bought Stinkweeds in Phoenix, put it in a truck and moved to Salt Lake.

I can't believe how much I like Salt Lake City now. Not that I could ever live there or anything, and it's weird how the whole downtown, everything, is closed on a Friday night. But these bright Western towns seem so cool to me these days. Shrunk by surrounding mountains, they are all so cute and homey, impermanent and toy-like with their trains and ranches on the outskirts of town, old downtowns and mountains always in the background, townhouses always in the middle of being built, everything conspicuously imported except the scenery itself. Model homes are being shown. Steeples and practice fields, refineries and mines of various kinds, dirt roads and Hobby Lobbys, phone lines or power lines head out into infinity.

When we showed up to the in-store, the seven-person MTV2 crew had all their lights and cameras set up in the only few square feet that we could possibly set up in to play. We were supposed to start in 20 minutes to make it over to the other show in time. The MTV2 crew wanted to get us mic'd up and do the interview immediately. They were annoyed when I pointed out that we had two shows to play and a big group of people had already assembled in the store. We went out to load in and they asked us to wait so they could get in position to shoot us unloading. We agreed to talk to them in the store after we played and they split.

Ecstatic Sunshine set up in the front of the store and we set up in the back. Our hosts had some good Bavarian dark beers for us. Having eaten only some roasted vegetables and a salad at the Wild Oats in Colorado, the beer made its small, pleasant happy-hour impact easily and immediately. They had a Joan of Arc *Guitar Duets* poster hanging in the bathroom of the store and I spaced out on it, really appreciating the work that Chris put into it now that I was removed from it a bit.

Ecstatic Sunshine sounded great. I was a little uncertain about how our energy as a band should be consciously adapted to the strange setting and watching them just go for it was inspiring. Reminded me how simple what we have to do really is. It only gets muddled when we allow our own perceptions of it to be corrupted by anyone else's ideas about what we're doing.

We started as soon as Ecstatic Sunshine finished. The store was packed front to back, people squeezing between every rack and aisle. We played only four songs, all new ones, so we wouldn't discourage anyone of age from attending the show later. We played well and it sounded great after a couple days of just driving and being cooped up together. So much driving, it's easy to forget why we are actually out here, but playing makes it feel slightly less useless. A lot of the kids were really young, like fifteen or sixteen, and we were even asked to sign a few autographs.

The MTV2 clowns returned and six of them bumped heads while setting up. One of them even accidentally started a fire in the background while another, never noticing the fire, gave us the scoop: *freelance production company, bands represent themselves, markets and marketing, etc.* We all stared at him blankly and drank quickly, Bobby occasionally interjecting, "Oh. Cool."

After suffering a good half-hour of their *Extreme!* cool-guy production-klutz idiocy, we were finally standing side-by-side in front of the lights, with three cameras on us: one handheld, another fish-eye. As if purposefully doing everything they could to make us as unnatural and uncomfortable as possible, they asked us to each re-state our names and our band name over and over to fit their format.

For the first fifteen minutes all they wanted to talk to us

about was our videos. They thought we were joking when we all kept insisting that none of us had actually seen them. Bobby knew them all a little bit, but didn't know which one was for which song. The interview guy couldn't wrap his head around us just not being interested in the videos.

The rest of the questions were lowest common denominator Band Interview. We stuttered and stumbled through as best we could. Earnestly trying to explain how we approach being a band, Nate ended up babbling a little. I had to pee so badly from having just chugged a couple beers, it must've added to how impossibly uncomfortable we must've all appeared. After another half hour I pointed out that we were now an hour late for loading into our show. The record store owner spoke up, "Everything always runs late over there." I shot her a look as we all undid our lavaliers. We practically ran to the van, all of us equally bummed out. It's real hard to talk about something that we obviously put a lot of thought and energy into in completely superficial, reductive terms, especially to someone who can't even pretend to understand where we're coming from. "How do you explain your Unique Sound?" Fuck you. We don't explain it. We make it.

Loading out of the store I went to pick up the suitcase of drum hardware and kept moving while the case stayed in place, total mime-style. I pulled my shoulder out bad. Every passing minute it bothered me more and more. By the time we drove the five blocks to the Urban Lounge, my entire left side was completely useless.

We were *seven* hours late compared to when they asked us to arrive, an hour later than we told them we'd get there, and still there was no one there yet to let us in. Califone, Pit er Pat, Wolf Eyes, and Glass Candy were all on the schedule, so it didn't seem too strange a place to be. Having played all ages shows at Kilby Court the last four or five times through town, we were worried enough about how a bar show would go that we bothered to set up the in-store. But then we worried no one would go to the actual show because they all went to the in-store.

Delicious seitan reubens and free Blue Moon. We won the dick soundman over by the end of our set. For some reason he played only Paul Simon and Simon and Garfunkel songs all night, including "Me and Julio" at least three times. I thought it must've been a limited jukebox, but there was no jukebox. The soundman chose the songs.

Sat around with Josh and Ashton and his lady. Ashton hadn't even had a chance to unload his truck yet. Pulled into town, straight to the in-store, dinner, then our show.

The room was medium-sized and poorly designed with the floor in front of the stage surrounded by waist-high bars, marking off a distinct area that people would have to consciously choose to cross a barrier to get into.

Twenty-eight people paid.

Taking the opportunity to practice, we played a strange set heavy with songs that we don't play often. We zipped through them and sounded great. My arm hung by my side in pain the entire time. Over and over I'd forget and instinctually move it a little and receive constant jolts of pain to remind me to keep still.

I like a show like that a lot. It seems like it just sucks. I mean it *does* suck, but we react to it by playing extra well instead of blowing it off. Makes us a better band.

The promoter was really nice and overpaid us. Kept insisting we have to come back and it'll be so much better, etc., and I thought the same thing that I'd thought a thousand times in the previous couple days; every time my expression went blank and I said "Yeah, sure, cool," I was actually thinking, "No fucking way dude. Last tour."

There was a fire going when we arrived at Ashton's mom's house to sleep. It had been 22 hours since we woke up east of Denver. We were all out quickly.

I dreamt that my shoulder blew up into a giant purple bruise.

I laid awake before anyone else was moving, listening to I-tunes on shuffle. "Over and Over" and "Storms" from *Tusk*;

first song from the first Jawbox album for the first time in ten years; Aki Tsyuko and Tower Recordings, both songs I didn't really recognize and liked a lot; Hot Snakes; live Gene Clark; lame Neil Young rock-n-roll-genre-exercise duet. Snapped out of it by hot pancakes being served. Sam and Ashton played video games.

Off to Boise. We tried to stop to see The Salt Lake twice and couldn't find it. It just wasn't there where the map said it should be. Got turned around in a creepy, *Children of the Corn*-type town.

Now it's northwest Utah towards southeast Idaho, most politically conservative area of the country. I used to always be freaked out that white power survivalist-types in Idaho would snatch us up *Hills Have Eyes*-style, until my recent decision to not allow myself to get freaked out by anything anymore went into effect. So now, instead, it's only that I love reaching the peak of even the smallest of these climbs, looking ahead and seeing our path laid out straight ahead of us, extending to the horizon without a single bend. Crossing Idaho, most of the afternoon passes only wondering, each moment, how far is it that I'm seeing now? Is that a mile? 20 miles? 100?

*

OCTOBER 29, 2006

Read more of *The Idiot* and more Ram Dass, swapping chapters between each and enjoying how they resonate together. Quiet for hours, I watched Idaho pass by out the window and loved it. Maybe it's just knowing deep in my bones that this is it, I'm done, last time I'll be passing through Idaho or wherever. Maybe it's all the anticipation of tour-misery still to come or maybe it's just that we're still only a few days in and it has yet to hit me, but yesterday was as simple and enjoyable a day of tour as I have had in years. Boise is beautiful, the mountains just a few blocks behind it in every direction.

I'm surprised over and over by how these Western towns move me: the air and light, old buildings and clean streets. Must be the time with Amy in Colorado and New Mexico that brought this appreciation out of me.

Got to town early and checked into The Doubletree. It's amazing how Priceline has changed touring. Instead of $85 for small shitty rooms we pay $60 for nice rooms. We suspected that we stayed at the same hotel last year, but each of us remembered a different detail and couldn't be certain if we were all talking about the same night or not. We compared memories and finally agreed in a dull way that we all knew we'd been here before. Walking through the convention center connected to the hotel—giant chandeliers and walls made of all windows—it all came back to me.

We got to the show an hour late after each settling in to different comforts the hotel had to offer. But even an hour late for load, we were still at least two hours early for anything to happen.

When we pulled up, a half dozen thirty-somethings were hanging out drunk and laughing, the few tables of the outdoor seating area all pushed together. The people were all vaguely Alternative in long sleeve Harley Davidson shirts and bandanas—that uniquely Western hippy-yuppie-hybrid with self-conscious flourishes of Boise Outlaw.

Early Saturday evening, walking in after Happy Hour and before the night, we were all immediately on edge. It was a Ministry-style Industrial/Goth/Biker scene. Industrial—what a resilient subculture. It really flourishes in these faraway places.

A woman dressed up as a sort of Bo-Peep baby doll paraded around in small circles swinging her arms wide back and forth, tilting her head side to side, smiling and staring at people until they'd give in and uncomfortably smile back. Her big, not especially tough, but creepy, straight-laced looking boyfriend sat and watched without expression.

A stocky guy in all black and combat boots and a bandana over braids-as-fake-dreads left his *Clockwork Orange* dandy posse and approached me as I tried to order a beer.

"*Loooooooooooooove* it," he said in a drawn out and heavily affected faux-dandy drawl as he fingered the brim of my hat, dragging his fingers as slowly as his long drawn out vowel sound.

I said thanks.

"Did you make it?"

"No, nope."

"Did your" — and here there was a long, long pause as he looked deep into my eyes — "*giiiiiiiiiiiirlfriend* make it for you?"

I blurted out the truth—"I got it in Tokyo"—and then immediately felt like such a jerk name-dropping Tokyo in Boise. I stepped away from him to lean in closer over the bar to try to get the bartender's attention.

"*Ooooooooooooooh.Tooooooooooooooh-key-yooooooooooo*!" He howled with implied menace as he spun to return to his table. For the rest of the night, any time I would occasionally pass him he would call out, "Oh *Tooooooooooh-key-yooooooooooooooo*!" and wave at me while looking away. I never have gotten flirting, even when both parties were reciprocating. Ugh.

Ecstatic Sunshine were spooked by the scene and it made me feel like I had to be a little bit stronger than I might've otherwise allowed myself to be. I've made it through plenty of creepier situations and I've been overwhelmed and paralyzed with anxiety in plenty of comparable situations. But I guess maybe that's the lesson so many hours wasted with worry teaches you: getting through it at the time isn't just *enough*, but *everything you'll ever need* once the worry finally passes. It may never even occur to you that some kind of lesson has been learned, but next time you end up in a similar situation, you breathe deep and keep your cool.

I talked to Ecstatic Sunshine about Baltimore and I think my age really hit them. It was fun to play The Old Man in a small way, naming clubs and bands long gone by the time they'd emerged from high school.

Next door was a flashy junk store, calendars and belt buckles, weird shit with Insane Clown Posse or whatever logos all over it. They had a small junk food cafeteria in the corner. Junk food at the kitsch store, get it? But what store encourages snacking while browsing? Hundreds of t-shirts with hundreds of band names or smartass dim witticisms.

In the back was a record store with a large and pretty good selection of used CDs. Lame vinyl selection: just garbage used and only Nu-Metal and Pitchfork-favorites new, but we were in Boise. And they had the Konono #1 CD used and Tania's first record and even a Joan of Arc section in the new CDs.

I put back a Southern Death Cult CD of two records that I already have on vinyl and bought only one of those Luka Bop comps, which I've come to trust pretty well. This one seemed especially cool: West African Psych bands from the early '70s. The guy at the counter commented how much he liked it and I told him I'd been interested for a couple years but had never seen it used before.

I indulged my credit card and while ringing me up the guy paused and looked me up and down suspiciously. Finally, after shifting my weight back and forth a few times and maybe even audibly gulping, he asked me in such a disappointed tone, incredulously, "*You're* Tim Kinsella?" as if he expected this "Tim Kinsella" that he knew of to walk around in Ziggy Stardust glitter or maybe P-Diddy furs? The poor guy was so demonstrably let down by me. I was surprised of course that a Black man in Boise, Idaho, a few years my senior even, would know me by name, so I just shrugged and said yeah.

"That's cool," he said. And I replied, "Sometimes, I guess" and he chuckled. He asked me if I owned Record Label Record Label and I explained that that was Bobby, but then I knew that he really did think I was me.

Having eaten only a peanut butter and jelly sandwich since Wild Oats in Salt Lake City that morning, I got drunk pretty quickly when I returned to the show. Curfew was 11:00 because of some DJs and it was almost 9:30 and Ecstatic Sunshine hadn't even begun yet. Sitting at the bar, Dustin was explaining Japanese conspiracy theories and Illuminati shit and Sam was engrossed and thrilled. The place had filled up a little. Maybe sixty people, fifty people maybe, but it was a big dark room with two dozen booths and tables, so it would doubtlessly remain insurmountably empty and that was fine. I'd watched Lawrence Welk on TV at the hotel a couple hours earlier, so I was excited to do a show on a tall stage far away from a mostly seated audience, try out some dance moves.

Walking through the dark room, people weren't visible until you were close up on them. Everyone was in costumes. And only then it hit me that it's the Saturday before Halloween. All the ultra-violence dandies and Bo-Peeps from earlier suddenly seemed so much less creepy.

We played the new songs first, opening with the AC/DC-sounding one—"Sometimes I See Sideways"—which we hadn't played yet on the tour and it sounded good. The second half of the set was again songs that could use practice,

The Show Tune-sounding one "Boom," "Amscaredica," "Temping," songs we haven't been playing much recently. We played well and it felt good.

Since I'm not eating ephedrine before these shows, I've been drinking a Red Bull before we play. It hit me only right before we were supposed to start that I hadn't done either. This realization made playing that much more inspired for me, knowing that the energy truly has been coming from inside me, and while the little pills or that syrupy macho-gunk can provoke or enable this energy, they might actually be placebos.

A young dork alone at the show, at the front of the stage, kept yelling out some Captain Jazz lyrical references that were almost familiar, but not really, and mostly corny and embarrassing. Not that I generally thought that that stuff was particularly cool, but I hadn't come in such close contact to any of its details in so long that I was surprised it was as lame as it was. I was as embarrassed for that kid as I was for myself. Sure, I may be responsible for it in some ways, but at least I forgot about it ten years ago. This poor kid was still seeing something worthwhile in it.

Joking easily with us, the soundman Larry made us feel at home. He said if we went over curfew a little bit *"we"* wouldn't get in too much trouble. I appreciated that he felt himself as one of us, on our side against the world, instead of on the club's side against us.

I got hung up a little bit on Lynndie England and talked about her between a few songs in a row. I never explained who she is, but I took a poll from the stage. Unanimously, everyone knew Angelina Jolie, and only two or four people knew Lynndie England. I again got hung up on introducing "Amscaredica": I guess just being aware of being in Idaho, I wanted to make certain in no ambiguous terms that we were in fact operating from a contrary mindset to that which we assumed to be the norm in their town.

Talked to a couple nice people after the show — one guy moving to the Virgin Islands, another doing some kind of specialized law that has him studying prohibition-era bars of Chicago. The room filled up more and more with ghouls and zombies and we decided we best load out quick before it got too crowded or we got too drunk or comfortable.

Driving back to the hotel, Sam, without clear provocation, went on a tirade against all these people we know who, according to him, "just improvise to make themselves seem cool." It was such an illogical, unreasonable, unfair, and ridiculous argument that none of us really even protested because we felt the idea of *Improvising Itself* needed defending, but more so because it was a good practice run for talking Sam down from a ledge. It was nice to get a dry run dealing with a 100% meaningless and inconsequential issue. In the event that he freaks out about something that he or one of us actually does care about, we will have had a brief refresher course on how to deal with him when he's at his most far-fetched contrarian.

All of us except Bobby went down to the hotel bar where a Halloween party was in full hop. The DJ was in a black-and-white checkerboard court jester costume. Two women that worked there were vaguely French maids and both were looking really good despite—more so than on account of—their costumes.

The dance floor was packed. Not that many people, but they were almost all obese. All Locals and Regulars—I confirmed it with the bartender. Sam and Nate couldn't believe it, but being myself a sort of semi-annual hotel bar regular in Amy's hometown, I knew it.

This one old man out on the dance floor never sat down once in the entire hour or more that we sat there. He wore a black t-shirt that said, "This is My Costume" in puffy orange letters. He was spinning and dipping his date. When she tuckered out, he hopped up and down with his friend, his arms pressed to his side. At one point we three were so stunned by this guy and his boundless energy that we stood up and stared at him and only a moment later became aware of feeling rude for doing so.

Every single costume was store-bought. Every single song was Top 40 from the last half-decade. There's nothing as depressing as watching people do their best to enjoy themselves and blow off steam and not know how to even approach doing so outside of very tightly scripted cultural parameters.

I was drunk enough to climb on Bobby and wrestle him while he was sleeping. I slept on the floor between the two beds and was never not aware of my shoulder hurting. The simple realization of its connection to the rest of me became apparent. By morning I hurt everywhere.

In the morning Daylight Savings bought us an extra hour of relaxing and doing nothing. I walked around the hotel taking a ton of pictures and loving it. The old health food restaurant that we would stop in Boise to eat at even when just passing through has been closed down.

Now on, across golden, rolling Oregon: teepees, trailers, telephone poles, and even an old wooden wagon, but nothing else along the side of the road.

*

ALL OVER AND OVER

OCTOBER 30, 2006

We gained two hours yesterday; Daylight Savings time and heading west into Das Homeland's last time zone. We had a leisurely morning, no hurry to leave knowing that we had plenty of time to make the nine-hour drive and get there for an 8:30 load-in.

Oregon's winding highways occasionally open up to a long straight path ahead, everything shades of gold and never darker than rust-colored in the deepest shadows. The wind tumbled us about the highway and I felt a little seasick, but happy to be so. We stopped at a scenic overpass. It was freezing out, but we all ran over to the gazebo at the edge overlooking shallow hills that stretched into receding waves at the horizon, flattened by perspective when actually at their biggest. Lovers pledged eternal devotion to each other and dated it over and over in the gazebo-wood's flesh. The wind cut past us and we laughed and laughed about it blowing us away.

After a few more hours of reading, sleeping, looking out the window, we were all restless. There was nothing in our Healthy Highways book between us and Seattle. I tried to eat a Taco Time taco and nachos a few hours earlier, but had to throw them both away after just a couple bites. Even going in expecting only Taco Bell, and figuring any variation of that formula would net positive results, it was far too gross to imagine actually ingesting and integrating into my life form.

We were still hours ahead of schedule. 150 miles to go, we decided to stop in some small Washington town and look around, sit down and get something to eat. The only choice at that hour on a Sunday in Yakoma, Washington was an Olive Garden. Having only eaten there once before, desperate in Odessa, Texas, a couple years ago, we all remembered being pleasantly surprised by it.

I went in and went straight to the men's room. Emerging

from the stall I found both Bobby and Sam also in there. When I got back to the entrance to be seated, Nate was stomping out, confused and frustrated. I caught up to him. He had thought that we'd somehow ditched him, sneaking out a side door or something.

It was truly a bummer even to just walk through that place, Olive Garden. Seeing young hicks on dates makes me sad for them. Older couples on a double date all look like animated characters to me; total cartoon blobs in their weekend leisure wear to live out the endless weekend that is the rest of their lives.

I immediately like these people, like I want to snuggle with any one of them, and I know that even *that* sounds condescending, but I do. Overwhelmed by them as a group, I can't help but try to imagine each of their individual lives, the totality of one's experiences, everything they may have ever been or will ever see or aspired to be beyond this moment—*my* Olive Garden experience in which they are all background.

I like them on principle and with a conscious effort and feel ashamed, knowing how cruel it is of me to do so. But I need to make that effort because they just don't seem like real humans to me at all, just Bubble People somehow. Thick-rimmed glasses and a bulb nose and a gray moustache? No, that is by no means a certain sentence for dehumanization.

Overhearing their small talk about their yards, we snicker. But what do we do any differently? Who do I think I am to be so judgmental?

And all at once I understood. It's really only that they were actually *enjoying* Olive Garden that bugged me and troubled me so much. I was so sad. How many disappointments does a life require before Olive Garden is OK?

At the very best, the most I could hope for was that Olive Garden could remind me of a meal that I would enjoy—red wine, linguine with red sauce. It couldn't possibly potentially *be* an enjoyable meal, but maybe it could trigger memories of superficially similar, superior meals. And I was angry at the world that it was somehow these poor fools' lot in life to think that this meal was in itself satisfying. I was angry on their behalf, and I was angry at them for not being bothered themselves and I was angry at myself for being so fucking critical all the time. I mean, Olive Garden gives you all the shitty breadsticks and shitty salad you want and there may be zero flavor, but it *seems* like a deal because you can get so much of all this shit that you really wouldn't even want any of unless it was made to seem like a deal because you got a lot of it. Great, right? Woo-hoo.

We figured we must've eaten lunch here before because this wasn't a deal at all, but was instead actually a kind of pricey bummer.

We all split as soon as we ordered to all go talk to our ladies. After working with Chris and then shooting all day, Amy did the charitable act of driving Steve to the grocery store. She's excited about assembling all the stills and cutting the *Orchard Vale* trailer. It makes me super-psyched, but doubly bummed to be away.

She told me a funny story about this woman she met that shot a documentary about Post-Traumatic Stress Disorder in veterans returning from Iraq. Amy might help this woman cut it, so they're getting to know each other. It turns out that the woman knows S_____ and Amy says, "Oh he's our good friend." The woman tells Amy that a couple years ago she was diagnosed with a totally debilitating social anxiety disorder. She confided this to S_____ at the time and he was very empathetic and understanding, responding that he occasionally wonders if he himself might not suffer the same troubles in a diagnosable manner. The woman doesn't see S_____ for a while, years maybe. Whatever it was they had in common, they no longer do, maybe a class or whatever. But so she doesn't see him for years until last week. Sitting down to lunch with a prospective investor in her film whom that she has never met before, S_____ walks into the restaurant and approaches the table. He smiles and greets her with "Hi, how's your debilitating social anxiety disorder?"

The woman is mortified and looks to the prospective

investor that she's just met. S_____ goes on with a chuckle, "Well, you're out of the house right? Things can't be that bad," and the woman decides that the investor must assume this is some kind of clever set-up. She can't get rid of S_____ but eventually his own social awkwardness wears him down and he leaves the woman alone with the prospective investor, who she will choke down a horribly awkward hour with and never hear from again.

I'm psyched for and proud of Amy and all her work these days and don't even bring up the Make Believe video that we need to get done soon. I know she'd feel obligated to do it and I can't ask her for anything that'd take up any more of her time or energy.

I return to the table to explain the situation to Bobby and he tells me that he just got word C_____'s sister is going to do it this week. She worked on *Me, You, and Everyone We Know* so that's cool.

Olive Garden food tasted like nothing, but did have a slight metallic aftertaste.

It was dark by the time we left and we were just on time for load-in. Sam was going to drive even though he can't see well at night and gets a little panicky in mountains or rain and we were going through both. We had less than a quarter tank of gas and were heading out into the middle of nowhere, but he refused to get gas before leaving town and I refused to be annoyed. Even while telling myself that tour is 100% about surrender, I still silently hoped that we'd run out of gas so I could be proven right.

Outside an old downtown building across from the public lot that we'd parked in, some kind of Mayan or Incan dance was happening. About twelve dancers were in ornate, but phony costumes and one man played one drum. Dancing and stomping and chanting, the performers weren't synchronized very well at all. It was sloppy and thrown together, but earnest. I didn't doubt for a second that these people were probably direct ancestors of whatever tradition and lineage this was, it just seemed that they didn't have access to the resources that their costumes required. A few of the kids acted like defiant, bored teenagers forced into doing this while they'd rather be doing anything else. We stood behind the 40 or so folding chairs set up in the street, half of which were occupied. Bobby and Nate stuck around longer than seemed necessary to me to be either polite or discern that this was in fact not that interesting or enlightening to stumble upon, even as much as the initial shock seemed to assert that it would be. I was anxious I guess about heading out through the mountains of *Twin Peaks* at night.

Sam drove about 20 minutes before stopping for gas and asking somebody else to drive and I agreed. While inside the gas station we heard that Snoqualmie Pass was closed, 90 West stopped completely around exit 50. Ecstatic Sunshine called and said they'd been sitting totally still for an hour near exit 70. We looked at the atlas, but could find no other way. If even the interstate was too icy, we couldn't make it through unfamiliar mountain roads at night. We considered waiting it out at the gas station, listening to traffic advisories, but then figured waiting for news would only set us back even more. It was 7:00 by the time we lined up at the end of the traffic jam at exit 78. We were supposed to load in at 8:30, 76 miles away.

The clock on the dashboard was still set two hours fast, so after sitting still a while it felt like buying ourselves some time just setting the clock right. It was cold and we were all feeling silly. The looping a.m. traffic advisory said there was no way to know when the road would open, *please don't line up*. There was a hailstorm earlier and they couldn't get through the 35 miles of stopped traffic to clean it up. Traffic was stopped in both directions and the eastbound side would open first. The prospect of missing a second show in five days because of an interstate closed for weather conditions that we couldn't even see was so absurd that all we could do was make each other laugh.

All the people in all the other cars looked so miserable: Seattle folk who'd gone off to the country for the weekend and needed to get home Sunday night to be up for work early Monday. Most of the cars were packed with camping equipment and lots of luggage. Many had trailers with 4-wheelers or motorcycles or horses. A lot of people were Asian. Everyone sitting in silence. One happy young couple passed a little kid back and forth to take turns bouncing it on their laps.

A woman in a red Suburban with a trailer hung her head out her window to stare at the sky. Eventually she was sitting in the window leaning all the way back and pulling herself upright over and over in a small, slow gymnastics routine.

Nate had an incredible fart fit and kept opening the door and sticking his butt out. Sitting in a traffic jam in an isolated mountain pass felt so surreal that it was hard not to feel a twinge of *Close Encounters* anxiety, like we were all being lined up for some fate none of us could imagine but would all be transformed by. But really we were all just sitting still. Thousands of people in thousands of metal boxes sitting still.

As proof of either collective consciousness or just too much time around each other in too tight of quarters for too many years, Sam said he felt like "the ghost-aliens were about to reveal themselves."

In the first 90 minutes we moved one mile. I imagine this was just the tense constriction of everyone pulling tighter, perhaps even subconsciously, to alleviate fear and attempt to create warmth. The doors were opening at the show.

The next hour we sat completely still. We listened to the West African '70s psych comp I bought and it sounded great. Two songs in particular I knew upon first listen would become my lifelong companions.

I thought of every traffic jam I'd ever been in: Germany, sitting still in a blizzard for ten hours, December 2001, second to last day of what had already been the nightmare Owls European tour; three hours with Auntie Linda and Uncle Gene going to Kalamazoo in 1997? '98?; every day of every year moving through downtown Chicago . . .

But mountains really somehow made it stranger. We settled into assuming that we'd spend the night parked there.

All the cars were turned off and the total darkness made sitting trapped in the middle of a mountain pass parking lot that much more surreal. There are robots so small that a thousand of them can fit on the head of a pin. Spider silk is harvested in goat bellies. Yet we were still all subject to an icy mountain pass. Snoqualmie Mountain Pass.

Finally Ecstatic Sunshine called and said they were moving, we'll make it to the show. But eight miles behind them, we remained still for another hour until all at once we began to move. An older tough guy-looking farmer had just gotten out of his truck and given the stalled rows a stern stare and saunter, hands on his hips, right before they all began moving. As he hurried back to his truck I imagined it was probably impossible for him to not be thinking at least a little bit, *well I should've done that hours ago,* as if his disapproval was just too much for the traffic to stand up against.

The roads were a sheet of ice through winding mountains dense with traffic. Slush and mist and dirt sprayed against the windshield in a constant blinding splash. Every second an incredible effort, it took two more hours to make it that last 70 miles.

We arrived to the show as Ecstatic Sunshine was just starting. Had to load in quick. My shoulder had been feeling fine, so in the hurry of the load I just grabbed something without thinking and with a jolt, I was immediately returned to the suffering of the previous days.

The club was small and filled, a great relief from our previous five years of Seattle shows. Probably the same number of people, they had just seemed more sparse in bigger rooms. Last time through the only all-ages option was a church in the suburbs, ugh.

Great to load in to a show at 11 after assuming we'd never make it, and actually have people waiting for us and seem excited that we made it.

As we pulled up, figuring out where to load in, a very familiar-looking guy approached. He had some kind of floating neck sideburns unconnected to any other hair on his head and I assumed it was some kind of unfortunate birthmark or medical condition. It wasn't even a neck beard. I don't know. But when I later realized it was a conscious fashion choice, it made sense.

"Hi. Remember me? I'm R_____. We met in Chicago. I'm friends with B_____ and you thought I was an asshole. Remember?"

I did remember him then and told him it was nice to see him again and I didn't remember thinking he was an asshole. He continued to insist that he was being an asshole one night when I was DJing at Danny's and he was sorry. He never explained what actually happened. I remember him being around town for a while and running into him a few times, but the asshole thing just didn't sound familiar. But now, as he kept insisting on this aggressive awkwardness, it seemed perfectly reasonable that I, in fact, may have found him to be an asshole in the past after all and had just forgotten it.

The club only had beer, so I ran down the street to an empty lesbian bar. The woman poured me a huge shot of bourbon and I gagged a little downing it too quickly.

Special J-2 was there. He's been living in Portland for the summer and drove up for the show. Always nice to see him even though he, by necessity, must be a bit of a mystery to me—always formal and polite and all I really know about him is that he spends a lot of his time doing his website about our bands.

We played on the floor and the audience surrounded us tightly, climbed on to tables and ledges to see over each other. Before we started they were all boisterous and then, with a few exceptions, everyone remained totally calm and cool while we played. A young Japanese man standing right in front of me kept shouting, "I take picture of such handsome man" and flashing his camera inches from my face and blinding me.

Special J-2 had an underage friend with him that I met

briefly before we played. He was a tall, blond, modest Utah kid visiting J-2 in Portland. As we played, throughout the entire set, I would occasionally catch glimpses of this kid standing outside the window of this place freaking out and dancing like a maniac on the sidewalk. A big hip-hop show—The Swollen Members—was letting out across the street right before we began. I kept wondering what that show's audience, hanging out in the street after the show, must all be thinking of this strange small town guy dancing with abandon alone on the sidewalk.

After the show, happy with how it went, but not happy enough to submit to an encore, the facts: sixty people paid. It was the fifth Make Believe show in Seattle. The zillionth Seattle show of my life, and sixty people paid is an *improvement*?

We made $160 at the door. Really hard to continue justifying this in any way beyond the immediate satisfaction of playing, and the immediate satisfaction of that one hour playing can hardly sustain the other 23 hours each day.

Two guys approached me at the bar to tell me how strange it is to meet me and I tried to settle them down and be cool and one guy was really nice and the other one remained weird. A girl kept insisting we go to her party and we'll have such a great time and it's no big deal and we have to go because American Football and Owen are her favorite bands ever. R_____ found me and continued to insist that he was an asshole.

The Japanese guy was fun to sit with for a while. He talked about moving to Seattle and meeting all the Northwest scene people of his record collection and thinking they were all "hicks from Tennessee." That's a funny enough thing to have repeated and insisted upon over and over by anyone, but coming from a high-energy, hyperbolic, 20-year old Japanese guy it was extra funny: *bloken engrish*, etc.

A guy with one leg was cool and liked the show a lot and we talked for a while.

ALL OVER AND OVER

Our hotel was downtown and very fancy. Gathering our belongings before pulling the van away to park, Sam dropped a twelve-pack of beer and a couple bottles broke in the van. Me and Nate cleaned up the broken glass and soaked up as much beer as we could from the carpet while Sam and Bobby brought everything up. Van smells like a loft the day after a party.

Fell asleep around 3:00 a.m., which would've been 5:00 where we'd woken up, but still I couldn't sleep past 9:00 or 9:30. Had a great time walking around the hotel taking pictures. The 28th floor, a pool and a hot tub, was all windows. Got a lot of cool Utopia shots for *Orchard Vale*.

Amy was obviously grumpy when I called: super-stressed out about bills and totally broke. I had to figure out how to get an advance and send her $150. No Citibanks in Seattle, so I finally just had Bobby overnight her a check he could write and I paid him. She'd shit if she knew we're only making about $150 a night and spending more than that each day to be out. She was as bummed, as pissed and annoyed as I've ever known her to be, and seemed only a little better when I was able to get a check off to her within three hours of her registering her complaint.

Did an interview on some college radio station. The girl was very sweet. Nineteen or twenty maybe, looked a little like a combination of a few different girls we'd all agree are cute. She had an endearing clumsiness and awkwardness to her that made her even cuter. The campus was beautiful. Brisk fall day, bright out, lots of trees and hills with all the familiar campus buildings, quads and yards, longitude and latitude. We must've climbed 200 steps to get up a hill from the parking lot to the sub-basement that the radio station was in. It was as easy of a four-way interview as we've ever done. We each talked a little and were all at ease.

Got directions to a vegan buffet and all freaked and ate ourselves overboard. I feel lucky to be a part of this funny bunch. Nothing gets us all as excited as a vegan buffet; not even one of us isn't into it. This was the kind of place to win anyone over—such variety and subtleties of spices. "Flowers," it's called. I wish a place like that could be more common; what a society that would be symptomatic of.

Now almost to Portland, my favorite American City (after Chicago of course). Even just the bridges entering it from the north on I-5 thrill me: always autumn, industrialized nature, bike-friendly, poor small town-big city. Can't wait to see Andy and Danny B. and Nathan and Drew, even! Drew!

What's Portland's magnetism? So overlooked and forgotten about except everyone knows a million people that live there. Veggie options everywhere.

And now to Powell's! Punk strip clubs! Veggie diners! The afternoon moon over the city, my vision blown out, white sky from all sides.

The land of Brautigan's youth! Mt. Hood beyond the old systems of bridges! Suicide Girls! Houseboats! Houses even! The eternally promising potential! Danny B. driving his DIY hearse conversion-van! And we've played a different club every single time we've ever played here.

*

HALLOWEEN 2006

Pulling into Portland around sunset last night we all agreed the city has such an intense effect on each of us, but none of us could name or identify this effect or its cause. There's something deeply sad about it that we're all always eager to jump into. Perpetual October 1973. Maybe some quality of the light here saturates colors in a way that reminds us of '70s film stock.

We went straight to Powell's Books. None of us knew exactly where it was or how to get there, but collectively we willed it and after a few short detours, we stumbled right up into it. We had an hour and a half until load and we all parted ways.

My semi-annual Powell's browse has become such a grounding force for me. These familiar spaces help me feel at ease when traveling—*Everything's OK, you've been here plenty of times before, right? And you were always OK then, so what's the problem?*

I checked my bag and headed up to the Red Room: General Metaphysics, Religion, Myths, etc. The crusty dude with barbarian punk style at the information desk was immediately familiar. But browsing the racks, pretty much everything I haven't read, and a good amount that I have, seemed corny.

I did pick up an Alan Watts book, *The Book*, which I hadn't read before. His books and lectures are always a great source of comfort when travel-anxiety creeps up on me. I packed a book of his that I figured I could re-read if I started to flip out, but it's still deep in my luggage and wasn't interesting to me except for its possible necessity. But a book of his that I'd never read before was exciting to find for five bucks.

I also got a slim book of lectures by Rudolf Steiner, *Fruits of Anthroposophy*, for five bucks. I recognized his name from him being referred to a lot in other stuff I've read. Flipping through it for a couple minutes, it looked promising. Nothing else caught my eye. I knew I wanted to find that *Cosmic Serpent* book but couldn't think of the exact title or the author's name.

Maybe because that guy was familiar as exactly the correct guy to be sitting right where I'd left him last year at that information desk, and part of me was let down that he didn't greet me, "Oh, you're back!"—maybe I just needed a way to touch base with him and say hello. I described the book and he seemed annoyed to be disturbed; he had no idea what I was talking about. I went overboard explaining how Totally OK it was that he didn't know what book I was talking about.

I called Kate and asked her to look around their apartment for me because I knew Ben had a copy of it, but was in France. Jeremy Narby—didn't sound familiar at all. Squeezed between two rude options—talking on the phone in a quiet bookstore or being short with Kate—I struck the perfectly wrong balance to maximize rudeness in both regards.

I found an expensive new biography of Cassavetes and an expensive art book of Herzog production stills. Some book of short stories seemed like maybe my thing, David Berman-y with a suburban-spiritual slant, but I already can't remember the author's name. Bought only *The Cosmic Serpent* new, never seen a used copy anywhere.

Talked to Amy. She's got Jonathan and Joe over going through footage for the trailer. They're all excited and psyched and it bums me out to be away and unable to be a part of that process.

Got lost looking for the club and ended up driving around some empty warehouse district/industrial area. Like the cartoon version of the middle class-white-paranoid nightmare of being lost in the wrong part of town, we got boxed in, trapped between two slow trains and strange long trailers moving through the docks.

Found Holocene and had the rare experience of showing up to a club and actually being excited to play there—tall ceilings, the show in a room separate from the bar, all clean lines, lots of wood, some quilts, some metalwork. Very European and kind of Manhattan, but not self-consciously cool. The soundman and bartender and doorman and promoter were all immediately friendly.

Andy and Nathan and his girl and Danny B. all showed up within minutes, and it was happy reunions all around. We skipped sound check to go out to dinner.

I rode with Andy and Danny B., both of them as happy and healthy as I'd seen either of them in years. Andy's working at a restaurant he likes a lot owned by a married couple that he likes a lot. Danny B., two years sober, strong and honest and as much himself as anyone ever has been, is so truly inspiring to me. It's super weird. Ten years ago I never would've believed that I'd still know this odd pimp-talking, gravelly-voiced skater kid that sold me weed. How strange to now think of him as my old friend. Who else could be a DIY mortician in an '80s conversion van, combing back his devil lock to appear presentable? He also works the door at Union Jacks. He'd been sitting there so much anyways they figured they may as well put him to work.

Nathan is working at a fair-trade organic coffee roaster and I'm excited to hear of him working somewhere that he's excited about for maybe the first time since I've known him.

Danny B. and Andy told me about Portland life and how cool it was and how it's changed them: dinner parties instead of bars, friendships based on honesty and trust instead of style and convenience. They were both genuinely surprised when I pointed out that maybe it also had to do with our ages now and not just the different city they'd both moved to. They assumed that I still live the life we all lived together as 22-year-olds, out until dawn every night, dizzy most of the time?

We ate at a Thai place, caught up on all the gossip of all the scattered friends everywhere. Flushing out rumors that we'd each heard barely overlapping halves of, we illuminated past circumstances that one or another of us may have always only been able to see in shadows. We all laughed a lot and it was relaxed. Didn't feel like being on tour at all, felt so at home and easy.

Walking back to the car, Andy, a step ahead of me uphill, had his head turned back towards me and walked his shin full-stride straight into a pipe jutting out of a wall. For the rest of the night, in between every other two sentences he would interject, "Oh god, my fucking leg."

Got back to the club still a little early, no one really around yet. Mojica texted me that he was at a secret Beck show at the Black Cat backstage; strange coincidence to hear from him while sitting with half of the staff of his café in Chicago ten years ago. We all got beers. Andy said Rosie was in town and might be coming. Hillary walked in.

When Special J-2 walked in a few minutes later, he was literally the only person present that wouldn't have been sitting at Jinx ten years earlier. A friend of Hillary's showed up that I didn't know, but she ended up being Bobby's friend from SAIC that he'd even gone on a couple dates with when they later both lived in Brooklyn.

The first band began. The singer looked like Jonathan, but done up with cowboy boots and a woman's winter coat a few sizes too small. He did a continuous buzzing poetry-thing while the band vamped like The Doors behind him, occasionally bursting out into obtuse math-metal. I know it's silly, but musicians I can't relate to often make me uneasy, like someone might mistake me for being motivated by the same impulses.

I ran out to the van for a minute, and the kid that had been dancing on the sidewalk outside the show last night was standing outside the club again. Tonight it was cold and he really wasn't anywhere close to being able to see or hear the show. We talked a little. He's from Utah. His parents are divorced so he flies a lot and had a lot of frequent flier miles built up. He only knew Special J-2 from the Joan of Arc message board and had come to visit him to coincide with these two shows that he wouldn't be allowed into. He was nervous, real shaky. I was surprised later to find out that neither Sam through Myspace, nor Bobby through the Joan of Arc site, nor Nate through niceties had any idea about the kid. None of them had noticed him or had met him. Strange for me to be the only one to meet someone. I'm usually the last one to know of these things.

Andrew, traveling with Ecstatic Sunshine, was only nineteen and he was inside tonight after having been sent away from a couple other shows this week. Made me think it wasn't impossible to maybe get the Utah kid in, something I've never been into doing before. Having worked at the bar for seven years, and having not been underage for longer than that, bar laws might be the singular instance of my sympathies lying more in line with The Power than The Underdog. Of course the kids that ask for help to sneak into a bar never understand the gravity of their request and the trouble it could cause. This kid didn't even ask, but I went in to sort out a plan.

The promoter woman had been so nice before that when we returned from dinner she told us that they actually served food at the club and would have fed us there, but since we'd split before we knew that, she handed us buyout money. She even gave us $20 too much that she refused to take back. We handed it over to Ecstatic Sunshine who were totally confused by the entire concept of a buyout. She then even offered to kick Ecstatic Sunshine out of the band room for us if we wanted it to ourselves and we laughed and told her No Thanks. So I thought she might not be offended by me bringing up the idea of getting this kid in.

Danny B. left and we agreed to meet him over at Union Jack's after the show. He ran home to get me a copy of the documentary some guy just made about him.

He said he missed acting a lot. Of course Portland doesn't have the deep theater scene of Chicago, but the rest of his life was so together for the first time, that he felt he couldn't leave Portland to pursue acting, however much it has always meant to him. He said Portland Theater is all special effects and hitting marks and none of the getting deep into a character that motivates him. He spontaneously and tersely lamented Abu Ghraib, then headed out to the strip club.

Rosie and Emily arrived. I'd been putting off calling Rosie to tell her we'd be in L.A. in a few days, because I thought she might be mad at me and she might be justified. We said hello quickly and then nothing else.

I searched the club for the promoter. She told me there was nothing she could do, wasn't her club. But I figured having admitted my intention to her, and having graciously accepted her denial, granted me a more covert cover. If she didn't know about it, there was nothing she could do to stop it. And she had told me No, so I couldn't get her in trouble. I told the kid to meet me by the side door in a few minutes and go directly to the stage and remain seated on it through our set. In the rare event of the cops showing up, we could perhaps play out the long-shot loophole that he was a part of the band.

I found Rosie and asked her to go to Union Jack's with us after the show. She made some small symbolic gestures of saying no, but she just needed me to twist her arm.

The room had filled up decently. It wasn't by any means crowded, but it was filled front to back, everyone with a little breathing room. We opened with the AC/DC-sounding one, a move I've found helps situate us a little bit when we might be nervous—big shows, weird rooms, or as in tonight's case, plenty of friends in attendance that don't see us play very often.

(In the immediate, Bobby almost just drove off a cliff and Sam got real happy. I can't believe I honestly thought to myself for a second, "Yeah, I'd rather die than have to finish this if the option were somehow presented." The silence policy of our van means more to me than ever today now that it's been contradicted by Led Zeppelin and Califone—two things I truly enjoy very much and often find great inspiration and satisfaction from, but today are proof of how miserable and trapped I feel on tour. When I was young, tour may have represented freedom, the open road, etc. But now that I don't feel oppressed by my home life, I sure feel oppressed when I need to sit in a van all day and at some shitty club all night and if I can't at least read or write because of noise I go fucking nuts—daydreams of suicide and murder.)

And this rant after the most fun night of tour I've had in years.

So, anyways, the show: it was a lot like they all are. I was a little more nervous, so I got a little more drunk. Drew showed up in the middle of the show and came up to the front of the stage. We said hello and hugged quickly in between songs.

Somehow, at some point in between songs, we ended up talking about V-necks and some woman called out "I've got a V-neck on" and then proceeded to very slowly and casually walk up on stage and just sort of stand there for a few seconds. Maybe she shifted her weight a little once. Indeed, she did have a V-neck on. Odd yawn in the show's momentum.

We played "Fumio Nambata" last and the kid who had been sitting on stage the whole show jumped up and lost his shit on the side of the stage in front of Sam.

We took a long time getting out of there, our whole big gang assembled and working out details, which all ended up being meaningless since we all just went over to Union Jack's. I counted on Danny B. working the door to be cool with getting the kid in and figured it would blow the kid's teenage-Utah mind to go to a strip club. I hadn't counted on the precise process Oregon law requires of doormen. I figured Danny could just wave us all through. The VIP passes he gave us not only allowed us to forego the $3 cover, but allowed us in the event of a line to cut to the front. Danny sat at a podium blocking the entrance and had to stop each of us: me, Sam, Andy, Nathan, all of us, and hold up our ID in front of a small camera so it could be projected on a big screen and recorded in the event of some kind of trouble. The kid kept moving along the line, but didn't even move to show his real ID. He just stood there frozen. Bobby slipped him Lauren's old college ID and the kid was in some kind of shock and just stood there. Danny B. winced and said, "Man, is this really all you got?" and the kid just nodded nervously. Danny rolled his eyes at me and waved the kid in. I had to grab the kid and settle him down so he wouldn't start jumping up and down in celebration and get Danny in trouble.

Our party filled up two big booths and I sat at the bar with Rosie. She's such a mesmerizing paradox. I've had such a crush on her forever—her bright and sleepy eyes and hilarious astute observations, shared in her lazy, nasal drawl.

(The bridges over mountain creeks through southern October Oregon sunset, the lumber stacked, the pines behind, sheep in the field, chimneys exhaling, campers parked.)

Rosie and I talked about *Budding*, about her character Dawn and Danny B.'s character, Danny B. I told her about the new necessity for a re-write since confirming that my dramatization of a long lost friend's present reality had in fact turned out to be a prophetic unauthorized biography. Neither she nor Danny B. could believe how strange this was. But we all agreed we're excited to see what it becomes.

Drew showed up and looked great. People had warned us, Drew is bananas, incoherent, etc. and we were all dreading witnessing him in that condition. It'd be devastating to see such a lovable nut lose his grip, spill over like a basket overfilled with apples. But instead, he shined, funnier and more articulate than ever. Same old story of course: broke, changing jobs, projects in the works, but vitalized by the process instead of being bogged down by it.

Over Drew's shoulder, more than an hour after arriving, I first noticed a bare breast across the room. I was surprised by it before remembering, *oh yeah, there's a center of attention to this place that I hadn't even noticed yet.* By the time we left I still couldn't say what a single one of the dancers looked like. Not sure I ever even looked up a second time.

ALL OVER AND OVER

I was excited to introduce Drew as our ex-manager to Special J-2. The Utah kid was in a daze, sunken deep in his seat with a faraway stare, perhaps suffering his first public hard-on. Special J-2 asked about the EP I was trying to get done before tour and asked if he could put it out. I said I'd be relieved if he'd do so and asked for $350 for one day in the studio to get it all cleaned up and put together. As a symbol of our contract I gave him the artwork for it that I'd been carrying around with me. I showed him the picture of my dad that I found stuffed in the same pages of this notebook. Seems strange to me today to have done so.

I was surprised to find us all walking to a diner at 2:30 when the club closed, Special J-2 and the Utah kid joining us. Stuffed into a booth with me and Andy and Bobby and Nate and Rosie and Andy's friend from Seattle, Bobby was complaining about the lap dance he got and how it was exactly the same as if it had not happened except it costs $20 more than not happening.

I sat across from Andy with Special J-2 and his friend next to us. Rosie was too far away to talk to. We were all drunk, laughing about *whatever happened to so-and-so?* and *what about such-and-such?* and *I remember—remember that?* Lousy food but no one even noticed, chatting through drunken dreamtime. Were me and Andy out-shouting each other or does morning's sober mind amplify the impressions of drunkenness?

I said goodbye to Rosie in the middle of the road. We'll see each other in a couple days.

Andy lives north of the city a little, still in Portland proper even though it seems outside. It's a long street buried deep in leaves, each house a different shape and size, and all in different color combinations.

(Mountains north of Medford, OR glow orange through fog at sunset as we wind back down the far side. Orange streaks through the sky's wide stripes of pale blue and gray, like oil in a puddle.)

Andy and Emily's small house is so cozy. Her paintings all over the house are cute and menacing and strange in perfect ratios: self-portraits in caves or looking some unseen danger in its eye just beyond the canvas, in animal skins, startled. In one she is a little princess so happy, unaware of the black smear in the background.

In his little turtleneck sweater Booser the poodle barked over and over, apparently thinking that his little yip might be made threatening if he repeated it enough. 4:00 a.m., we climbed around each other to pile sleeping bags on the hardwood floor, flip open a futon, bend up onto the couch. An air mattress slowly deflated under me. At first I tried to continuously shift my weight. Drunk, shoulder-ache spread over me like a web, I lay half-asleep for hours, concentrating on how to lie so completely flat that my weight wouldn't settle anywhere like a long, slow game of *Light as a Feather, Stiff as a Board*-solitaire. The sun came up before I'd even had the chance to give up on sleeping.

Read the first chapter of *The Cosmic Serpent* before anyone else woke up. So immediately pulled in. Ram Dass, half reread, will be put aside for now. I needed it to transition into the shock of being removed from home, but it's so hokey as soon as it isn't completely necessary.

Great breakfast at a veggie diner place. One last meal with Danny B. Met his woman for a minute. Andy's off to the airport to pick up the other Chicago Hillary whose old car Amy is now trying to sell for parts, four months after leaving it at the garage for the afternoon.

And off into the long day off, south through beautiful, poor Oregon.

Later in the day, our leisurely start will make it seem dark early.

Long way to our hotel room in Redding.

It's twilight.

ALL OVER AND OVER

Redding. I drove the last few hours through Mt. Shasta, beautiful, etc., northern California. Listened to the *DaVinci Code* book-on-tape that my brother left on his laptop when he gave it to me. Absorbing in the same way that I devoured all the *Hardy Boys* books as a kid. In a van loud with road-hiss and wind, the narrator gets difficult to understand when he falls into different characters' funny accents. We got through the first half of the book in the last 140 miles. Must be an abridged version, otherwise how can this entire book be read out loud in two and a half hours? That's part of its mass appeal?

It's fake-smart. The plot devices are all simple and effective cliffhangers, which only suggest greater depths because of the esoteric references. But so far, those elements are only superficial decorations. It could just as easily take place at The Super Bowl instead of after hours at The Louvre.

Healthy Highways book paid off big time, found a whole new town none of us had ever heard of: Ashland, OR, fifteen miles north of the California border, home of The Oregon Shakespeare Festival and Southern Oregon University. We drove through the small town square area, hundreds of kids out trick or treating. Bobby was overwhelmed, flipping out, loving it and Sam was creeped out, both in response to the same Norman Rockwell/*Groundhog Day* vibe. But its natural foods co-op was a treasure to find, reminding us all of Weaver Street in Chapel Hill.

Packed with old hippies in costumes, one man wobbles in an over-sized troll head, but just a smidge of white face paint is enough for this other guy. And this old man is dressed up as a young boy dressed up as a cowboy? I got a stuffed squash, BBQ tofu, black rice and cashew salad, and a big salad for $7. The biodegradable utensils were made out of potatoes processed to make them indistinguishable from plastic. Reading this, Sam insisted on eating a spoon. We all flipped out.

It's bad for us to leave too much of the drive for after dark.

And, not yet adapted to Daylight Savings Time, it's getting dark early. And, not yet adapted to tour, it also means none of our spirits are entirely crushed yet, crushed in the way that's necessary to survive it. We each still have a little kick-back-against-it left in us. None of us are ready to fully submit to the group's momentum.

Headphones on and eyes closed, Nate stood for the last long bit of the drive. Sam had to stop to shit every 40 minutes for the first half of the day, and that's an obvious sign of panic attack or at least chronic restlessness setting in. And once it's dark out, but still early, you can't read or write, and not yet tired enough to fall asleep, those are the torture hours, the hours psyched to find a *Da Vinci Code* book-on-tape to pass the miles. Nate said it sounded like an adult voice from *Peanuts*. Sam said he could hear it, but couldn't follow it. That made me sad for my dearest old friend who's always been so extraordinarily bright, but so reckless with his brains. These days, his fixation with Myspace, his bias for sitting hypnotized by portable video games for hours on end — it scares me. These things must be in direct proportion to his inability to follow a book-on-tape, its complexity the literary equivalent of a summer blockbuster.

Redding always reminds me of the girl I met from here seven years ago, M_____. She lived in Chicago for maybe two months tops. We hung out together only once, a pathetic only-a-date-in-my-mind kind of hangout. Never spoke to each other again even once after that one afternoon. She'd never remember me.

K_____ was my neighbor and my ex-girlfriend's roommate. M_____ was her cousin or her cousin's friend. There were two of them in Chicago: K_____'s cousin and the cousin's friend. Whichever one wasn't M_____, the other girl, stayed in Chicago much longer. I talked to her all the time. Saw her around everywhere, but I don't remember her name or her face. I must've only been being nice to her so that she would possibly pass on to M_____, without really even noticing she was doing so, how nice she thought I was.

But now, recalling that strange, mostly celibate and totally isolated year, and that one stray afternoon attempting to reach out, I have to wonder: who do I think I was?

I was platonically living with and spending every day with a beautiful woman that I was afraid to have sex with because of all the obligations and expectations that doing so would inevitably tumble down on me. Circumstances were weird enough, I guess repressed me enough, I had to lash out every couple months, indulge in stupid, reckless, and irresponsible sex.

I was trying to avoid the relationship baggage that my deflated-self never would've had the strength to carry. But by restraining from the positive aspects of the relationship (i.e. sex) I ended up living out only the bad parts: the squashing fatigue of every mumble. I now know that I may as well have at least gotten laid. At least when I see her around every so often now, I have to think that for a second.

But truly, in a year or more, only that one afternoon with M_____ did it ever occur to me that here is some lady that I want to be my girlfriend and I'm willing to be whatever kind of klutz she might need me to be to make it happen.

Her and the other girl must've been in Chicago because K_____ was pregnant then? Some kind of family spy sent out to lend an eye or a helping hand?

But what crazy egotism on my part to have ever thought it possible I might've had some kind of chance with M_____.

K_____ set it up. The three of us went one crowded August afternoon to the public pool near Fullerton and Western. Some people we knew were doing some kind of synchronized swimming thing some afternoons there as a kind of guerrilla theater. Those in the know knew what time on which days to show up to see the Mexican mothers and all the kids all made fools of by those cool kids spontaneously swarming in synchronized public swim. There wasn't one of these events that afternoon, but they'd been happening a lot and people we knew were organizing them and the Park District was trying to figure out strategies to combat it, but no defense mechanism had come together correctly. So it was hot out in a way that demanded dealing with, but beyond that we all had the pool on our minds.

It was one of those busy Saturday afternoons where there's no room to move in the pool. M_____, me and K_____ swimming. I imagine now that I must've been strutting some. This must've been August 2001, not only before the great American humbler 9/11, but also before 30 or 40 more pounds of me materialized.

I don't remember anything except that I must've been high. I don't remember that either, but I know I was always high then.

It was too crowded to move in the pool. The girls decided we should go see some movie instead so we could sit in air conditioning. They made fun of me for not knowing what *Ghost World* was.

But here's the whole story of this story I remember whenever I'm in Redding, knowing only that this one lady came from here and assumedly returned to here and wondering if maybe I'll run into her.

And the story, it's a simple story.

It's a simple bummer how crowded the pool is. I'm pretending it's totally normal for me to be hanging out with my ex-girlfriend's roommate K_____, and she, to her credit, plays along for my sake. The girls get out and towel off, decide we'll all go to a movie. I hang on the side, still submerged, as we talk. They're done, dried off and ready to go and getting impatient but I can't get out of the pool. I need to remain submerged until my boner dies down. They're confused and in a hurry and I don't have any idea what litany of explanations kept tumbling out of me for a good five minutes, stalling while they keep at it, "Come on, we're late." And I hang on the side of the pool, my arm on the ledge.

That specific afternoon hard-on is all I think of every couple times a year that I pass through Redding.

Nate, Sam and Bob walked across the street to a casino's Halloween party. Been alone in the room for a much needed couple hours of quiet. Traveling, always in such close quarters, practical dormancy usually overcomes my sex drive. But of course, every one of us beats off whether aware of any urgency or not, any time one suddenly finds one's self left alone—*won't get this chance again soon and don't know how long I'm gonna have it for now.*

Watched Sean Hannity interview President Bush with and without the TV muted and it's totally fucking insane. They both have these arrogant smiles while they slap each other's backs and seem to even be winking at each other over and over. By what standard anywhere could this *possibly* be defined as journalism? I thought Fox News could no longer surprise me, but I was wrong. This time no spin was even needed to get me enraged and scratching my head. It's so offensive, their lack of enough respect for the audience to even bother hiding things a little bit. Shouldn't they at least have to agree to submit to that?

Today's Danny B. text correspondence—

"My girls 5 year old daughter is down wit Make Believe. Album Sounds Great! Gd 2 C Ya my friend!"

To which I responded that we had a great time, and if he ever wants to ditch his van of stiffs and jump into our van of corpses and tag along we'd love to have him.

To which he responded—

"Fuk Yah. That van is sweet. We could stack more and make more money. But Sam aint allowed 2 fuk any of em!'

*

ALL OVER AND OVER

NOVEMBER 1, 2006

Grampa's ex-birthday. Day of the dead, exactly one month since my Jade Tree check was sent out and still hasn't arrived; sent to the coach house, where my mail has been forwarded from since June, lost somewhere in the Chicago postal system. Haven't asked them to send me a new one yet because I know they'll be weird, since a distant associate of mine asked them to do that years ago and then tried to cash both checks. After all the royalty excuses and fiascos and never getting paid any more, it really must be only vanity that makes me even pay attention or count on it at all anymore.

The one guy, it's been all pink Fred Perry shirts and diamond studded earrings ever since losing a lot of weight quickly gave him the nerve to finally act like a college freshman at 37-years-old. In his suburban house where everything is cable TV and "Punk" like *The Blues Brothers— we like both kinds of music, punk and hardcore*. And always laughing at us with his condescending laugh, like we're such losers. He shouts and shouts everyone down and talks and talks and talks, but if you ever get him to sit still for one second, if he's ever quiet for just one second, you look into his eyes and it's just a blank stare. Just the static of suburban cable television and a career in "punk" bouncing back and forth between those studded ears. And his partner: loveably riddled with hip insecurities, bullied into submission. What a bummer power dynamic to witness.

Anyways, November 1st. We were going to go for an adventure to the nearby waterfall, but it's raining and we aren't so adventurous as to deal with that. No one else is up yet to notice that our plans will be cancelled.

I walked down to the lobby to wait for a phone interview to call. Down the long halls of these sprawling-winged hotels, it's funny to walk past someone. It's silent and you each see the other approach from 100 yards away, *'Incoming! . . . Incoming! . . . Still Incoming!'* and it really seems like it may never happen. You look for a second. You look away for a second. Do I say hello? Good morning? It's crazy not to. I'm not playing that game. God damn good manners are nice. *Here it comes and finally almost. Almost, not quite yet. Still not quite yet.* And you just cannot fucking believe it hasn't happened, but here it comes and then we cross. I always say hello, every fucking time this happens and the other asshole is always looking down and away. Happened half a dozen times this morning already in just one walk to the lobby.

In one long hall, the two plastic patio-furniture chairs from the balcony had been pulled in and placed on opposite sides of a door, facing the wall three feet ahead of them. A young guy, must've been a full ten years younger than me, sat in one chair staring straight ahead. He had the shave and black suit only CIA or some kind of creepy Religious Right conspiracy would require. I figured that he must've been a guard for whatever whoever was doing in that room. As I got closer, 20 feet away maybe, he stood up and turned around towards the door. An old man stood in the doorway dressed in an identical impeccable suit. They shook hands and the young man introduced himself. Must've been some kind of interview. A cryptic neat cardboard sign was hung on the door, but there was no stopping to try to make out what it said.

Passing back 20 minutes later returning from the lobby down the same hall, two new young men each sat in a seat. They both sat up perfectly straight and stared straight ahead. They appeared perfectly symmetrical and identical. Neither even blinked as I walked past them and I considered it entirely likely, if not probable, that whatever it is they are doing there, whatever the specifics and whoever the sponsor, they each must've given me one glance as I passed and thought to themselves that I was exactly the kind of thing that they'd be working to eradicate.

Last time in San Francisco, a couple months ago for the *Ladies and Gentlemen* premiere at the Frameline festival there, was such a joy: being in the same place for a few days in a row, just me and Amy. As filmmakers, we got the VIP treatment, the best of which was access to a party at the hillside mansion of Tom and Jerry—naked young guys in the hot tub, open bars and hot hors d'oeuvres galore. Mid-party The San Francisco Gay Men's Choir suddenly performed, thirty or fifty of them lined up along the steps. The mansion was built into a hill, the whole city spread out below. Its back was turned as if turning to look over your shoulder, you find the entire city has crept up on you. It felt like access to The Gay Illuminati and even knowing no one there except each other, it was such a blast. One of those splitting-a-cab-with-strangers-and-not-remembering-the-ride-home kind of nights.

We spilled red wine on the white carpet in the living room. Only the line for the bathroom through the sliding doors was hanging out inside and somehow in those few steps we managed to act out our destiny as the straight klutzes. A very cool and sympathetic young house boy or handler-type guy flew right into action and knew exactly what to do and the proper order in which to do it.

Not much later, walking down a flight of stairs, Amy recognized the middle-aged and buff, maybe Greek, man that was pointed out to us earlier as Jerome, the Jerry half of our hosts. Wearing only an apron over his wife beater in the cold Bay night air, coming up the stairs, he balanced a wide platter of something that he was en route to serve. Amy, feeling a little bit princess-drunk in this situation, a personally customized utopia from her perspective, opened her arms out wide into the wingspan of a pre-embrace, and descending the steps, bellowed a long, slow, impassioned, *"Jeeeeeeeerooooooooooome!"* to our host that she'd never met. His eyes popped open wide and he gave the distinct shocked look of, *I don't know who this straight bitch is, but I'm getting the fuck out of here,* and stepped aside. Amy, perhaps assuming their embrace would've functioned as her brakes, instead tumbled down the stairs. Letting her pass, Jerry stepped immediately back on to the footpath and proceeded to deliver his platter upward and onward. I let him pass at the top of the stairs before taking flight to Amy in a pile in the garden at the bottom of the stairs.

The time before that when we were here, we were in Berkeley, across from the Indian restaurant Todd had taken us to years ago when he lived there. I talked to my dad on the phone for perhaps the longest and easiest phone conversation of our lives. We were both drunk. I had missed a big family dinner that day, maybe a christening of a cousin's kid or the triplets had a birthday or something and I called him to get the scoop. We scooped. It was only fifteen minutes, but it was sort of an unexpected exhale after a lifetime of breath-holding.

So: Amoeba, burritos, Jill, hopefully Leroy who's been living out in the woods across the Golden gate bridge in some kind of artist's residency. Amy has a long Amoeba list I'm happy to hunt down.

Playing The Hotel Utah Saloon, our ban from Bottom of the Hill apparently still in effect. San Francisco might perhaps be the ideal case study of our touring career:

1996—Bottom of the Hill, to no one

1997—Bottom of the Hill, half-full

1998—Bottom of the Hill, sold out

1999—Bottom of the Hill, sold out

2000—Two nights Bottom of the Hill, sold out

2001—Two nights Bottom of the Hill, one night sold out, the next half-empty

2002—Two nights Bottom of the Hill, both half empty

2001—One night pretty full

2003—One night sold out but Hella was opening and everyone must've been there for them

2004—One night half-empty

2005—One night, no one there

Ah, such a neat decade career arc. The 2004 tour she had given us too big of a guarantee, I think a grand to play to fifty or seventy-five people. I tried to get her to take it back, insisted we didn't want it. But she preferred to make us take it and forever banish us to the back-rooms-of-Mexican-restaurant-type clubs of the world.

Eh. Pfft.

(The MC of The Miss Outdoors Competition says, "Without further to do –")

*

ALL OVER AND OVER

NOVEMBER 2, 2006

My first thought waking up at Shay's in The Mission was that George Segal was never a very good actor, no matter how much I like a lot of the movies he's in. Don't know why.

I dreamt there was some kind of event at Chris Connelly's house and a big bunch of us were there. Everyone was outside, but I got trapped in the basement. Eventually escaping after a brief panic, I ran to catch up and hopped up on to a long banister to slide down like a hotshot teenager in a movie. But my balls got hung up on a sharp ornamental handle. I arrived at this party—maybe we were about to play—with shredded pants exposing my bloodied testicles.

First thing this morning I looked at a book from a Dutch museum, 15th-16th century paintings. A lot of the paintings were familiar to me, more than I would've expected, and it was good to sit with them before even speaking out loud yet. Maybe it's because so many of these paintings were specific examples in Berger's *Ways of Seeing*, but I was aware that I could admire the compositions and occasionally a subtlety, but none of them could really hit me. I had to force the mental leap, *Oh right, 450 years ago a man made this with his hands*. I also learned that this short beard and feathered hair that I've passively acquired would've been very chic in 16th century Netherlands.

We arrived in San Francisco yesterday around 5:00, a couple hours early for load-in. Deferring to each other over and over, none of us would articulate where he'd prefer to go to spend that time, and ironically that caused a bit of a flare up between us. Approaching the city, it was getting later and later to decide and we needed to change course according to what we all agreed on. Finally we chose Haight-Ashbury — Amoeba for me.

We laughed a lot then pulling into town, dusk descending on the bay. We tried to figure out together: they must've built these bridges before the town could really be built, right? Or everything was brought over by boat? Sure, the 1849ers and all, but what a strange, crazy-young city.

With San Francisco as our spontaneous case study we were stunned, how insane—the 20th century. The earth transformed. And now, with the disconnect from history that that century's means of production has inevitably created, exploitation ubiquitous, of course paranoia is the norm. Suddenly, even more so than ever before, what is it to be human? Everyone's apocalypse-obsessed because there's no other alternative to consumer capitalism in any vital and present way—Consumer Capitalism or Total Obliteration. The structures of capitalism isolate every individual both through flattery and alienation. Pulling a vegetable from the ground and eating it shouldn't be the shock that it is. So of course no one can imagine the world continuing on without him or herself present as a witness. Their own isolated perspective being the only way that they've ever experienced the world, it's simpler to imagine the total spontaneous destruction of the world than to imagine the world continuing on without the continuity of one's perspective. It's common sense.

Anyhow, we arrived in Haight-Ashbury after an afternoon invested in *The Cosmic Serpent*. Ha, funny. Is that a thing: people become kind of hippies after 30? *I arrived in Haight-Ashbury after an afternoon invested in* The Cosmic Serpent. Ah, well. The book is well written. He makes connections between genetic science and deeply intuitive shamanic knowledge. It's mysterious stuff and a less well-written book wouldn't be able to hold all of it. It unfolds in a personal way. The story of these connections, the results of his own research shocking him, grounds it well.

Browsing a Tibetan Buddhist shop that we parked near, I bought a ring of coiled DNA or serpents, some twisted ladder without beginning or end. After browsing super-expensive bells, a ten dollar ring seemed like less of an impulse purchase than it normally may have.

In Amoeba I did a quick mental inventory:
Shoes—hand-me-downs from Mike.
Socks—gift from an old girlfriend years ago.
Pants, undershirt and shirt—all-hand-me downs from Dad.

My jacket—free from Levis, years ago in case Owls ever became cool.

My current credit card debt is $3500. What's $3570, right? I don't spend money on clothes. I could DJ and pay for the records in one night, right? Putting two-thirds of what I picked up away, and leaving with only the exceptional bargains or finds, it ended up $70.

- Used Popul Vuh, "Sei Still, Wisse Ich Bin"
- Xhol Caravan reissue
- Marissa Nadler
- A cheap used Stockhausen CD
- Cybil Baer

I realize that my Books-and-Records Rule of only buying used or exceptional deals sets me up in a way to always find an exceptional deal. This is a sneaky way to not only justify any purchase, but I also get the satisfaction of feeling like I collect these things despite myself. But honestly, where was I going to find any of that stuff as affordable? And I walk out of places all the time without buying anything.

By the time we all met back at the van Nate was agitated. He told me that he bought a Bollywood comp and I blurted out without thinking, "Yeah, a lot of that stuff is great, just gotta be careful to stay clear of the '80s." He looked. The collection he bought was all '80s. I tried to backpedal, pointing out that I generally trust Luaka Bop comps, but he still gave me a look of *you're such a fucking know-it-all* and I did feel like a dick.

Later I'd realize that it wasn't me. He was already buried in something, his own head or something else going on unknown to me. I kissed his ass a bit as he stomped around and pouted through the night, but he seemed most happy to be bummed.

ALL OVER AND OVER

Sam explained that some girl that he used to go up to DeKalb to sleep with now lived here. To discourage her from coming to the show, he'd told her an elaborate lie. He said it was his birthday and his girlfriend was flying to town to visit him. So he asked us to all play along that #1—it's his birthday and #2—if any random woman is somehow immediately contextualized in any small way as his girlfriend, we shouldn't be surprised or confused and we should instead please gracefully confirm his front.

The Hotel Utah is a cool old room. The doorman says Joe DiMaggio used to sneak off with Marilyn Monroe there. Smallest room with a balcony that I've ever been in and it's a cool effect. All old, ornate wood. Dark wood compounded like that has such a great rich-warm-strong-soft-deep-fragrant quality to it. Lots of little details carved into the woodwork. A couple tables and some connected booths wind around the entire strange and fluid shape of the room. We had to load into a hallway far too tight to fit all of our stuff into. It began to rain softly.

Strange how even in these cities that I've been to 25 times, even with their familiar details—that same security guard at Pancho Villas—the overall impression is still sometimes so profound. I feel as strange as if I'd never been anywhere before.

Nice half-hour walk from Shay's to Pancho Villas this morning. Misting rain, but not enough to make the walk uncomfortable. I counted my steps out to the constant rhythm of those lines from that Lee Hazelwood song, "some weeks in San Francisco, subsisting on Nabisco cookies and bad dreams . . . something-something and paranoia." We passed an insane ratio of facial tattoos per capita. Sam pointed out the number of people with scarred cheeks, and explained that it was because of the Mexican tar heroin common here that's most efficiently shot up into the cheeks. Saw a few midgets.

We took a detour down a community-sponsored graffiti alley. It made me totally reconsider what I have always superficially considered graffiti to be. Without giving it much thought, the philosophy behind it has always appealed to me as a democratizing force, re-appropriating public space. But I usually assumed graffiti wouldn't be stylistically engaging to me, whatever skill may be on display or not. But in this alley, these were such thoughtful and fleshed-out works of art dealing with their contexts—the alley itself and the neighborhood—in articulate and surprising ways. Each piece was striking as its own unique self, while simultaneously being amplified by its proximity to all the other pieces. The alley as a whole was a different, more complex experience, like a salad versus each berry or nut or vegetable component. We took our time sauntering through it, hardly bothered by either our hunger or the rain.

Inside Pancho Villas the line was long. The suspense was building even more so after the long walk. A man with Down's Syndrome walked up to the door at Pancho Villas and halted, demanding loudly and tersely, *"Door!"* The man at the end of the line standing closest to the door was shocked to realize that it was him being addressed, but he smiled widely as he opened the door.

The burrito hypnotized me. I sat across from Sam and after a couple minutes I looked at his plate and couldn't believe how quickly he'd eaten his burrito. Then I looked down at my own plate and realized that I'd eaten the same amount. No mindful-eating meditation could stand up to Pancho Villa.

Walking back to Shay's, we stopped in and browsed this weird store. It had taxidermy and fossils, bones, owl pellets, crystals, shark teeth, peacock feathers, "The Living Jewels"— bugs of every size and shape and color — Crispin Glover's weird little books like ($30!) spooky hardcover zines, a staggering variety of plants and flowers, lotus, bonsai, complete skeletons of small birds and bats and turtles, shark teeth, penis bones of a few different species, petrified wood, the fake eyes used in taxidermy for a huge variety of species. How delicate the bones of all these small species are. Like dental floss synchronized into bulbs and delicate curves, they hardly seem like they could possibly function as we assume bones should. We ducked in the pirate store next door, but after what we'd all just seen, even a fucking pirate store was a letdown. Sam announced the store's promotion to the new first place he'd go if he ever became a millionaire.

Walking the last couple blocks, there was a big crew shooting a commercial in a small park in the light rain. Shay picked some rosemary from a bush and I thought, "how strange it's just growing there on the street." But actually it was the only thing within my view at that moment that it wasn't strange was there. How strange I even thought that it was strange. Everything I see on a city street has been filtered through a human mind. Nothing is as it is. It has all been purposefully designed by *someone*.

Nate laughed and told us about the time that he'd visited San Francisco as a teenager having never been anywhere but on the farm and Minneapolis before. Having no way to comprehend hills, he found the entire city distressing, alarming even. He said that he thought at the time that it looked like someone had just spilled Legos in a big pile and called it a city and left it instead of finishing it.

I liked this description of San Francisco from the introduction to a Green Day article that I read in the paper here this morning: "San Francisco is a European-style city where beauty and creativity are always just a few steps away from danger, demanding constant engagement instead of allowing passivity." A vaguely Situationist summation.

When we arrived to the show last night Pearsall was already hanging out. Sam had said on the ride over that he still hated seeing him because of the ambiguity of *did he or didn't he ever rip us off when we were all kids?* I pointed out that Jade Tree ripped him and Corley off worse than those two ever could've ripped us off. And if they did cheat us, at least they were young, disorganized, eighteen- or twenty-year-olds, overwhelmed by the responsibilities of their ambitions. Any bigger label would've ripped us off worse. And those two got all haughty only when Jade Tree re-released the Captain Jazz record, so why wouldn't some young guys in that situation get a little righteous? I was glad to hear later that Sam had enjoyed hanging out with him for the first time in years.

Still working at a print shop, out of everyone he'd moved out there with, Pearsall was the last one left on the west coast. Still the same: endearingly ornery, in a way that no one else that I know could pull off; lots of talk of Midwest-representing and weed and skating and the good old days of Heart Attack and emo. He got a ticket for peeing in the alley next to the club.

(Rainbow high across the golden hills an hour outside the city. Yesterday the hills we drove through were all charred black. We missed a turn and had to take a two-lane country road a few miles to make it up and it really did feel like being alone on a scorched moon. All we could figure was that it was some kind of harvesting technique?)

D____ was there too, all hipped up in a floppy hat, recently married and recently sober again: nice to see him and chat for a while. Always interesting for me to hear about any Chicagoan moving somewhere new. I listen and think *They're mad, who could leave Chicago? What were they thinking? What did they ever expect?* And they all always talk about how much they love Chicago and miss it.

In that same ten-minute conversation about starting over and a fresh start and all, D____ lamented the pile of old four-track tapes that he needed to sort through and organize, but how he's being lazy about it. That reminded me of him re-issuing all his five- to seven-year-old zines a couple years ago, pseudo-profound poetry motivated mostly by thinly veiled attempts at vengeance. Dense language as an attempt to make simplistic ideas appear heavy really is the worst. Half of his zine anthology was a big cryptic *Fuck You* directed specifically to me. I had forgotten about that until we were hanging out there on the sidewalk together smoking in the light rain. I didn't stick around.

Leroy showed up and we sat at the far end of the bar together. He's just completed his one-month residency at some ex-military base isolated somewhere up in the hills north of the Golden Gate Bridge. He got an extension on his stay but needs to crash at his friend's small apartment with a newborn baby until the place opens up again. Then he hopes to stay beyond that into their off-season and get an internship. Sounds amazing: a cabin to live in, a gymnasium-sized studio to work in, all meals provided and a $500/month stipend. He wakes up and hikes and lets his mind wander and then returns and puts his mind's wanderings to music. I'm excited for him. He's always been such a super-cool, deep, thoughtful guy with a ton of daring and talent. A perfectly flattering sideman in so many contexts, he's always made whoever he was accompanying sound so much better: Liz Phair, 5-Style, Wilco, Beth Orton, or Marvin Tate.

Marvin: whom I last ran into at the grocery store where he'd just started working his second job. Teaching poetry in the Chicago public school system wasn't getting him by.

We sat for a long while after the show. Leroy said that me and Amy's wedding was one of the funnest nights ever. His favorite part was seeing people dancing over here and eating over there and here's the bar and people are milling about and then there's the smoking room across the hall where my dad and Azita would meet or Jimmy and Dee would hold court and Leroy said he was aware for a moment of having such a great time and standing alone taking it all in, when he saw me and Amy in a corner. We were laughing together and no one was bugging us and he said that's how he always remembers that night—the surprise of seeing us and remembering *oh yeah, this is their center-of-attention night, I forgot.*

Jill and Shay showed up. I was surprised to hear that Shay had moved. He seemed so immersed in his art restoration job in Sarasota. He'd given us and Need New Body the back room tour of the museum a few years ago. What a crew being told to tiptoe cautiously through these art labs and listen closely like little kids on a field trip. He and his partner there, Dave, talked us through all the sensitive minutia of their processes and all dozen of us stood stunned, hanging on their every word. Raising his hand before asking a question, Jeff made us all laugh.

Hella missed it. They'd gone to Disney World for the afternoon. Hella, Need New Body and Make Believe: "The More is More 2004 Tour."

Later that afternoon, alone in the sculpture garden with a full-size bronze replica of Michelangelo's *David*, I had to concentrate to keep myself from breaking out into a screaming mad dash flight. For a couple years there, this had become my most common reaction when facing a powerful work of art: Fear. In that case specifically, David was obviously as alive as anything else ever had been or ever will be. The privilege that such perfect beauty and size granted him, what was to stop him from pouncing on me, squashing me like an ant with a single, thoughtless step? I realize that sculpture gardens depend on the immediate impression that they may come to life at any second. Anything less than striking that fear in me would always leave me ho-hum. But my Fear of Art phase that couple years was different than that.

Cave paintings did it. *Cave paintings!* What prompted that initial impulse to attempt to represent the world in a subjective and stylized manner? Did that buffalo on the cave wall make the same impression on its contemporaries as the panic that evacuated the first movie theaters of the early 20th century? *The train is coming straight for us!*

The sky in Renaissance paintings: demons and angels do battle up there, ducking between black clouds. What fear and paranoia such a cosmology demanded of its subjects. And what intensity of stylization that fear and paranoia instilled in the paintings. Heavy.

The meticulous patterns of Persia, Mesopotamian pottery, the perfect never-perfect spontaneous circles of Japanese monks, the evolution of armor—all these things strike the same profound Beautiful-Fear chords in me, make me feel like some storm on a beach lives in my stomach. I am alive as part of a continuum. My consciousness, whatever it is, is the same consciousness that countless before me have praised and suffered; its eternal mystery is never any closer to any tangible answer or solution, but these objects survive as proof. Praise and wonder will find expression. This expression rolls on on its own accord. At our very best potential realized, we are each nothing more than simply an infrastructure for this expression.

*

All Over and Over #2

SAN FRANCISCO—HOUSTON

ALL OVER AND OVER

NOVEMBER 2, 2006

Shay and I greeted each other with hearty handshakes, but didn't talk much immediately. Jill gave me a big hug and a big smile and it hit me how much I appreciate the ease that our decade-old lazy friendship has acquired. We've never sought each other out, have never attempted to keep in touch, but always fall right in with each other whether it's been a year or three years since we'd last seen each other.

She glows. She's truly radiant: mellow, southern, and stoned. She greeted Leroy sitting next to me by putting out her hand and smiling big, "Hi, I don't know you yet," and no wonder everyone always thinks she's flirting with them. Who wouldn't want to think so? When is anyone, especially a woman that looks so good, ever able to speak to a stranger so easily?

It was Jill who first brought Bobby to check out a Joan of Arc show when he moved to Chicago and they met in the art school dorms. And it was Jill who first introduced me and Bobby when I ran into them at Earwax one day in what, 1997? Sam remembers me being excited about her after the one date that we went on back then, telling him, "I've met the coolest girl. She eats even sloppier than you do." Bobby remembers that Jill hated Ann because ten years ago Ann said she looks like a mouse.

She's still working at the bookstore but now also assisting a blind, deaf sculptor. She lets herself in and the woman will be sitting in silence in the dark at the kitchen table. Jill puts her hand on the woman's arm to let her know that she's there, but it doesn't scare the woman because she's expecting it. I don't know how she'd know what time it is.

On a few occasions Jill has forgotten something and needed to return to the house. She's afraid of frightening the woman by showing up unexpectedly and touching her. So with no other way of making herself known, Jill decided it's better to just walk through the house and past the woman and complete her task without making her presence known.

One time the woman was standing at the sink with both hands at the faucet, simply standing there while the water ran over her hands. Another time she was standing in the hall sideways, just standing perfectly still and silent while Jill picked up the laundry she'd forgotten.

They communicate with their hands. They write out words using the other's pointer finger as a pen on her palm like a piece of paper. I couldn't understand until Jill took both my hands into hers and showed me, *H-E-L-L-O*. She picks the woman up a couple times a week and takes her to her studio where the woman sculpts for hours without breaking concentration.

I told Jill that I'd had enough of traveling and I'm staying home for real this time. It's so nice to confide that to someone and get a smile in response. She told me she was proud of me and happy for me.

The Hotel Utah Saloon filled up pretty well. It was a show dynamic unique to that particular room: people all sat tightly around us, up close to the stage. Behind them a lot of people stood to watch and the back walls were then filled with more seated people as were the steps to the bar. The balcony was right above our heads and a few rows of people deep. It was a tight, intimate feeling, but more relaxed than a small space like that would usually provoke. The same population density at any show in any small town would have had more familiar and self-conscious show rituals, but here everyone could just be cool. It should've been an excellent setting to relax into.

But Nate was having trouble with his kick drum. Still grumpy and pouting, he stomped off stage between each song. The whole first half of the set we couldn't build up a head of steam. Only after placing both Ecstatic Sushine amps and a giant Canola Oil container that we'd found in the storage room next door all in front of the kick drum did we finally get any sort of flow working to our advantage. And I had eaten a great messy veggie burger too late before the show. So, plagued by belches, I fumbled through my call to those slippery primal forces that occasionally condescended to allow me to channel them.

As we began to pack up slowly after the last song, the sound man grabbed the mic and announced that a band from New Mexico on tour with no show that night had showed up and was about to play. We thought our night was over, but instead we had to pack up quickly and backline, trapping ourselves in behind their equipment which was already beginning to fill the stage. They were astonishingly loud Death-Prog? We were all bummed, already pooped and then had this dropped on us. But having been in their shoes before, I was happy to meet those guys and chat a bit after their set.

Sam A. was in town visiting a friend. We stepped outside to talk and he immediately jumped into apology-mode. "I never said Amy wasn't pretty enough to cut her hair short!" and I had a hard time talking him down and making him understand that I know better than anyone how she can get defensive sometimes with a drink in her and I knew how she was that night. It's funny to be laughing while someone is so desperately and earnestly pleading and apologizing and you can only laugh because you know it's such a no big deal that how could anyone get worked up about it. I just like the way Sam talks so much that I don't really even care what he's saying. Is that objectifying my friend's voice? He sounds just like the singer of The Dead Milkmen.

A cop was being a super pain in the ass while we tried to load out. The New Mexico band's van was in the way. The cop insisted that I drive around the block until we could load, and then I had to sit in the car watching a street cleaner slowly approach in the rear-view mirror. While I sat in the driver's seat with the car running, Shay helped us load out quickly, only to find a ticket on his truck parked just up the street from us. No good deed goes unpunished.

Sam told me that he's now hit the point where nothing that any of the three of us could possibly do could annoy him. I told him that I hoped it wasn't just a phase at the one-week mark. The hard part is nurturing that outlook once it's achieved, like our old motto about getting high being easy, but staying high being a life's greatest achievement.

We parked across the street from Shay and Jill's in a spot that we'd need to move from by 7:00 a.m., which of course we slept through. Shay and Jill live next door to each other and as we walked up Shay announced, "Night caps over here, beddy-bye to the left." None of us knew whose home we were stepping into, but it turned out by volunteering for a night cap that me and Bobby stayed with Shay.

He had a beautiful long apartment, one hallway wide front to back and a dozen doors along the walls. It was meticulously clean, no dust in the corners. Me and Bobby found this so impossible that we tried to think of scientific reasons that there just might be no dust in San Francisco. Seemed like every wall had been freshly painted. We dropped our stuff in the room in the far back of the house and trotted off through the rain.

Went to the same bar that we'd been to before when staying with Jill. Real classy looking old-timey place that doesn't seem hokey in a martini and cigar kind of way, just a nice old wood bar with lots of glass that's been kept up nicely. Even though it doesn't correspond directly to a specific location from either, it seems like it could've just as easily been a location in *Love Streams* as *Casablanca*. We each ordered a whiskey and the bartender was beautiful in a plain kind of way, lots of personality and immediately friendly without being overbearing or phony.

We laughed telling familiar stories that one or the other of us may have only partially remembered. We compared our loves for friends in common, often agreeing that the obvious shortcomings or frustrations that each dealt with was exactly what made each of them so loveable. The bar was quiet and the lights came on soon.

We walked back through the rain. The streets were empty at 2:00 a.m. and I couldn't believe this cozy upscale neighborhood was the same Mission District I thought I had a vague impression of from early-90s punk bands. Shay said his roommate has lived there for twelve years and they have rent control at $1200. The identical apartment upstairs was renting for $3000.

We sat in Shay's room and looked at a book of paintings by Alexis Rockman. Shay knows someone that works for him, so he had a little insight into the processes of these strange vegetal and organic collages. "Organic matter," a vague enough term that some might consider it a given in most paintings, was made the central priority in these—almost-chimeras, decay and organizational modes of rain forests. It all set my mind reeling.

We watched an absurdist YouTube music video about a German man with bananas for hands; made me miss my decade of always being high.

Shay showed us what he's been working on and calling "painting with pure paint." I couldn't understand the concept until holding various small examples in my hand. He would swirl the colors together. They aren't mixed. There are no blocks of color and no canvas. Just the paint itself and the small folds and bends the colors negotiate between themselves. He has many of these swatches and from them he takes the most interesting parts and cuts them out into whatever shapes the colors provoke. With these swatches he then puts together images like a patchwork quilt. From there, once the subject is determined, he flushes out the scene by painting in the details. This binds the complex patterns of the "pure paint" with more traditional brushwork.

A painting of three birds in a small tree really struck me, the surface of the paint perfect as the textures of the birds. It was all such an exciting example to me of the purity of one's practice—trusting it and surrendering to it, allowing it to lead you—achieving surprising and deep results. A skull-and-crossbones, some eyes, flowers, and an insect were all familiar forms made new by the process, but none were as developed as this bird painting. Their feathers and beaks and the bark on the trees all had textures that seemed truer than what the eye can usually catch. And I don't mean impressionism or psychedelia. They were flat and hyper-glossy, no more textured to the touch than a thick pool of coagulated dish soap.

(Just named the tour "Road Trip with Friends 2006")
(Hell is a Guitar Center in Fresno)

So what struck me so deeply in Shay's paintings—knowing that his work for years as an Art Restorer must've required an infinitesimally refined touch and keen eye—is the depth of his knowledge and concentration regarding this singular, specific medium. When he described the process of these paintings to me, though I immediately recognized the connection to my own approaches towards writing, however much I wanted to prove and demonstrate that our approaches were somehow parallel, I couldn't put together a coherent analogy.

(G.W. School Supply—how ironic. Doesn't everyone think of Bush?)

It was so on the tip of my tongue and I was drunk enough to not hold my tongue—*But I mine words in this way too*—or something. But it all seemed like vanity to try to ingratiate myself and my work, however apparent the connections seemed to me.

I was humbled. Years ago I must've decided that I'd be a Generalist, do what I enjoy and get into what I get into. I always knew that I could never think of myself as a professional musician because as soon as I ever did so, the requirements would warp and then what? The music could never be for its own sake any longer if my livelihood depended on it entirely. The true lover of music working in service to specific, personal sonic-visions could never be a *Professional*. And in that regard I've certainly maintained my obligations dutifully. I'll never confuse pouring beers or carrying equipment around for my passions. I love odd jobs and the strange glimpses I get a day at a time of other people's lives. That's always interesting. But even when I hate being at work, I know that I could never play my songs for a living. I especially can't understand the hired guns that play other peoples' songs for a living. I mean, going on tour solely as a job, if you didn't have an investment in the music; what a nightmare job. But so, we've made these couple short films and now shot the feature. I've written some whatever articles for various magazines. But I can't really play guitar well. The way I practice is putting it down for a couple months at a time so that when I pick it up again my dexterity may be compromised, but my approach is refreshed. I can't read music and I don't know any sort of formal arranging skills.

I've never been a specialist in anything and now I feel like a phony. I've spent years at a time dissecting songs. And I've dug through my own guts and rearranged them in countless variations for fun. But I always stray and move on.

My Life as a Generalist—a fine dilettante's biographical subtitle. My last couple years living at the loft, I'd play guitar for an hour, get bored, write for an hour, get bored, make some weird computer music, get bored, leave my room for a minute, see Dave cutting up laundry detergent bottles and sculpting and stitching them into nine-foot robots, or Rob Roy looking for the perfect circuit board design deep in the patterns of the Persian rug he'd pace, and then I'd get excited again and start the process all over again playing guitar. This constant variation and the sense of community kept things fresh, kept me moving and working.

But now I wonder if perhaps I've never been able to get deep enough into any one thing. It seems so impossible to me. A month or a few months at a time, I can't help but do so, but the sustained attention . . .

What are the analogous approaches of the pure painting to music?

Mike and I are on the cover of the *Newcity* in Chicago today. It's extra embarrassing to not even know what the picture looks like. I read the thing online and it's not as bad as it could be. Boring, but boring is hardly the worst I've come to expect.

I like that Mike admits that his songs might sometimes come across as mean-spirited. I never knew that he knew that. Not sure if it makes it any better or worse that he knows it, and I don't think it effects my reaction really, but it pleases me to know that he's not blind to what he sometimes does. He can't be as mean-spirited of a guy as the frequent persona in those songs if he can recognize how mean-spirited the songs can sometimes be.

*

ALL OVER AND OVER

NOVEMBER 3, 2006

Winning lyric of last night — opening band, all the music drops out and the guy rattles off in an urgent, dramatic whisper: "It has been said before that love is incomplete without you. Today, this I do not believe."

Pulled into Fresno and checked into our hotel. Only had about half an hour before heading over to the show. From Portland to San Francisco, every single person that we mentioned we're gong to Fresno to responded with, "White Trash." All protests to the term fully acknowledged, everyone who said so must've never been to Bakersfield before. Fresno seemed like just a giant strip mall like Colorado Springs or Sarasota or everywhere. Unlike Bakersfield, which is inhabited 100% exclusively by speed-freak White Power-types with rotting teeth and the glaring gazes of trapped animals.

Except for an Art Walk going on, Downtown Fresno was desolate. The show was in the big back room of an Irish pub. An Irish band played in the corner of the pub and we were told that we were getting dinner from there. An Irish restaurant really seems like the worst idea on earth, but maybe in the context of Fresno . . . ?

The room that the show was to be in was painted green with lots of tables with green tablecloths and a big green stage with a big green curtain. It was set up like a wedding reception was about to begin. Would I be expected to throw a shamrock bouquet from the stage? One wall was covered with dozens of autographed promo photos of traditional Irish bands and folk singers. The only exception was the photo of a U2 cover band recreating the cover of *Joshua Tree*. We all stared at it and felt weird, like seeing Bizarro Superman.

As we loaded in and set up, I went to the bar to get a menu and a beer. The bartender was a very big and tall, arrogant oaf with a gray, Prince Valiant haircut that defied all sense. The haircut was *so* cartoonish. The arrogance that the man exuded while looking so totally silly—silly in a way that required such specific choices, if not effort — was incredible. He looked like Richard Gere in a fat suit playing the role of the sheep-herding dog from *Looney Tunes* in a Notre Dame jersey.

Upon first interaction he was immediately a prick, not only protesting my right to a menu, but going so far as to suggest: *who do I think I am to even ask for a menu?* He confirmed every negative stereotype of the Irish. I think I must be the only self-loathing Irishman on earth, which is exactly what makes me one.

I mean: I like my aunts and uncles. They're cool. And one time Dublin was super-fun. Patrick came and we hadn't seen him in years, but in the meantime he had become a superstar skateboarder. That was weird.

But the Owls show in Dublin, the promoter let us into some grimy apartment before leaving town to go visit his girlfriend. He left the six of us one potato, one carrot, and a pound of dry spaghetti and told us to make dinner ourselves. A guy lighting a cigarette at that show, when I asked him for a light, responded in all seriousness that he couldn't help me out because his lighter was low on fluid. And the JOA show in Belfast, the promoters stopped us halfway through the set because they wanted to go home. Is it fair to feel that the Irish have not been entirely supportive of my artistic efforts?

Me and Bobby split an order of fish and chips which were like *Long John Silver's*, gross: greasy fish with potato chips—not "chips" in the British sense of the word, fries, but just potato chips. Even eating as little as I did, I felt horrible for a while afterwards.

While eating, the doors weren't even open yet and I noticed this kid B_____ that we'd met before sitting in the doorway photographing me eating. I tried to ignore him and choke down a couple bites of the garbage quickly.

He followed us around being a general nuisance at our Bakersfield show last year. I mean, enough of a nuisance that we all remembered him. He had e-mailed me a few times and I responded, which seems like a generally appropriate response when e-mailed. Unfortunately he took this to mean that maybe he could come live with me and we'd start a band together. Apparently he was a pretty ingratiating Myspace friend to Sam at this point as well. After the Bakersfield show that he'd followed us around and bugged us at, he sent Sam and Nate links to photos that he'd taken that night. In every photo one of us is on the phone or turning a corner or stepping out of the van, surprised to find him standing next to us smiling real big with his hands out in a wacky faux-*Fun-Times* gesture. Best-case scenario: this kid is a brilliant performance artist making some project at the expense of our nerves.

The promoter, a friendly guy named Tim, told us that B_____ was "very disappointed" that we wouldn't be staying with him. He had told everyone that we would be and invited everyone over after the show and was so confused about why we got a hotel room. Now he'd be embarrassed in front of all of his friends if we didn't stay with him and he was mad at us and demanding an explanation.

This kind of shit, specifically, is the *exact* kind of shit that makes me understand in a very deep and real way the potential, dormant ability within every person to strangle the life from someone else. I slipped out the back door and went for a walk, truly dreaming of murder. And even though I was self-conscious of how crazy it was that I was actually, literally fantasizing about denying this kid of all his future breaths, it didn't blot out any of the satisfaction of imagining this in detail.

The happy hour Art Walk was wrapping up. I strolled the few blocks peeking quickly at things. A lot of people were out, mostly affluent hippy-types in their middle years. The art was all variations of stuff you might get when you buy a new frame: soft focus photos of toddlers with dogs and water color sunsets so shamelessly clichéd that they threatened to zap the life from the sun itself. But the people all seemed really happy to be out walking around downtown.

Besides Fagan's Irish Pub — now a mob of smoking, posturing kids — there was nothing downtown after the Art Walk closed except for a big casino. All the pawnshops and bail bonds places, the big old brick hotel and the old theater were all boarded up.

As I was talking to Amy on the phone, B_____ walked up with a bunch of his friends behind him, strutting like The Pink Ladies, and started yelling at me, "I wrote you on Myspace and said you could stay with me! Why did you get a hotel?! It just doesn't make any sense!"

After getting him to shut the fuck up and acknowledge that I was on the phone, he skulked off. Amy had to go but I held the phone to my ear and talked to myself as I turned the corner to explore another block.

An interactive Children's Museum was still open for some reason. I was pretty bored with most of the exhibits for a while, but then I remembered that I'm a grown man. Even so, the few exhibits that were potentially interesting, I couldn't understand what they were trying to say—just lots of sand and water and wind machines and a small tornado and pendulums. Some optical illusions were pretty cool and granted, this stuff is targeted towards nine-year-olds, but I was pretty underwhelmed. I was excited to spin myself around on the perpetual motion machine and happy to be a clown for some little kids that assembled to laugh at me. The room was spinning when I climbed off and I felt a little funny about all the parents gathering their kids and scurrying them away from me. Guess my hobo-style doesn't translate as Style to new parents, and might just be mistaken for plain old hobo spinning himself around the perpetual motion machine downtown at The Children's Museum.

Went back to the show and the music was familiar but slightly off, a little discomforting. I sat with Dustin and we talked about our families and growing up and all. B_____ was across the room and took photos of us hanging out and I wanted to go punch him in the fucking face. It's one thing when we're performing, but I don't have the right to sit around and hang out at the show without having to feel like I'm on display or something? Is my performance supposed to begin the moment we arrive and continue until we're loaded out? Ugh.

("Cowshwitz"? Totally uncalled for.)

After a few minutes it hit me what this strange music was: a U2 cover band. It never occurred to me that cover bands recorded and it seemed even more odd that someone would listen to it. Andrew and Dustin and I figured that the only possible way that it could make sense was if it's done as a historical re-enactment—like the Civil War guys do or maybe Ren-fair-types. Maybe if the band reads a bio of the production of a particular record and then acts out each argument, follows every tangent of production that they'll eventually ignore or throw away. But then there has to be a behind-the-scenes cover version of the entire supporting cast: engineers, wives, managers . . .

Otherwise, why on earth do records by cover bands exist? They've already established the ideal. Everything will be considered a success or failure according to how closely it can approximate this ideal, even though everyone involved at every level knows that it can only fall short of this predetermined standard of excellence—assuming of course that the cover band members don't secretly feel slighted on a cosmic level and believe that they are in fact the superior version. Are there people that prefer the U2 cover band's versions to the U2 versions? I guess U2 does evoke such unrivalled depths of repulsion in me that maybe anything would be an improvement.

This labyrinth that the cover band uncovered inspired me to tell Andrew and Dustin about "Pierre Menard, Autor del Quixote" and get excited about a few Borges designs.

Three meals and six beers later, the combined tab for the four of us was spent. Oddly, when the prick bartender told me this, he wasn't as enraging as earlier. I just felt sorry for the bloated old dork.

Some guy at the bar asked me if I was musician and I said yes. He wanted my opinion: he'd never booked a show before, but he's signing a contract this week to pay Big Head Todd and the Monsters $20,000 to play a 700-capacity room. I tried to offer what I thought was a rational response based on some simple math, but it turned out he was more bragging than asking advice. Turns out he's been on a Big Head Todd and the Monsters-sponsored cruise and has met the guys before, so he figures he *owes* it to them to bring them to Fresno.

It was cool to be playing the first all-ages show since Wichita and for all the junior high talent show vibes that the first couple bands exuded, it was still nice to be around a big bunch of kids hanging out and their resonant energies.

The local bands seemed really popular. The second band introduced one song as an instrumental and then the whole audience sang along to some long chorus during it that they all somehow knew even though no one in the band was singing. Can't really understand what that was about or how that comes together, but it was cool to see.

People didn't know what to make of Ecstatic Sunshine. They played great, me and Sam both up in front loving it. Matt played with his ski mask on and very few kids seemed into it at all except for the couple dudes that were totally flipping out.

Wandering around before we played, using the men's room and stepping outside for a smoke, the kids were all weird to me. They were all super young and not that I wanted to befriend them or not, but one kid told me I was a *"Legend"* and another said he felt like when a little kid meets Mickey Mouse and they get afraid because "that's the real Mickey Mouse himself." OK. Even if my humility might otherwise come across as somehow feigned, we're getting paid $150 to play the back room of an Irish pub in Fresno. That seems like pretty sound and concrete evidence that one has probably not acquired *"Legend"* status.

Setting up to play, I asked the soundman why he was listening to a U2 cover band all night instead of U2. He said because it was around and a U2 CD wasn't. That was probably unique in all the expanse of the multi-verse to this immediate situation, but it seemed reasonable enough. But then, I had to ask, why did he think cover bands even record at all? He said he guessed that it's kind of weird, but he hadn't ever thought about it before. After a moment's pause and some stage mannerisms of pondering acted out—a chin scratch and a shift of his weight—he suggested that the cover band probably records in this case "because the band still exists." He darted off immediately before I could point out that that explanation made zero sense and zero difference.

The energy of an all-ages show surprised us after a week of being dulled down to a bar crowd's standards of energy. But I felt uncomfortable the entire time while playing, misunderstood. After all the confrontation—grabbing blindly into and aiming straight for the audience—that I've been doing the last few years in this band, it's strange to feel as if I'm actually trying to hide while on stage. A similar thing happened in Wichita, but that was more intuitive fight or flight instincts kicking in. Those kids were going crazy *with* me. Here in Fresno, the kids kept cheering when I'd walk to their side of the stage and it wasn't like a communal guttural excitement, it was a high-pitched teeny-bopper *Tiger Beat* scream, the kind of screaming that I imagine Kirk Cameron or Jonathan Taylor Thomas must get a little uncomfortable entering a room without hearing.

The sound was good on stage and it felt good except for those strange kids. One really cute Asian girl that I'd seen earlier that seemed super cool and together and above it all was losing her shit to one side of the stage and it was funny to me. Even as a 32-year-old man, I see a 19-year-old girl like that and think she's *so* cool, she's got it all figured out. I regress at a molecular level into a teenager trying to impress some girl. It's surprising later on to see her freaking out, smashing up against everyone at the front of the stage when we play. Some other young cuties were all dancing on the side of the stage together in that way that young girls like to make up dances together with their friends. So funny to me to do that to us, of all bands—synchronized cheerleader dances to Make Believe? I guess, like the U2 cover band's CD, we just happened to be the band available at that moment to choreograph something to.

Ended the show with "Fumio" and "Temping," a standard show closing a year ago, but now a real breath-drainer. Had to walk around the block choking and coughing. No one was out except for a few people leaving the casino. The old California streets were silent and dark. I caught my breath, stunned by the old theater that I stood across the street from. Its marquee had only some vague message about a sale for something. I assumed that whoever needed to know what the cryptic sign meant did know. I bet it's beautiful inside that old place. It was huge. Its ornate details had fallen into disrepair and it seems to have been forgotten about or at least not kept-up for a long while.

All the locals had warned me about walking around the abandoned city center. And I'm not tough about those kinds of things. I don't walk around outside my own apartment at night and I'm totally open to the advice of locals. But this was only sad, not scary. The only scary thing about this was how this emptiness is probably more typical than not.

Luckily I saw B_____ approaching before he saw me and I hopped the few steps to the van and hid. I ducked low in the back seat in the totally likely event that he might peek in. After what seemed like definitely more than long enough, I braved stepping out and he seemed long gone, not even his cackle left dangling in the air behind him as it so often had earlier in the night.

Back at the show I talked to these three kids, maybe

eighteen or so. We were talking about the central valley and its water issues and I was telling them about *Chinatown*. They'd never heard of it. One kid kept calling me "Sir" over and over and it was really irritating me. One guy was cool and calm and the last one was kind of a smartass. I understood from everything else that the kid calling me "Sir" was saying that he meant it to be polite or whatever, but it was hard not to ask him a third and a fourth time to please stop doing that. I'm not Ian Mackaye. He was very soft spoken, monotone, and stared just above my head without blinking.

Finally, the "Sir" shit was bugging me enough as the conspicuous subtext to an otherwise cordial and engaging-enough conversation, that unable to see the point in a fifth or sixth request to please stop calling me "Sir," I blurted out without thinking, "and what are you staring at anyways?" His friends both grimaced and moaned. He replied, "Well, I just regained my sight last month, Sir, after not being able to see for a few years. I apologize, Sir, but I haven't quite gained back control of my eyes again yet, Sir." I am such a dick.

I pulled the van up and the club was completely abandoned except for us as we loaded. All the other bands gone, promoter and his goons gone, club owner woman that had been walking around all night announcing to everyone within hearing range, "You all seem like a really great bunch of good people," she was gone. Soundman gone. Dickhead-bartender gone. No one on the streets anywhere either, very strange. We loaded quickly in silence and locked the door behind us and we split.

Back at the hotel we tried to order a pizza but nothing was open. We drank warm beer that we had in the van and all made each other laugh. I ate peanut butter with a spoon, kept it on my tongue and closed my eyes to hear the ocean-sound that pouring beer over it provoked deep within my ears.

I finally got the *Orchard Vale* trailer open and watched it. I was pretty bummed. This Smog song seemed so 100% totally inappropriate that I was stunned that they could use it even as a guide for a rough cut. Went out for a smoke and took a long shower before e-mailing Amy and Jonathan, knowing full well that I'd make them both mad first thing in the morning when they'd each wake up and read it. I considered my language very carefully and considered the time that they'd put into it and considered how busy I know that Amy is. I took a long time writing it and fell asleep quickly afterwards.

   Can't believe I asked that kid what he was looking at.
   Woke up to find out that both Amy and Jonathan are indeed as mad as I'd imagined.
   Whole Foods hot bar lunch before heading out.
   Mmm-money.
   *

ALL OVER AND OVER

NOVEMBER 4, 2006

Getting to town with no real direction or ambition, none of the L.A. things that we traditionally do interested us. We've driven by Peter Falk's a few times, but have never gotten a glimpse of him. After years of tossing dozens of copies of our records over the fence on to Danzig's porch, we've still never gotten a response. Had no money for Amoeba and no time to see *Borat*. Drove past "The Manly P. Hall Center," but half of us weren't interested in checking it out. Edgar never got back to me and Rosie said she wasn't feeling well.

Amy wouldn't talk to me all day, every time I called, she just said she was busy and didn't have time and was all terse and "pass-agro" as Rog would say. With nowhere to go and none of us excited enough about anything to insist on it, we went to Nate's old neighborhood Las Villas to eat at a cheap noodle stand that he recalled fondly. He must've been as broke as he said he was when living out here, because I would've much rather paid $2 more anywhere else and not gagged on every bite. The Yakisoba reminded me of that disgusting Japanese delicacy of Osaka that all the locals are so excited to introduce newcomers to—Okonomiyaki. That shit is my standard of things that could, in theory, physically be eaten—it can be placed in one's mouth and chewed—but that does not make it edible. Noodles and squid fried into a pancake with mayo and thick oyster sauce. In theory it sounds kind-of-bad, but in practice it has a density and richness nauseating even to just recall.

Pulling in through the mountains of its outskirts, L.A. seemed beautiful to me. As many times as I've been here and as much time as I've spent here, I still never know how I'll respond. I've had a few good friends that have fallen in immediately and felt right at home. Edgar especially has always shown me around and made me feel welcome.

One time I stayed alone in his studio in some far-flung, super-ghetto neighborhood. Right after he dropped me off, I broke the key off in the lock. I spent the night alone with a door opening directly out onto the sidewalk, struggling to balance half-sleep and security. Another time, at a small house he was living in, we stayed up through the early morning hours drinking and laughing on his back porch. The next morning, we found a neighbor's annoyance with us expressed through a Santeria ritual involving chicken blood on Edgar's porch.

A few years ago he and M_____ let me and Tania stay at their place for a few days. They were out of town. Her name was hanging from banners on the streetlights through the whole neighborhood. It took me a couple days to notice that a caricature of her was on the cover of *The Believer* on their coffee table.

First time I had met her he brought her to an Owls show at The Troubadour. Alyssa Milano had come to our only previous show that we'd ever played there, so needless to say, we were psyched. Ms. Milano's boyfriend or husband or whatever complimented our "intriguing song titles" to Andy doing merch.

But this time at The Troubadour, this young kid B_____—whom we'd never met before and I've since only bumped into at an airport once—was tagging along for a few days and had a lot of mushrooms. He tripped for a few days straight and a couple of us dropped in and out with him. So when Edgar showed up to The Troubador's big elevated telephone booth band room with M_____, they were a bit unnerved, she more so and he for her sake, to find shouting drunks throwing deli trays and giving teenaged girls piggy back rides on their hands and knees. It was probably determined at that moment that none of me-and-M_____'s conversations would ever get further than *Hello*.

One time we pulled into town and Edgar immediately took us to see a Latino Smiths cover band play in a gallery. It was the opening of a photo show: audience members at Morrissey concerts in Mexico—all sensitive tough-guys swooning and weepy. The cool and collected affectations of the Morrissey in that Latino Smiths cover band made such an impression on me, that—besides maybe Ben Gazzarra as Cosmo Vitelli—there is no other Ham that I recall as often for inspiration any time that I hit a snag with the public vulnerability that singing in front of people requires.

Edgar and M_____ had walked me around through all the Chinatown galleries. None were open but they know all the owners and managers and we were greeted everywhere and shown what each person was most excited about. We talked with one guy for a while about his campaign work for John Kerry that was just getting underway. This guy seemed to be really out on the streets and working hard at a fundamental level. When we left him, Edgar told me that the guy had just lost his bid to buy HBO which had seemed was going to come through for a while, and he was throwing a lot of time and energy into other things to keep his mind off of his disappointment.

Last time I was in L.A. and saw Edgar, he took me to lunch at the hotel that Belushi OD-ed at — The Chateau Marmont. He bought me a sixteen dollar tuna sandwich. We dined poolside and it was, in fact, the most fucking superior tuna sandwich of my life. They'd just had their baby last time we came through town, so we couldn't hang out. Today he's out of town.

With Teo and Little Andy both now in New York, Rosie and me agreeing we've seen enough of each other this week and Edgar not around, I felt pretty aimless.

We didn't have enough time to go to Observatory Crest as we often do. That Beefheart song always gets stuck in all of our heads as soon as we pull into L.A. But even my first time in L.A., nineteen years old and not yet familiar with Beefheart's worst phases, I was certainly psyched enough about *Rebel Without a Cause* to head over there. But our van couldn't make it up the hill.

That van: in which it somehow seemed completely

reasonable to pile four people in the backseat and two up in the loft if anyone wanted to tag along. We'd have to leave after the show and drive overnight if any mountains were between us and our destination, knowing that we wouldn't be able to go over 25 mph uphill. We put that old-fashioned hamburger-container luggage rack on the top; Chumbawamba had left it at Southern. We never did remember to avoid parking garages.

Amy still wouldn't talk to me. The air had that anxious charge of dusk. The constant helicopters and sirens weren't helping my nerves. Everyone zipping around past each other, each floating a few feet off the ground in his or her own little glass-and-metal bubbles, always in a crowd and always cut off from any contact.

In the window of a bookstore I saw for the first time *How Japan Created its Own Lost Generation*, whose author I had heard interviewed on World View a few weeks ago. I'd been obsessed with the story ever since, talking about it with everyone I'd seen—"Did you know that millions of Japanese people never leave their rooms? No one even knows how many people they're talking about because they can't count them because they never leave their rooms." These people have been shamed somehow; not getting a job right out of school marks them as useless, or the silent treatment taken to the furthest degree by high school classmates negates one's identity to such a degree that it becomes impossible to recover. Their families support them, but don't speak of them outside the house. I stared at the cover for a while, but never went into the store. Maybe I was afraid that the idea seems too appealing to tempt myself with.

I decided to go sleep in the van. As I crossed the street a dog barked at me out the open window of a passing car, almost giving me a heart attack. Now I really needed to lie down.

We once spent an afternoon walking around this neighborhood when Don still lived here and Dale and Jeff were visiting with Ashton and Darren. At 38 years old it was Darren's first ever couple nights away from home and he was taking to it well. Darren's band, Muscle Factory, takes a little explaining. The band played while two guys bench-pressed on stage. Darren was the singer and his vocals would coach the guys through their workout—"Six more reps. You can do it. Work those arms. Five more reps." They broke up and now he's doing a new band: Tantric Polyamory Sexshop. That's cool. He walked in on Bobby sitting on the toilet that afternoon and Bobby never really recovered from the experience.

The four of us—Make Believe—together with Ashton, Dale, Jeff, and Darren were quite the freak show to Don's roommate Joe, the Icarus Line singer. He sat back and watched us, relaxing his sneer only once when his little dog jumped on my lap and licked me all over my face. I submitted to its will and Joe said with a smile, "It just ate its own shit." Yep, real cool guy.

We headed over to the show. Passed the *Grease* Ridell High, and the Seven-Dwarves huts from *Mullholland Drive*. Nate told us the story of why these strange buildings were originally built, Disney studios, etc. and none of us cut him off or pointed out that he's told us the story a couple times before. Sam played us one of his Garage Band songs, a deeply layered paranoid creeper with him acting out both sides of a 911 call. It sounded incredible. After hearing both his and Nate's solo stuff that they're each getting into, I feel extra-ok about bowing out. Make Believe may actually be holding each of them back.

When we arrived, no one was there except a video crew and ridiculously smoldering, ache-inducing hot rockabilly girls with tattoos and dyed-hair and skimpy outfits and bodies like Betty Rubble. A thuggish Rancid-type punk with tattoos all over his shaved head was immediately suspicious regarding our arrival, until I talked him through point by point: We are a rock band, This is a rock club, It is time to load in. As we also were there to meet a video crew, none of whom we knew or would recognize, I felt justified in my curiosity into their doings. Apparently that's super-square and in L.A. one should always expect to find two separate video shoots in any one room at one time and I was a country bumpkin not to know so.

The bartender N_____ showed up and I was happy to see her. I remember every time that she has a man's name, but I never remember what it is. I'm always happy to see her and she never remembers me and I think it's kind of cooler that she never does. We can hit it off all over again, a greater testament to her character than if she always remembered me as her buddy. She's cute and tough in a way that makes her even cuter and it always feels a little bit like she's letting you in on something when she talks to you. Like she knows better, but will make an exception this one time.

I can't count how many times I've played Spaceland. First Joan of Arc tour it was one of the five shows in three days in L.A. and the show that I remember the least about. A year later I remember berating the audience from the stage. No one was really there and I just mocked the few people that did show up for being so L.A. The next year the only people at the show were a dozen sexy young fashionista ladies that danced at the front of the stage and made eyes at all of us and then *zap*—disappeared. What an unlikely party line-up that was—Mike, sure, but me, Jeremy, and Todd? Not exactly guys out cruising for wild times.

A couple more times we played to no one. One time our bar tab for the five of us was the same as the bar's ring for the night. And that was one of our better shows there, as much a testament to our quantity of drinks that night as to the density of the crowd. Sam went home that night with the hot cocktail waitress and we were all stunned, but not as stunned as the next time we showed up to town and he called her and she said she didn't remember him but would come by the show anyways. Then he ended up spending another couple nights with her.

That time we ended up doing a Gwar set. Bobby sliced his

ALL OVER AND OVER

head open on a cracked cymbal. Nate jammed a drumstick down his throat bumping his accordion into it while holding the stick in his mouth. I guess the big difference is Gwar's violence happens *during* the songs and the Joan of Arc violence was all while switching instruments *in between* songs, the stage too crowded to move around.

One time I played here solo opening for Elefant, and even that was half-empty when I played. Never played to more than a half-full Spaceland, even on tours in between shows at a filled Troubador.

We soundchecked for the sake of the video crew so that they could get close-ups on the details of each of us playing the actual song to intercut with the hundreds of live photos that people have sent in. D_____ L_____ is directing. None of us have ever met her, but she's C____'s sister, so it came together easily at the last minute. Besides being M____ L____'s daughter and whatever worldly or cinema-language clout that translates to, I was excited that she is doing it because of her work on *Me, You and Everyone We Know* and a Will Oldham video she's doing.

She was certainly standoffish. She didn't remember Amy, even though just two weeks ago they went out to dinner together two nights in a row and a show together one of those nights and Amy had told me that they hit it off. Her boyfriend was working with her. Nice guy. Used to assist the infamous Mayo, worked on some tape loop installation with him.

A very young, super cute, skinny, and buck-toothed girl was with one of the camera operators, his girlfriend from back home. She looked so good in such a unique way that it really made me nervous.

We met Eastern Youth from Tokyo, who were playing tonight in between Ecstatic Sunshine and us. They were formal and friendly. We sorted out our friends in common and felt immediately connected. Each of them had seen different shows that we've played. The bass player even saw me play solo with a dazed Nate improvising along in an Art and Design Library in Tokyo.

I paced out front of the club trying to think of anything to do but eat at the Thai place next door. Doing so meant remaining stuck around the club with nothing to do and that seemed too easy. I was anxious, felt like I should *do* something. For the sake of all the nights in Boise and Salt Lake City and Wichita, I should take advantage of the L.A. night. But everything is far away from everything else. There's no getting anywhere easily. All I really wanted to do was laundry.

B_____ from J_____ and S_____ walked by. I don't know him, had met him maybe twice over the years, but we'd never said anything to each other to make any impression. In my agitated state, restless and thinking out loud, I called out his name as he walked by then felt weird about having done so. He turned around surprised.

I introduced myself as a fan that had seen him play a dozen times when I was a kid. Nate told him that he'd seen him play in The M_____ in Madison, which I didn't know that he'd ever done. We pieced together that it was the tour immediately after the tour The M_____ did with Joan of Arc, and we compared stories of being witness to their adventures: laid, laid out by a punch, sneaking off with panties, endless conquests of proof of virility. I certainly didn't envy being The New Guy in that situation, ending up on tour with those guys without any warning of what you were getting into.

Knowing full well that before the end of the night, as always, the Spaceland's toilet would overflow and its functionality would be abruptly halted, getting my mental game in order to deal with that, I ate that same fucking Pad Thai as every other time that I've ever played there. We talked the entire meal about how our dads had probably never tried Thai food. Nate told us that his other grandpa, the one that I don't know, retired from the same factory that he started working at when he was sixteen years old. Of course our parents have some mental leaps to make to meet us halfway, if that's the generation that they have sandwiching them from the other side.

Michael called and I put him on the list and told him to come over, but I never saw him. Guess he opened a new gallery in Chinatown, was looking forward to hearing about it. Funny how similarly we've turned out, or seem to have turned out from our brief tri-annual conversations, always in a different city. My best friend until I was six years old, a poet that's now opened a gallery.

I sat on the street with Matthew for almost an hour, talking Baltimore and the young bands there and stories of Ecstatic Sunshine's first tour out west. The highlight was a house show in Missoula, Montana. The guy who had set up the show moved to Alaska a week before the show, but told the two young secretaries that wanted to rent the place that they could have it, but only if they agreed to put this show on. So they invited some friends over, all of whom were friendly enough, but completely confused as to why these guys from Baltimore wanted to show up and play music at their house. And how did these few pothead teenagers know to come over? They promised the next door neighbor that there wouldn't be a party; he had to be up early the next morning.

I finally reached Amy and immediately knew that I'd have been better off if I hadn't. She was offered a cool job, editing a movie that's supposedly already been accepted to Sundance and gotten a DVD distribution deal. (How you get these things in place before even hiring an editor beats me, but that's how she was selling it.) She had to turn the job down because she wouldn't have time to do it with her job at the university and she can't quit that because who knows if another good opportunity will come up again soon. So she was lamenting being the one with the steady income allowing me to pursue things and I couldn't blame her. I'm waiting for checks from T_____, Jade Tree, and Showtime, which should total about $2500, and now all of them are late while I'm out here on a tour that's losing money.

She was pissed. "Orchard Vale looks like shit but it doesn't matter 'cuz it's just another stupid movie anyways and who cares 'cuz it'll never be enough for a feature anyways." Co-producin'. Cool. Kick ass.

She hung up and wouldn't talk to me for the rest of the night.

Talked to a cool guy named K____ while Eastern Youth played. A very southern California dude, he'd seen Owls play at Koo's years ago and recalled it fondly. I told him about Sam's dad deciding to surprise him and coming in from Vegas, not to the capacity Troubadour show, but the next night instead at Koos, a condemned house with no stage in the ghetto. K____ is a janitor at a museum and enjoys it because he doesn't need to carry it around with him at all.

Eastern Youth was *Intense*. I missed the first few songs and walked in on an a cappella section complete with guttural screams and lots of tears, the guy convulsing. Little blips on his high E-string occasionally punctuated the lines, all in Japanese and with a very traditional-seeming Japanese cadence to the melodies. This section went straight into a rock song, not very punk even, just like straight-ahead rock. Cool, subtle bass playing moved the song along, the bass player occasionally interjecting weird little percussive runs with all of his fingers like Steve Harris—really cool.

Half of the audience was Japanese so I expected the place to empty out by the time we played, but it didn't. By far our best Spaceland show ever, by no means close to capacity but certainly closer to full than half-empty. The audience seemed psyched and the energy was reciprocal, very unlike any Spaceland show before.

J.J. was standing at the front of the stage when I looked up for a second late into the show. We waved hello. Haven't seen her in at least five years and things weren't going so well for her when I did last see her. We'd met the first time we played L.A. She and Hopper had walked up to us at the Huntington Beach Library and Hopper introduced herself to us as our publicist, which we were all surprised to hear since Jade Tree had never mentioned it to us and none of us knew that we had such a thing. J.J. was her pal and we all hit it off quickly. Skeptical as we all were about a *publicist* — back in 1996 it was hardly the common word that it now is — we were all psyched to arrive in mythical L.A. for the first time and be greeted by two young cuties offering hospitality.

Sam took an immediate liking to Hopper and it seemed mutual those first few days we were there, which of course now seems *so* insane. She was just 17 at the time. We'd been camping out in her living room for a few days when her mother arrived to visit her for the first time and found us six stinky guys there. Oh, poor mothers of the world.

Unlike Hopper, J.J. was a life-long L.A.-kid. She was a hairstylist to the stars, which landed her brief gigs drumming for weird famous people. It was rumored that she had been in Hole for a few practices, but it didn't stick, and she would neither confirm nor deny the truth of the legend, satisfied to let it linger as a possibility. Hopper, too, had these vague rumors surrounding her of having been crashing at Kurt and Courtney's when he killed himself, supposedly one of the last few people to have seen him alive. She was already infamous as the girl that had broken the mainstream media ban Riot Grrrl had all agreed to. So we were all a little extra-excited that she'd be our *publicist* after we all figured out her scene-infamy.

The two girls had driven up to Bakersfield with us for a show. A kid hit another kid over the head with a pitcher of beer and he was covered in matted gore. This was a strange turn of events for a Joan of Arc show, but over the next couple years we would learn that this was not such a strange occurrence for Bakersfield, the place on earth that I have most dreaded returning to the three or four times I've had to.

As soon as our show was over I instinctively headed out the front door and down the block to breathe deeply and catch my breath. A few blocks away I ran into J.J. and we sat against a building and talked.

She had followed Hopper out to Chicago maybe eight years ago. That was a time when it seemed like everyone we knew anywhere all moved to Chicago in a short period and suddenly touring was no good because everyone we expected to see anywhere was absent and now back in Chicago. She ended up moving in with T____ in his big apartment on the boulevard that Paul and Amy would eventually live in. Her room was later Amy's. She ended up playing in a few different bands citing me as a character reference. When she relapsed into a dormant junk habit that I never knew about, she spun out of control and took down a good number of people around her with her. And though I had very little to do with her on a day-to-day basis in Chicago, I was still called in for a good amount of the fallout, having vouched for her character to some different people. She's been back in L.A. since. I haven't even heard of anyone having seen her.

She seemed happy and healthy and even after so long, we fell back in with each other quickly and easily. She'd had a "spiritual awakening"—her words—almost a year ago as a means of getting her out of some "dark shit," which we never acknowledged by name. She had been hit by a car. Breaking her collarbone finally snapped her out of it. After a long stay in the hospital where she had hit it off with the staff, as she did everyone else, they talked her into working with them. So she was now a probation officer of sorts, dealing with L.A. County dudes just out of jail or mothers trying to kick. I'd forgotten how short she was. The tough-guy act that she explained she had to put on was funny. She worried that she was getting too attached to all of her cases.

By the time I returned to the club, our small posse had assembled out front, slowly developing a plan. I talked to A____, K____'s old roommate in Chicago that I never knew too well, but always liked. He has that gay-pirate vibe that I'm a sucker for. Last time I had seen him, a guy had broken into his apartment that afternoon while he was stoned and half-napping. The guy held him at gunpoint for a few hours before he came over to the bar and we sat for a drink to calm his nerves.

B_____ was around now and L_____ and his new girlfriend and all of us going to R_____'s. K_____ called L_____ while on his way to the Continental back home and L_____ handed me the phone to answer. L_____ was drunk enough to not believe I was me, but instead L_____ doing a really killer impersonation of me, so we didn't really talk much except for me convincing him I was, in fact, me.

We had all spent such a long time standing around on the sidewalk negotiating our options that we were running late to make it anywhere. I'd been feeling bad all night since talking to Amy. Feeling guilty about my entire lifestyle. She wouldn't answer again, so all I could do was say fuck it and get on with enjoying the rare opportunity of my present company.

R_____ had moved to L.A. about nine months ago. He was offered a job that he couldn't turn down. We all later noticed that he had announced he was going to move just a day or two after N_____ and S_____ announced their engagement. Probably not a coincidence that any one of them involved would've noticed, but striking to those of us on the near perimeter.

We'd known R_____ since forever and I'm not certain if we were somehow involved in orchestrating this, but when he got to L.A. R_____ moved in with Nate's old friend J_____. And I couldn't think of a more perfect Odd Couple.

From what I can tell from my limited exposure to the type, J_____ is very much the new breed of young L.A. artists. When he lived in Chicago a few years ago we got off to a pretty undeniably rocky start. I couldn't believe the forced awkwardness and the young art students' insistence on seeing the Art in everything in the most simplistic and obnoxious manners. I so greatly appreciate that quality in those who've refined it and have achieved a sense of mysticism with the impulse, but that wasn't the case with J_____. He was more into things like barging drunk into a recording session going at full steam at 1:00 a.m. and insisting everything halts until each person can thoughtfully answer, "Why are you doing this?" about every minute detail.

We can all argue the Art in porn or Nikes or whatever. But once such a perspective is integrated naturally into one's worldview, there's no need to go around imposing it on everyone when they're all just in the middle of doing whatever it is they do. Since he's moved to L.A. it's been a lot easier to see him just a few times a year, L.A. or Chicago, and spend a little time together knowing that he's not going to be around constantly.

He's been making kind of gross-out paintings that don't appear to be gross-out paintings. Lots of science-talk behind his pretty color-fields made from fly puke after feeding them food coloring. He's been in negotiations with us about commissioning a song about himself. We told him $500 was the friend's deal, because we stayed with him every time we're in L.A. these days. But this time he was out of town helping his sister campaign for some state representative in Florida. This was the first time we'd been here since R____ got to town, so we still had the same familiar apartment to stay at. We all went over to Little Joy, directly down the hill from their place.

As we were leaving Spaceland and saying goodbye to A____, C____ said, "All my best friends are in Chicago or New York," and A____ shot back, "That's so L.A." Funny and repulsive in alternating waves.

Outside Little Joy I ran into E_____, ex-Chicago straight edge guy and political activist who ditched all that and left for L.A. to be a male model soon after his first drink. It was too crowded, so we were all held outside. Nice to have a minute to see E_____, his continuous, monotone commentary occasionally interrupted with sudden chirps of excitement. He was coming from the Rise Against show and couldn't believe that I didn't know those guys, and then grew enraged that I "insisted on pretending" that I'd never heard of them. I don't know. I'll remember the name now I guess.

We were at the bar to find B_____ Jr. who we never have to track down. When we toured with him, he had a cooler on wheels like a luggage, rolling it along behind himself as if the world were his airport. Teo's old-beau R_____, who was at first, years ago, extremely tough towards me until finally realizing that I was no threat to him and just her old friend, also worked there. We always hit it off easily enough. The Kalamazoo emo-scene—destined to haunt me forever I guess?—was personified there by Joseph, ex-Constantine Sankathi.

Walked down the street to a bar owned by the guy from the Afghan Whigs. It was also packed, but at least they let us in. The whole place was dancing and too loud for us to hear each other. They played that Journey song, "Don't Stop Believeing" and I got sentimental for the Chicago White Sox World Series title. They played "Take on Me" and R____ got sentimental about Captain Jazz. It was crowded enough that N_____ was able to pull his pants half way down without anyone noticing. But he pulled them back up quickly because he said he hasn't been with his new girlfriend long enough yet to know how she would deal with it. Fair enough.

I guess Sam mostly doesn't get punched because everywhere we go most people assume that he's retarded? He jumped up and down waving his hands in the air and charged into groups of people screaming, "Awesome!" at the top of his lungs in a chicken-lady voice.

As the bar let out and the crowds jammed up the sidewalk, Kirsten Dunst left the bar. A few dudes were shouting at her as a security guy led her up to an apartment next door, some kind of backroom holding pen for the stars. Before being whisked away, I heard her say mockingly to some guy, "Yeah, that's her. I'm me," her tone deeply implying, *Duh, Asshole*. She's cute; looks like Amy.

ALL OVER AND OVER

I fell asleep immediately in J_____'s bed, thinking, *Gross, I can't believe I'm sleeping in this guy's bed.* Maybe it's just his moustache, but something freaked me out about it. Everyone else had gone out to a party with some fashion-types a few years younger than us. I slept with the patio door open, loving the breeze.

*

ALL OVER AND OVER

NOVEMBER 5, 2006

Everyone but me had been at a party until 4:30 a.m., so they were slow to get moving once the sun flooded the place and left us no other options. I'd been sitting on the back porch, Echo Park spread out below me, reading and writing for hours before Sam called me in to tell me that they were all up and didn't know where I was.

It was a real tight fit for all of us. Even with me in J_____'s room, Sam had to sleep in the kitchen and Bobby in a hallway.

Everyone else had watched a video R_____ made in Japan: Kaori interviewing Mike. It has already become the source of endless Kaori quotes for us to drop on each other all day.

We've eaten breakfast at the Coffee Table most times we've been in L.A., but feared the Saturday morning crowds. We all figured we'd get to San Diego early, drop Sam off at the border, eat a burrito and see *Borat*. So we all agreed to just eat a bagel or something quick now to save room for the awesome place in San Diego that's in our *Healthy Highways* book. R_____ decided to drive down with us for the day. Bobby rode with him. Me, Sam, and Nate followed in the van. They didn't stop for food before getting on the highway and then switching highways, and finally after an hour of L.A. highway traffic we ended up stopping at a Quizno's because it was all we could find—in L.A.! All we could find was a sandwich that I'd only eaten before in truck stops across Wyoming or Arkansas. We were all frustrated and pissed.

Nate drove. He made it abundantly clear that he was going to insist on a silent treatment all day, swelling every necessary movement into its biggest possible expression of passive-aggression. He made fast turns in tight spaces, anything that he might need to pick up, he slammed down hard, slamming doors, not responding to questions directly addressed to him. We were going to drop Sam off at the border, meet Bobby and R____ back up in La Jolla for the 4:00 p.m. *Borat* screening.

Driving along the coast was beautiful. Mesmerizing waves, so perfect in such a deep, instinctual way that it's impossible to not try to get at what it *means*. Of course there's the expanse of the ocean beyond our comprehension, waves beating against the beach like the patterns of our own breath. But this magnetism happens at such a primal level, it's hard not to feel like ancient, timeless man, part of an endless continuum—backwards and forwards—that will never be able to help but look at this source of life, the ocean, with terrified awe.

And then it's downtown San Diego, always seems like a little Matchbox Cars play-set city to me. I love it. Almost without exception, every time we've been here we've had free time so we go downtown to the park complex and the zoo. Only paid to actually go in the zoo a couple times, but the parks and museums surrounding it are beautiful. Many a stoned afternoon I've wandered those parks with headphones on, ducking into this museum, then that one, each for only a few minutes. These were often my favorite days of a west coast tour.

Last time there, about two years ago, we finally went in the zoo, coughed up the $20 each. Sam, Nate, and I took one of those small trolleys that carry you over the zoo suspended 100 feet in the air. We all freaked out regretting having decided to do so as soon as we got on and the door closed behind us. We hooted and hollered non-stop for however long it takes to fly over the zoo.

First time we ever played San Diego was in a coach house behind the house The Locust lived in. It was Tristeza's first show. I'd known Christopher from Kalamazoo.

Constantine Sankathi again. Like a lot of my friends at that time, I was super into San Diego bands: Antioch Arrow, Heroin, Drive Like Jehu, and the whole style that went along with it — black turtlenecks in July, etc. It was one of the most anticipated stops on that first tour. We all expected a land of high and beautiful rich kids that fucked all day, only stopping occasionally to play blast beats and eat a burrito. And these impressions were generally confirmed at the house party. We just hadn't anticipated everyone being so standoffish. It did, however, begin a long-standing casual camaraderie with Tristeza, most recently playing with them at the Promise Ring reunion show last year, but not hanging out much. And we hung out for a night in Tokyo with Jimmy that used to be in the band.

With a few exceptions since that first show, all of our shows there have sucked. We'd always play the Casbah, generally to thirty people. Last time we played there, B_____ showed up. I hadn't seen her in about eight years. She looked very much the same, still a spaz and affectionate and quick to get angry.

She'd moved out there the year before, after leaving S_____. None of us could believe she'd married him, but then everyone felt that much more surprised to find out a year later that he'd gotten another woman pregnant and pleaded with B_____ to raise the baby with him. A lot of sabotage ensued, people's bank accounts and mailboxes broken into and shit, until finally she moved out to San Diego to start over. Her parents were back in Europe or maybe Florida and her sister somewhere on the east coast and she was fighting hard against being lonely.

We stayed at her house. She started playing drums at 3:00 a.m. and the police came over. Her roommate got fired in the morning for sleeping through her alarm. We'd been in the eye of a drunken storm and didn't feel much responsible for it, even if just our presence was somehow enough to provoke it.

In all those years of playing a Casbah show once or twice a year, always ho-hum no matter who it was with—Hella, JeJune, etc.—only once did we play an all-ages show at the Che Cafe. We always *wanted* to, every time, but it was always hard to set up because they were too Anarchy or whatever to call our booker back. When we finally did play there, 400 kids showed up and couldn't all fit in the room at once. It was great. Next time through town, we insisted we should play an all-ages show again, but the Che couldn't be worked out. So we ended up at a youth center 40 miles outside of town playing to half a dozen twelve-year olds there with their moms. And that was the *Gap* tour, hardly our closest moment to crossing over to adolescent appeal. So back to ho-hum Casbah shows for another couple years, until a mediocre return to the Che last year and now again last night's show.

We pulled into town by around two and brought Sam down to where I-5 ends. We didn't pull all the way up to the border this time, but instead dropped him off at a fancy mall a few blocks away. There was a Polo store. After having gotten turned around and lost in the neighborhoods around the border before and seeing the poverty close up, the gall of building such a ritzy mall in such proximity was shocking. This was a different kind of poverty than familiar urban ghettos. It had a rural, southwest vibe—dry dust and chickens in the city.

Confused, but relieved to not have to come face-to-face with border-reality, we headed back to meet Bobby and R____ at *Borat*. The irony of our choice of movies when directly returning from the border was not lost on me. I saw a car pulled over just back on the highway north on the 5. Not more than an exit or two from the border, a few cops stood over a woman who lay flat on her belly on the shoulder of the road. The cops all had their guns drawn. Two little kids stood a few feet away and watched. We drove past, Nate lying down in back, so only I witnessed the quick scene.

I was alone with Nate. He was treating me to his silence and it was annoying. We got to La Jolla an hour early and bought tickets and walked across the mall to where the line was just beginning to form for the 4:00 o'clock show. Having never really been to a sold-out screening of anything before,

ALL OVER AND OVER

I got nervous about the crowd, claustrophobic. There was that Jarmusch thing we played, that was a capacity theater, but I had a little bit of a privileged role that night and wasn't stuck choked in by hundreds of people.

(Now driving through the desert east on 8 towards Phoenix. Through all the rocks and mountains which eventually open up into Calexico and Mexicali desert, trailers abandoned and left to rust in the sun.)

The Borat movie was pretty exciting to witness as a part of a big group of suburban rich people, the audience flattered by both the portrayal of backwards Borat himself and all the American subcultures he mocks. There are a lot of layers to dig through for a movie in which the funniest moments involve wrestling a naked obese man and breaking dishes in an antique store. Being among the first ones in got me the back corner seat closest to the door, which allowed me to relax.

Bobby's friend S_____ met us at the movie. He had only gotten to San Diego six weeks ago for an MFA at UCSD and offered to put us up for the night. To say he mumbled would be an understatement. I've championed plenty of eccentrics and I've appreciated plenty of people specifically because of their quirks. And I understand that stuttering is a medical condition. But this wasn't that. S_____ was so kind and gentle, but the full-on fucking refusal to enunciate was maddening. He spoke at $1/8^{th}$-speed, like a shy kindergartener forced to talk in a second language or a squirrel with a concussion.

R_____ left us to pick up a friend. We had a lot to coordinate between leaving the movie and getting to the show. Me, Bobby, Nate and S_____ had to get from La Jolla to downtown where Sam had gone to the House of Blues just to be at an easy landmark, then over to the restaurant that we found in the Healthy Highways book. R_____ gave us directions from the theater to House of Blues and they were written on my hand. It took fifteen minutes to even explain to S_____ in a way that he could understand that we needed to get from House of Blues to this restaurant. Once he understood that, he handed me the phone and someone on the other end began giving me directions while I was at the same time trying to navigate Bobby through downtown towards the House of Blues. It felt like some kind of Russian astronaut stress test—trying to read one set of directions from my hand while transcribing another.

We got Sam, couldn't find the highway, knowing all along that we were continuously within a few blocks of it. An hour and a half after we'd left the movie, having changed plans twice and already late for load-in, we jumped out when we drove past a Whole Foods. Nate wasn't speaking to anyone. The brain-dead kindergarteners had each other to baby-talk together. Sam and I figured out how to break up the best little variety pack goody bag for my dollars—six Xanax and four Vicodin, the Xanax in bars of four for ten dollars, the Vicodin 10's, five bucks each.

Sam was ahead of me in line at Whole Foods. The woman weighed his food and rang him up: $9.12. He stood and talked to me while she weighed my food and rang me up: $9.12. We all paused. She started gushing about how super-weird it was and we shrugged and walked off.

Talked to Amy. She'd just come from a *Ladies and Gentlemen* screening at Chicago Filmmakers, all the trannies, her and Krakow at dinner beforehand. J_____ showed up and Amy remained aware of her through the entire Q-and-A. Now she was off to endure a Scritti Politti set at the Double Door to get the guy to talk about Mayo. In the morning she'll be hosting the Chicago Indy Media TV show, before working on the Bobbie Conn thing with Usama, and before doing the Scritti Politti interview. Tomorrow night she'll try to get in a couple hours work on finishing up the trailer. No one can say we don't work hard for the no-money that we end up making. That was actually the funniest thing about that Say Anything guy's letter in response to me. He called me "lazy." *Lazy?!?!*

We went to the Che and loaded in. They had vegan mac and cheese for us, which is delicious, but of course not a meal for anyone except a vegan toddler. The toilet had an aerosol can jammed down into it and shit all over the outside and back of it and all over the walls. S_____ agreed to take me over to his studio across campus. He needed to pick up an inflatable mattress there anyways and I needed to use the men's room. Walking around with him I felt so bad about fantasizing violence on him before. He's so super-nice, he just can't communicate a single sound to anyone and prefers to play along as if he is somehow communicating. We walked a lap of the Bruce Naumann building with the flashing neon, *Vices* and *Virtues* alternating.

Back at the show I really wanted to find a place to sit and be alone and read and write. I knew a few friends would be coming out and I wanted to sneak off before being sucked into conversation and not getting the little done that I need to each day to not feel like the day's an entire waste.

A lousy, no-wave Hella rip-off duo with no clue or ideas played. They were young guys. Maybe they'll stick with it and find a reason for playing. But it didn't seem to me that they had any reason to not break up.

Next an L.A. garage/punkish band played. The girl on lead was a super-ripper playing cool leads and using a wah pedal. Tsk-Tsk they're called. The rhythm section is sloppy and rocking and the girl singing was absurdly cute. They closed with a cover of "I Wanna Be Your Dog," and most of the set preceding that was variations on that theme.

Ecstatic Matt and Dustin Sunshine were planning out their trip to the beach to eat shrooms, but really didn't seem to comprehend the time commitment, talking about eating them in the morning before leaving for Phoenix.

It was a full moon. I took a couple beers and walked through the beautiful wooded campus to find anywhere to sit. I ended up staring at the thick trees; some with bark like fur, others with splintered exteriors revealing entire other trees inside of them, everything densely layered and intertwined. Hard to believe that moonlight alone can illuminate everything so brightly.

R____ had shown up with some girl.

(Mexico is just to our right. Nate, continuing his passive-aggressive trend, is driving like a maniac. It seems like we are about to flip over, over, and over, and I don't care. I hope we do. It'd be better than having to continue on tour.)

The side door of The Che where the vans were parked turned into a sort of lame party. Everyone was standing around with Miller Lites talking about how they despised their lame jobs and despised their long commutes and hated President Bush, but no one could make the obvious connections that their lifestyles depended on their lame jobs and their lame jobs depended on their long commutes and all of it depended on George W. Bush as the hideous cartoon logo of the entire global bullying system. The system was closed and locked and eating itself.

(I wonder if Nate has just invented road rage in the desert or if this is some kind of thing that happens.)

Besides the yuppie-talk there were a few teenagers milling about. One heavily acne-scarred kid with his silent sidekick asked me for an autograph. I signed his CD and then he asked all coy, "You smoke?" And I wasn't sure if he was offering me weed or asking for a cigarette. He laughed and looked incredulously to his friend who looked as surprised as he did. He laughed and said, "No man, crystal."

I laughed and said, "No." He couldn't believe it and told me that he's had us wrong all along. He was positive that we all must've been into crystal meth. I told him that was gross and he was truly shocked and offended.

ALL OVER AND OVER

Dan showed up. We'd met years ago when he used to live at Speak in Tongues in Cleveland. We'd play there on our way to or from New York over and over for years and me and Dan hit it off, but I always got the impression that Dan was the kind of guy that just hit it off with everyone. I was surprised once Speak in Tongues closed down and he'd moved first to somewhere in North Carolina and then San Diego that he sought us out and made an effort to keep in touch. I always appreciated it. He never drank or smoked and was always happy, always good to see and up to something new, like a big teenager. In my more cynical moments I wondered if he maybe wasn't an ex-junkie or secretly born-again Christian. But I think he was just really that cool and easy-going.

Last year when we played San Diego he brought his young friend Ian, maybe twenty, twenty-two, neck-tattooed and excited. Ian brought us a painting he'd done and he was as striking a guy as I ever meet for a night: a twenty-year-old suburban southern California messiah, unable to tone down the energy, manic with his deep hybrid of hip-hop inflection and Old Testament vocabulary. Not sure what hour of the Karmic clock he'd been reborn into or if it was just the too-easy access to acid with nothing else around but the Dead Sea Scrolls, but the kid is deep and cool, himself completely, take it or leave it. Ian brought us a new drawing, my beard manifesting from a strange collage like a Genie's bottle and some recordings of his band packed in a diorama packed into a music-box.

Of course there's no monitors at the Che. I blew my throat out. Soon as the show was done I had to run straight outside to puke in the bushes. Kept puking and puking a long time after it seemed like I should've stopped. My throat burned all the way up to the top of my nose between my eyes.

I had loved wandering the acres of forest near the club in the full-moon-lit fog. But driving with baby-talking S_____ shotgun as navigator, not even sure where he himself lived, the fog demanded to be understood as my externalized emotional state drifting through the downtown streets. His neighborhood was beautiful, impossibly descending to a valley and peaking again each block in every direction. But by the time he recognized his small apartment at the top of a hill, it was obviously pretty ghetto, not a safe place to park the van overnight.

Any other tour of my life I would've slept in the van. But this time, knowing this is it and I'm done, I didn't. I set up my sleeping bag between S____'s kitchen table and oven and fell asleep on the tile. The stark apartment was entirely tiled, so sleeping in the kitchen was no better or worse than sleeping in the living room. S_____ insisted on curling up on the floor so one of us could take his bed, refusing to be more comfortable than what he'd expect his guests to tolerate. I lay awake praying that the van would be stolen so I could just go home.

Every tour this realization happens—every single time—but I never remember. How could it be that I never really recognized this drift for what it actually *is* before? I always only focus on what it *could be*, everything wrong with it. How do I always get so turned around and fucked up and backwards?

We all woke up with stiff backs to head off to Phoenix. Nate still imposed his mood on all of us, making us all sort of pretend that it wasn't happening and ask ourselves: is this a clumsy attempt to ask us to acknowledge something? But what? Or will this dark cloud just blow over? In the immediate it was easier to ignore it.

I skipped showering at S_____'s knowing that we had pricelined a room for Phoenix. After our first Stinkweeds show in Phoenix, which had been the biggest show in a few days on that first tour, Phoenix had repeatedly become a let-down until settling into just a Nothing Day once or twice a year, a place on the way in between places. We could consistently play to 75 or 100 people and break even for the day between Austin and California. It had zero impression, positive or negative, on us and that was its most distinguishable characteristic.

(Beautiful drive across Tatooine moonscapes of boulders and desert, opening slowly at first then a space-station city on the moon.)

Me and Bobby talked about it and considered that maybe it was only Phoenix's distance in every direction from anywhere else that we'd ever play that imposed limited time to get to know it and that made this indifferent impression on us. This idea made sense. Portland and San Diego were two of my favorite places and each always had a short drive from Seattle or L.A. on one side or the other of it, so we had time to get to know these cities. Maybe if we ever had a chance to get to know our way around Phoenix and could dig into it a little bit, it might become a place that we looked forward to getting to. We've had plenty of afternoons to detail the course we'd plot for San Diego or Portland. But whatever benefit of the doubt we tried to give Phoenix, it just didn't work. No iota of me ever considered wishing that I had more time to get to know the place.

The few times we've played Tucson I've loved it. Solar Culture and the old downtown, Union Pacific railroad running close past us, raw feasts prepared by beautiful young women. I've never had more time to spend in Tucson than Phoenix, but couldn't deny which one drew me in more.

The best I could say is that we were able to load in late enough and there was no local band, so the show passed quickly. My throat hurt bad, swollen big. I knew I wasn't going to blow it for Phoenix on a Sunday. So I wrote a set that erred toward as little stress on my throat as possible. The room filled up and we played well and who cares?

*

ALL OVER AND OVER

NOVEMBER 6, 2006

Election day tomorrow, falling asleep after a long shower pondering the common, but mythic plight of Borat's fixation with Pamela Anderson. How often I assumed as a younger man that I alone had some rare insight into the beauty of a young woman that no one else could recognize only to later have it hit me, *Oh, everyone knows she's smoking hot. I alone am dumb enough to allow myself to get caught up in it.*

Flipping through all the pundits on the news channels, it occurred to me that of course these secret forces that govern us—that determined the last two elections and prefer that Iraq descends into chaos and *Das Homeland* devolves into medieval feudalism—of course they'd want Bush to serve out his term as a lame duck. The agenda is all in place, all set in motion. The majority of people are disgusted. The whole world over, everyone is shocked and offended. If in his last two years he is unable to further his agenda, the illusion of democracy is restored and the system of checks and balances *appears* to remain strong and healthy. So, the projected Democratic victory fits nicely as the next piece in the puzzle.

Leaving town today north up into only Wile E. Coyote and *Hills Have Eyes*-style desert all day. Glad to be able to get back into *The Cosmic Serpent*. Once my tour momentum is hit, it's funny how I prefer the long drives, less of the not-enough-time-to-do-anything to have to figure out what to do with; more time to get into quiet things—reading, writing, sleeping, headphones.

120 pages into *The Cosmic Serpent*, it only hit me after putting it down and picking it up again a few days later, how my own drawings of the last couple years have directly paralleled the serpent/DNA/ladder/helix of Shamanic artwork. Maybe I've been channeling this thing common to

people all over the world through all of time with no contact with each other. And my own drawings, the way they close on themselves, could also be seen as the serpent eating its tail—another commonality making it all come full-circle. Ouroboros pun!

These drawings I've been doing when I want to summon the second attention are all the same and each unique: Belfast 2003, Midland, Texas 2005, Tokyo 2006. I've never given much thought to them. I just always enjoyed the challenge of trying to redraw the same simple patterns and appreciated the ways that they'd always end up different. It's a lot like the other drawing I used to do over and over, but it's paradoxically more sophisticated and more organic. And now this parallel emerges that I never even considered before. I always knew that my drawing-mind was just an antenna. But why would I have ever assumed that I alone was receiving the message? There might be millions like me, all drawing these same patterns.

Of course that would change everything about what I think this meaningless drawing means. Every specific aspect of how I draw the pattern would take on a new implication. The looping ladders cross over themselves at different points. I've always left only these intersections blank. Everywhere else the parallel lines have perpendicular lines connecting them. Four years into this compulsive doodle I now recognize the implication that by leaving these intersections blank, the spaces within the intersections open up and each create a variation of the different possible angles. It implies something is in there. Only at the intersections of the helix is something there. But by leaving this blank instead of drawing right through it and creating a grid — which would be the obvious first instinct that for some reason I intuitively dismissed upon first doodle years ago—the Something that's there gets represented only by Nothing while all the Nothing to most people is all that can be shown. It makes perfect sense!

So, anyways, good day to drive the high desert.

Disappointed we have no time to stop at Montezuma's Castle.

I drove into Phoenix last night, the last couple hours through the long, slowly changing light of the desert sunset. The full moon hung big and low over a state highway early. It looked totally flat; just a big white disk cut from tissue paper and hung up flat on the dark wall of space. The state highway was clogged with traffic although we didn't pass a single building for 30 miles or more. In the distance around the bend, hundreds of bright orange lights hung at the same height. For miles approaching it, I couldn't guess what it might be, just vaguely "military" somehow. Ended up being the long series of yards and small buildings and towers of a maximum security prison. The lights receded into the rearview mirror and we were again into nothing darkness across the early Arizona desert evening.

The last few times through town we'd stayed with M____. When she got out of rehab a couple years ago her parents wanted to get her out of Chicago. At the same time her brother had happened to drop out of college in Tempe. He'd just signed a lease on a new place that his parents were paying for, and they decided to fly him home and send M____ in there in his place.

Over the years, she seems to have gotten her act together, relatively speaking. She still always *seemed* high and flighty. And every time, one of us would get stuck in the living room chatting with whichever boyfriend was living with her at the time while she'd be fucking Sam in the other room. But I guess that's getting it together for a sultry, young heiress. Her drug of choice these days tempered her constant hummingbird energy down to a mellow constant buzz. It was better than tantrums.

But now she was back in Chicago for the first time in years, seemingly in every corner of the city at once—working at a record label and a cafe and a restaurant, breaking the café's record for the number of drinks made in an hour. Running into her everywhere I'd go, she was somehow always able to pull the exactly right item out of her bag to loan someone. No matter what conversation she overheard, it was like she'd just been waiting for the appropriate moment to make an entrance with this perfect loan. It was uncanny.

J____ and J____ told me of a night after the bars had closed when she invited the two of them and S____ over to her new place for a drink. She let them in and made them each a cocktail before sneaking off for a second and returning in lingerie, carrying a tank of nitrous. She offered them all whip-its and they politely declined. She helped herself to a dozen in 20 minutes while they protested that maybe it wasn't such a good idea. Scoffing at their protests, she put on a VCR mix-tape she'd made of gang-bang scenes and gang rapes complete with lots of cum shots. They all downed their drinks quickly and split.

With M____ and Stinkweeds both gone we had little direction. Stinkweeds was of course just a cover or a codeword. None of us actually cared about any more record shopping. But we did like to go ga-ga over the sublime bosom of the waitress at the Mediterranean place next door to it. But without a cover story, none of us could really justify going over there, however much all of us may have wanted to. That waitress was a lighthouse for this desert town and I felt lost without her.

Nate had made it clear that he planned on ignoring me when I spoke to him. When we got to the show they were showing a movie in the space, so we had to wait to load in. The Ecstatic Duo and Andrew pulled up a minute later. Matt got out of the car wearing boxer shorts with his shirt tucked into them. They'd all tripped the night before and were still a little woozy. I imagined the soft afterglow still surrounding every noun and verb, the unity of being still apparent in its infinite ways.

We loaded in and set up. Only the two bands, which we always prefer. Sam rode with me to Safeway to get some whiskey and beer. Last time we'd played there with Chin

Up and Paper Chase, we drank shots in the band room with Greg. The next morning when we were all waking up and getting moving at M_____'s, he announced with the biggest smile while stretching, in perhaps the most cheerful sing-song tone to ever say these words, "Boy, I feel like shit today."

Sam told me not to worry about Nate and I already pretty much wasn't, but it was nice to hear. We all know we're all going through the same shit: sick of being away, cooped up with each other, making no money to at least justify it in that way. We're bound to each have our frustrations manifest differently. I had a hard time, by way of explanation, not telling all of them that I plan to quit. I feel a little weird when things come up about the future and everyone talks about it and I just nod along. But I don't think I'll be surprising anyone. I'm going to suggest four options:
- I quit and they all continue as a three-piece.
- I quit and they get a new singer.
- We break up immediately.
- We record a new record and don't tell anyone but we all already know that we're going to break up before it comes out.

I don't really care which one we do.

Bobby said that he sees both my side and Nate's, which I thought was an inclusive variation of not taking a side.

L_____, our hostess at the show, was a little standoffish, but not in any way I took offense to, more just practically minded, task-oriented. After tapping into our whiskey while we played, she had a profound Jekyll and Hyde swing: flirting with all of us, telling me my belly was just because of my wedding ring and if I lost one the other would follow, and following me around asking me about my "sexy ass hair." Weird. She kept constantly shouting out my full name like some kind of gym coach standing over a student that was falling behind while running laps. But I was just standing there.

The show itself was fine, one of those that when we start the room somehow spontaneously fills and we don't know where these people just came from. Once we were set up and the music was turned off and people had surrounded the stage, we took a long time to start. Nate got into doing some kind of routine of stretching and flexing while the room was silent and waiting for us to begin. It was a little silly. I let the room in on me and Bobby's jokes with Dustin—"Camping is intense"—get it? *In Tents.* "I hear the circus is too." Nate got confused and annoyed, and asked, "Is this an inside joke?" which compounded the pun without him knowing that he was doing so. After milking that for all its worth, we all stood around for another minute or two of silence. There were only two bands and we'd been back-lined since before Ecstatic Sunshine, so it seemed a little ridiculous to me when our man Nate, insisting on the long pause, complained, "Ok, well I haven't had time to stretch." As if we should tell the audience to take another half-hour break. And he said it with this accusatory tone as if I was somehow responsible that he hadn't found time to stretch in the 135 minutes since we'd loaded in.

Show was fine. Played a strange set opening with "Wild Science, Wild Signs," "His Short Quip When Eddie's Bothered," "Say What You Mean," then playing the new ones before ending with a few more old ones. My throat was blown already and would later keep me up all night, but I made it through the show somehow, which I'm not certain I could do again tonight. Hurts so bad now I can't even speak. My nose is stuffed and burning, sucks.

After the show I ended up surrounded, talking to a bunch of kids. I gave them the long, detailed economic breakdown of our day-to-day existence as an explanation of why they will likely never see me play again. It was hard to make the distinction in their minds, between the simplistic, *he's just in it for the money* and me trying to explain that it's not a matter of just *wanting* more money, but that this could not be sustained. We are losing money to play there and we cannot afford to continue to do so. They were all up in arms—"But you were in Captain Jazz! That's so *influential*! You must be rich! Blah-blah." Ah, Tom Thumb's Blues. A guy walked up and asked me to sign a record. Those kids had all read about *Orchard Vale* online and asked about it.

A kid pulled up in a brown Pinto and asked us all to autograph the hood and we did. Wonder if he regretted the idea as much as we considered he might.

Watched *Sixteen Candles*. Molly Ringwald still so sickeningly hot 20 years and a whole lot of corny cultural baggage later. As much as all of that retro romanticizing provokes an immediate gag-reflex in me, I still could not believe how great she looked. Jake and Long Duck Dong were like Owen being interviewed by Kaori.

(Trains across the long flat open states.)

Ordered Domino's Pizza before lying awake all night, sick and unable to breathe with a swollen throat and plugged nostrils. I lay awake wondering, as always, what this is that I'm doing, what it makes me, who I am in relation to it. Makes me even happier to walk away from it. The last couple years the traveling has become nothing more than one more means to reconsidering my spiritual ponderings. I hit the brakes a year ago. These last tours are just the inevitable skid after ten-plus years of momentum.

Even before hitting the brakes, what happened to allow me to hit the brakes was a reorientation of my sense of self within the cosmos. I had to hit the absolute bottom of paranoia and dementia to be forced to look at things differently. What a cliché. Drug addicts quit and have spiritual awakenings. People escape destructive habits of all kinds by turning inwards. But now the traveling is only a confusing stress that forces me away from my good life at home, makes me reorient my life over and over.

ALL OVER AND OVER

(Shantytown factories of Northern Arizona)

Oh, and regarding my drawings and their subconscious and unconscious connections to shamanism—the poetry of the Shamans, their secret languages didn't surprise me. The Shamans are just Lacanian post-structuralists.

(What building could've stood there now reduced to rubble, not even a road to get to it?)

Clusters of buildings, a boat in the desert, RVs galore, they all look as if they've fallen from space.

One windy day shooting "A Lover's Discourse" in Champaign, we'd hooked up the car mount and I lay hidden in the back seat. Paul and Rosie drove a stretch of road over and over under a canopy of trees at noon. When we finished and returned to the remote field where Tomasz, Armene, and Chris waited for us, they stood with a giant inflatable raft, big enough that it could've seated all of us.
"What's that?" I asked.
"A raft."
"Where'd it come from?"
"It blew into us from across the field."

At Wild Oats this morning a 50-something-year-old man who must've just gotten divorced, walked the produce aisles, unsure exactly how to get back out there and jump back into the game. He stood mouth agape, staring at the butt of a 20-year-old woman in sweatpants bending over to get to a lower bin in the bulk section. She just remained bent over and he just continued to stare.

All day desert, the occasional low bridges over dried up river-beds, houses without a means to connect them to any other houses, sheds shredded, red soil, yellow straw.

*

NOVEMBER 7, 2006

Election Day in the USA. We're driving thirteen hours without passing through anywhere but the big old wide-open Texas panhandle.

I screwed yesterday up a month ago. It was supposed to be a day off to drive from Phoenix to Austin. Only at the last minute did Santa Fe get in touch offering no money. I figured it was Monday and would've been a day off anyways, so why not play? Anything would be better than nothing. And I love Santa Fe so much that I was excited to get an opportunity to visit.

Unfortunately, I didn't look at a map before agreeing to go and Edwards must not have either or he never would've suggested it. We drove from 10:00 a.m., as soon as we could get up and get out of Phoenix, and got to the show at 8:30 last night after the first band had already finished. Nothing to look at all day. The last few hours through the New Mexico desert, a full moon hung straight ahead and huge over the road, hypnotizing and confounding all of us. The moon, like Led Zeppelin or olives, is one of those things that I had to grow into. Its ubiquitous familiarity builds a tolerance, but that also deepens its mystery. I guess it's easier to forget about the moon in the city and that's probably just about at the heart of every country person's superiority complex.

Me and Bobby listened to more of *The Da Vinci Code*, just fifteen minutes left of it. Reminds me of one of those old fashioned Lone Ranger-style cliffhanger serials. It's fun in that way, but I can't really imagine any other circumstances except for a restless long drive in the dark that would get me to listen to it. It's funny: all the esoterica and Secret History books that I've read and walked around thinking *I am in on some shit that would Blow People's Minds*. But I never even realized that last year's biggest blockbuster was about all that same stuff. It's like finding out that Make Believe actually sounds exactly like some super popular MTV band

and everyone knows it except for us.

Talked to Amy. She was having Jonathan, Joe, and Chris over to import Jonathan's song into the trailer and re-cut it by committee. S____ and B____ and L____ all had to stop by to drop off or pick up different things, so it became a little spontaneous Monday night house party.

We got to the show and loaded in. The young promoter was very sweet, provided all the details of the contract that most people, more often than not, don't even notice that they've over-looked—batteries, socks. His mom had made two big pans of veggie enchiladas and some beans and New Mexican fried bread. It was so *exactly* the New Mexican cooking that I'm super-into that I got actually, literally sad that I couldn't taste anything because of my stuffed-up nose. With my throat swollen and nose so stuffed it's hard to even eat anything, can't breathe well enough.

I feel like I don't have a cold, but like a cold snuck up on me in reverse by reading the signals that my body was sending and misinterpreting their context. My throat was so blown from San Diego and no monitors. I could feel the muscles pulled in my throat and the restricted opening to breathe through. It's like my nose heard the alarm going off in my throat and responded, "Looks like we're sick. Places, everyone! No warning, I know, and it's been 75 to 80 degrees in dry air for days, but oh well. Let's stuff this fucker up!"

We see nothing of Santa Fe but the club, and I end up having to play on what should've been a night off that I ended up really needing. The club was cool, an all-ages teen center kind of place that must have a grant from the city. It was very European to have been there at all and very New Mexican in its design and details. There were some graffiti murals and positive reinforcement posters around that give the whole place a bit of a *Mr. T keeping the kids off drugs* kind of vibe. But with that magic sky over the parking lot, drugs must already be less necessary than they are for most teens in most places.

A band called Yellow Fever from Austin played. They were a trio, two young women, maybe 20 or 18 or 22 years old, and a young guy playing drums. They were super good, really tight, creepy harmonies through just about the entirety of the set. Simple and laid-back and cool, they had a bit of a dated Riot Grrrl feel on the surface and superficially may have sounded a lot like Quixotic. But it was executed so well that the reality of what they did far exceeded those immediate impressions.

I drank a couple hot toddies as quick as I could and wandered the parking lot attempting to summon the ancient energy of the New Mexico moon to rise up through my every molecule and reveal my body to be the hologram that I know deep down that it is. How can my throat really be so fucked and sore if I don't really even believe that I have a throat? But my New Mexico-isms were a bit too self-conscious. Even standing on stage about to start, I was still completely unsure how the show could possibly happen. It all sounded under water and in slow motion. I asked the audience if anyone knew who Chris Griscom was and was disappointed to find out that no one did. And no one there lived in an earth-ship. So much for my New Mexico illusions.

Two summers ago me and Amy spent a few days in Santa Fe. We went out to Teo's mom's Institute of Healing Light in the desert just a few miles outside of town and each underwent an "Exercise in Consciousness" led by a beautiful Indian woman named Navjeet. While each of us went in alone for an hour, the other one wandered the grounds and looked at the clouds and the brush and the dust—a perfect hour for either before or after an hour with Navjeet. Amy went first. I sat in the magical yard. Surrounded by the desert, four buildings came together at their corners to leave this yard in the center, lush with plant life.
The hour with Navjeet was the ideal blend of a guided

meditation, seeing a shrink, and tripping. In response to her questions, animals spontaneously blossom in your mind. Parts of your body glow with different colors and when she asks that body part directly, it knows exactly why it chose the color that it did.

We browsed the shops of Santa Fe's old Town Square. Crazy neo-flamenco guys played, reminding me so much of Sam's playing that I called him to tell him to google "Flamenco." I felt a little old and square enjoying myself browsing the galleries, but I didn't mind it. On the outskirts of town we found The Church of the Magic Sky and another old Western Santeria-type church.

We spent a couple nights in earth-ships twelve miles outside of Taos, alone with the colors of the sky hundreds of miles wide flashing as if in conversation. Despite the ornate doors, and knotty trees and winding walls that opened up into skylights, I remained on edge the entire time, anticipating *The Hills Have Eyes*.

At the end of the trip when we had to head to Lawton for her brother's wedding, Amy's dad gave us directions. They involved 30 miles down a two-lane road through tall fields without a single intersection. The road was on the map only as "Other Road." For that brief period, while I sped straight ahead and, reclining shotgun, Amy pretended to sleep, I was granted a brief reprieve from *The Hills Have Eyes* and thought only of *The Texas Chainsaw Massacre*.

Got back to the hotel early and lights out by midnight, up at 6:30 a.m. to head to Austin. Up all night the second night in a row trying to breathe. Coming into Amarillo: signs for Fried Rattlesnake and a 72-ounce steak, rusted out train cars and everything is golden straw in all directions. Cops and truck stops, everything appears menacing.

460 miles still to go, across Texas on a state highway. We pass abandoned gas stations and cafes. The parking lot of a veterinary clinic is packed. At the rest stop there is a pen for "Utility Animals Only—No Pets Allowed." In a small town,

a "Steak Buffet" has a sign with a chef holding a steak the shape of Texas.

Amy tripped last night with Chris, Joe, and Jonathan and they all watched the trailer on 'shrooms. I laid awake all night worrying about the trailer online and these posters hung all over town and now these postcards sent out. It's like we're trying to draw all this attention to *ourselves* instead of to the film. And the film isn't even done yet. Makes me feel like an asshole show-off, totally embarrassing, like I somehow need my name hanging all over town all the time. Wish we could finish it before even telling anyone about it.

Memphis, Texas: Home of The Fighting Cyclones and The My-T Burger, Cotton Capital of the Panhandle.
Did you know that wide swatches of America have been abandoned entirely to rubble? Hundreds of miles at a time, whole towns left to rot.
430 miles left to go. Sam has accelerated over 60 mph for the first time in two hours. Maybe he's exhausted his own current manifestation of passive-aggression.

One chapter left of *The Cosmic Serpent*. Not as into the second half as I was the first. Hopefully it'll wrap itself up interestingly. I'm excited to return to *The Idiot*, hopefully remember what's going on.

When Dustin showed up to the show last night, he thought Isabella and Jennifer from Yellow Fever worked at the club. When he introduced himself as Dustin from Ecstatic Sunshine, they replied, "We're in Yellow Fever," and he, being Japanese, thought that they were hitting on him.

Four more hours to go, I guess, going bananas sitting in the far back. Sleep for half an hour, read for half an hour. Repeat. Actually, that part is pretty good. It's just the being trapped part that gets to me.

*

ALL OVER AND OVER

NOVEMBER 8, 2006

Had the TV on this morning all ready to check out election results, eating eggs that Vernon had scrambled with peppers from his garden when the breaking news came on CNN: Rumsfeld resigns! Amy is excited to have a baby today. Today Mike is crossing Iowa by himself, driving home for a night off between Kansas and Indiana, screaming along to the radio. Mom is giddy, dancing in the hall at work. It is 75 degrees, bright and breezy, a perfect spring day in Austin.

Yesterday we were all stir-crazy and none of us said much to each other. Our already low morale coupled with a fourteen-hour drive was a real fucking lobotomizer. Not even tense between us, just nothing.

Emos must be the place that we've played the most times ever and like everywhere it's always hit or miss for us. We've sold it out and we've played it empty and every ratio in between. A couple years ago we did a few support tours in a row that happened to all go through Emos and so we played there four times in five or six months. I recognize everyone that works there and none of them ever remember us ever having played there before.

Austin is a city where we always know a lot of people, but just don't know who it'll be. If cities were airports for bands, Austin would be a major hub. Smog hung out a couple times ago when we played there. Har Mar was wrecking the place once, climbing all over a minor celebrity and forcing her into his awkward *Sean-partying-what's-the-big-deal* agreement.

For some reason we usually have hours and hours to kill there. I walk back and forth between the yard and the TV in the bar, walking up and down Sixth Street and all its gross Mardi Gras frat-boyisms, Red Bull signs in every doorway, tattoo shops, three dozen live music venues, pizza on the street, airbrush art as performance art, creeps all over. And retreating to Emos, everyone's always super friendly, but in a macho *drinker's-drinker* kind of way that I can't entirely relate to.

A veneer of cynicism shades every conversation with drinkers like that. People use cynicism to imply "Critical Thinking." It's a lazy shortcut meant to give the impression that a certain depth of character won't allow the person to believe anything anyone says. But when coupled with heavy drinking, it usually comes off to me more as if the person's brain has gone a bit soft and it's going to take an extra second to process things. But the vanity is always the last to go, and they remember to *appear* as if concentrating. Strange how people get most proud when at their worst, but I guess it makes sense. Shame kicks in and they lash out at it.

I've dreamt about my dad four or five times since traveling, very vivid dreams in which nothing happens except that we're together. In one he was giving me some advice that I remember listening to carefully and appreciating, but not being able to remember by the time I woke up. In another dream we were laughing together. I don't know if we knew what was funny even in the dream.

So heading out to familiar Emos almost feels like home, if home had piss all over the floors and was just two functional boxes, one big and one little, and a yard with broken bleachers and theater seats strewn about.

Fourteen hours through nothing, I finished *The Cosmic Serpent*, got a little lost in the technical details of the last chapters, but didn't try too hard to keep up. I figured it's a matter of if you're gonna buy it, you're gonna buy it. And who am I to refute any of his data? I've never lived in a rainforest. It all made sense to me as it was explained, but it's not like I *understood* it well enough to know how to look for what the counter-evidence would be.

Sitting up shotgun I slept a deeper sleep than I have in days. Woke up to all the variations of Lawton, Oklahoma, zipping past us. We would cross each through its Main Street. Maybe a gas station has survived. One "Odds and

Ends Shop" advertised "Clean Restrooms" on its big sign.

Read the first 40 pages of Zizek's *Iraq: The Broken Tea Kettle* and got immediately wrapped up in it. Even being two years old, it doesn't read as dated because it's focused on the initial attack and the grotesque aspects of the global subconscious of which the war is a manifestation. He ties things together from all over in such a brilliant way, makes things make sense.

Listened to iTunes on shuffle through West Texas dusk— Red Krayola, Bert Jansch, Aki Tsuyoko, Angus Maclease, Xhol Caravan, Michael Hurley, weird Talk Talk EP, Will Oldham. Maybe it was the desperation of my restlessness, but everything sounded real good.

I drove the last 200 miles. Me and Bobby put on *The Da Vinci Code* and listened to 20 minutes until it just stopped without resolving anything. Turns out there must be a Part 4 that I don't have. It never occurred to me that the mp3 version that Mike gave me might not be complete. We laughed about our media savvy and pretended to be know-it-all types who insist, *Oh no, that's how it ends.* I remember Chris seeing *Magnolia* for the first time; he put the second tape in first and watched it from the middle to the end. He then switched tapes to watch the beginning back to the middle. Not recognizing his mistake until we talked about it, he gushed about how awesome it was, how he couldn't believe how it was structured, so bold.

Loaded in after 10:00 p.m. and so little was going on that it still seemed like we must've been hours early. The Rapture was playing next door and it was packed. Took me a long time to find a place to park and must've been gone another 45 minutes doing so. Ate the single worst piece of pizza I've ever eaten. Even sent it back to re-heat it and it was still just a cold slab of coagulated white cheese.

I watched the band opening for The Rapture with Dustin. We weren't sure if we could call it a band or not. It was just two guys and a couple keyboards, two mics and a drum set. I said I felt like it was a cartoon band and a second later Matt walked up and said first thing, "This is like a caricature."

But 500 people were pumped. The little guy stood at the keyboard while the taller guy waved his arms around and struck some poses that seemed like the Ali G. gay fashion designer character. It was like being at an MTV Spring Break Beach Party Special. My cold blown up into full effect, hardly able to breathe even while concentrating solely on doing so, I was in no mood for a Texas November beach party. But when I heard the crowd roar I had to turn back and see. The tall, dark dork had walked over to the drum set and was standing behind it, his cheeks sucked in and an intense stare straight ahead like a cheetah at the disco. He twirled the drumsticks. For all the attitude and posturing, you'd think that this guy was demonstrating the grace and coordination of an Olympic figure skater. The crowd cheered.

After a good, long 32-bar pose, he finally sat down and played a straight-ahead mid-tempo 4/4 beat that did not contribute to or color the pre-recorded track in any manner whatsoever. He wiggled his shoulders back and forth in time to the beat, nodded his head. The crowd went so crazy it was like he was a toddler and he had 500 mommies and daddies seeing him sit down at the drums for the first time.

L_____ showed up. We sat for one drink together in the yard before peeking in at our show inside. A one-man karaoke electro-clash guy in a dumb moustache disguise was basically doing exactly the same thing as the guys outside, except it was supposed to be funny. It was vain and overbearing, but probably meant to be a critique. That kind of thing though can be so tough to pull off when the required audience enthusiasm is lacking. The band outside, being serious, was actually funnier.

L_____ was doing well, likes Austin, like his job doing social work at the city's worst school, helping to coordinate after school programs. Not so excited by the Austin gay scene, but said he's meeting a lot of people and everyone he's meeting is friendly. One of the most striking memories I have of my wedding is L_____ and my dad in a corner, both lit and hitting it off gang busters, both cracking up. So I never doubt L_____ can get along anywhere. We talked about the Democrats winning the house and how it made us feel each good *kind of*, but not good in any way that you can believe in, or trust to be anything more than just passing relief.

Drank whiskey hoping it would help clear out my head and comfort my throat. Walked to the van and did tons of breathing and throat exercises, but nothing opened my nose. I'd already been eating some West Texas truck stop cold medicine all day and it did zero. And I had drunk a Red Bull as soon as we'd arrived because I was zonked from the drive, which actually doesn't make sense to me. There's really nothing tiring in itself about driving. Must have to do with air quality and cramped space? I ate a half of an ephedrine pill hoping that it would clear my head, but nothing helped. I'd eaten a preventative Imodium AD knowing that with The Rapture in the good dressing room there'd be no using the restroom if I had to. And the cumulative effect of all of these meds was cold sweats and nausea. Felt like a fever breaking.

A_____ from Chicago showed up and surprised us. Looking fit and positive as ever, buff, I dare say. He might be the only person on earth that could conceivably be called ex-Make Believe as Sam and I did have the name in mind already when we got together to play with him once. (Though to clear, the name has always been a compromise to me, vastly inferior to my original idea: Make/Believe.) We were excited about the blast-beats he'd played with his old power-violence bands and he was excited to play with us because he wanted to play mellow music. He was teaching a spinning class at the time, psyching up a room full of people facing him as they all pedaled. He had this idea of making music for spinning classes and was convinced that we could all just sit back and live off the royalties.

One time his old band and JOA played Emos together. We all went out for burritos together before the show. As the meal was winding down A_____ disappeared. After a few minutes we spotted him in a corner talking to a waitress, not even ours, that we'd all noticed from across the restaurant and thought was cute. Later, while playing, I looked down and she was sitting on the stage at my feet with her back turned to me. Her legs were spread. A_____ was leaning in and they were making out. The kid is good.

Anjala also showed up and was kind enough to bring us a bottle of Maker's Mark for the road. She had five days off from Cursive tour and spent them in Austin with an old friend that she grew up with. Cursive has been out since July 4th when we met up with them, and has had three five-day breaks. They leave again tomorrow for the last month. It will have been five months straight by the time they are done, and although I'm sure they're all getting paid well, which must make it easier, I sure don't envy them.

Before the Cursive tour that we were on, Anjala had never been on tour. And at that point she'd only met Cursive three days prior to meeting us. We all got along swell and quickly with her, but we perhaps meant more to her than we otherwise would have since we were the opening band on the first tour that she'd ever done. She's 26 or 27, classically trained, and maybe a little self-conscious about not really being a Rocker. It was great to see her and talk, but really all I could focus on was not puking.

I watched a few songs by The Rapture and it sounded pretty good. I could see why a lot of people like them.

Our set may have been the toughest show to get through of my entire life. Even while setting up, I was overcome by coughing fits and was convinced that I'd never be able to get through the set. I could barely speak, let alone sing and bellow and bray. The room began to fill up a little bit. It was still sparse, but spread out, the room was filled, people in clusters in different corners.

By the end of the first song I thought I'd puke if I kept going. I was aware of singing with less force than I ever really have before, like I was just singing with my mouth, not even my throat, let alone my stomach. I couldn't breathe fast enough to keep up with the songs and skipped entire phrases. I was dizzy. I kept my eyes closed and feet planted and the mic in place and just went down the set list checking them off as they came up. Nate kept dropping sticks and I couldn't believe how he'd pick them up without missing a beat. Bobby ended up out of tune and not noticing. All around perhaps the sloppiest Make Believe show ever that we didn't abandon halfway through. I noticed a familiar-looking guy watching us that was later pointed out to me as the singer of Spoon.

A few wasted stylish kids were freaking out in the very front, jumping up and down, back and forth, dramatically pounding their fists on the stage and throwing their heads back to howl. One of these freaking-out kids grabbed the base of the mic stand while I was singing and jammed it back up towards me so that the mic banged up into my mouth and I bit my lip. Another night, more people going crazy and not feeling like shit, it might not have been a big deal. But frustrated as I already was, I responded as if it was a deliberate act of sabotage. My intuitive caveman reflex, I swung the mic stand back at him to crack open his head with the base. I missed him and the mic stand lay smashed in half at the front of the stage. It had all happened in a second and I was so glad that I missed him.

I had met this kid earlier when he offered to sell us Xanax and I sent him to Sam. He had a young, hot Latina girlfriend that earlier had run up calling my name and hugged me. She held me tight a little too long and asked, "Isn't it weird to have girls you don't know run up and want to hug you?" I told her that doesn't really happen all that much and felt awkward. Now I scolded her boyfriend, asking him to please not grab or swing anything.

Vernon and Angela waited for us to pack so we could follow them back to their new apartment. They'd been married just a month and were now both out of work, worried nothing was coming together. I told them they were lucky to be unemployed together as newly-weds, like an extended honeymoon. And though they both laughed a little and riffed on the idea, I could see the worry that their glances to each other betrayed.

Lee from American Analog Set came over. We hadn't seen each other in about five years and it was really nice to catch up. I've always liked their band as people and musically. One of the few bands that we toured with that long ago that I still occasionally listen to.

We dropped Vern and Angela off at Vern's truck. It was after two in the morning and still it felt like we'd somehow gotten out of there quick. Strange the number of times that we've been to Austin and played there and who are these people? We know Vern and Angela. We know the few other friends that pop up where they do. But I mean all these *other* people, not just Austin, but anywhere. Have they all seen us all these times? Or all of them see us sometimes? Once each?

After such a long day and a shitty show we were all snappy with each other. Vern lives about fifteen minutes north of downtown on the outskirts that seem like consumer-desert anywhere, but is in fact still in Austin.

(What a day—Rumsfeld! Spring weather, Jade Tree check!)

Vern might be the guy that we all know and like the most but have the least in common with. He's a life-long Texan from a small town who moved to Austin to get to the big city and write about bands. We met when he interviewed me about five years ago. We needed a place to crash and I asked him and he seemed shocked, but then got really into it. He might secretly be a giant Owen fan that uses us to feel a little bit closer to Mike. He's sent us all Christmas presents and at their wedding last month they even walked down the aisle to Bobby and Nate's guitar duet. He never comes across as a *fan*—he is our *friend*—but it can be a little like visiting a parent's house when we stay with him. It's always clean and there's snacks and TV and he fusses over making sure that we've got everything we need. He is the only guy we know who is still shocked that we're vegetarians and he can't believe we don't bring at least one gun on tour with us.

A year ago in Austin with a free afternoon, we were sitting at an Indian buffet when Vern insisted on taking us to the firing range. After a good amount of protest, we did all have to admit that we were curious. So we went back to his place, grabbed the rifle and the handgun and headed over to the range. I can't say I enjoyed anything about the place, a Texas vigilante/sporting good store hybrid. I was nervous just being close to the other people firing down their lanes. I did shoot each gun once, but then just hung out outside for half an hour. The actual physical brutality of it shook me, made me nauseous. Of course it's not clubbing someone over the head, but it was enough to creep me out.

We were all happy years ago when Vern showed up to a show with a girlfriend and she was smart and cool. We befriend plenty of loner-types and although Vern never really fit that standard in a lot of ways, he did live alone in a suburban apartment complex and we never met any friends of his. So we were all happy to hear of the engagement and now to see them together.

Pulling into their new neighborhood last night a few deer were running around the lawn outside the gate. Bobby was feeling argumentative, which I'd never really seen before. Sam was passed out, which I'd seen all too much of, and Nate still wasn't talking to me. I had to enjoy the deer on my own.

I passed right out in my sleeping bag behind the dining room table while everyone else hung out and chatted.

Today, this perfect beautiful spring day after the Democrats have taken the house, promising at least the *possibility* of a check on Bush's power, Rumsfeld resigns, I finally get my Jade Tree check, Mom gets an offer on Dad's condo.

In Houston, across the street from our usual haunt Mary Jane's, which we always dread but always return to. Ryan and everyone else that works there are always super cool and friendly. There's just nothing to do and nowhere to go. And the shows are never any good. Maybe the Owls/Need New Body show in 2001 was good. Since then, opening for Good Life was good, but Hella, Need New Body, Cex, JOA—nothing really, just another place on the way to another place.

First time that we ever played here—I would've been 22—we stayed with L____, the 41-year-old CPA and world's unlikeliest JOA fan at the time. L____ drove an old orange Corvette, hosted a college radio show and had XL condoms left out on display in his bathroom. He's since come around to say hello now and then, but it's been a few years. Last time I saw him he told me of going to the club that we were playing the night before to be in the audience recording overdubs of applause for a ZZ Top live album. Seems the recording of the show didn't quite capture the gusto of the crowd, so ZZ Top hired some dancers to strip to their songs and gave away free beer. They pointed mics at the audience to layer the cheering over the recording of the show.

I did once also meet the man—in Dortmund maybe, some smaller German city—that insisted that he was the guy sitting back stage that played James Hetfield's solos live. The soundman hits a switch and that guy rips from an undisclosed location. That was his job.

Which reminds me of Felix one time at a party—in Berlin or Cologne — can't remember where he was living at the time. He met a girl. She was cute and he was excited. She didn't seem familiar before he approached her, but became immediately familiar once they started talking. She told him that she was the German voice for Bart Simpson.

The helicopters over Houston. P____ out of town for a week doing some Home Shopping Network gig.

Ryan the promoter has joined the Smoking Popes. He's very much the Latino Rob Roy.

ALL OVER AND OVER

The owner of Walter's tells us her version of the riot here a couple weeks ago, a cop tackling a band onstage because of noise complaints, pulling his taser out on the audience. Through the back-channel small-worlds of Texas politics, it's now all straightened out.

Listening to Cat Stevens as we sat in Houston rush hour I almost got weepy. It *is* a Wild World! I *am* on the road to find out! I *do* listen to the wind of my soul!

Everywhere is home to someone.
This rush hour is familiar.
*

All Over and Over #3

CROSSING LOUISIANA—
BOWLING GREENE

West Coast = "The Hypnosis of the Zigzag Open Drift versus Impossible Deadlines"

East Coast = "Between Strange Friends and Friendly Strangers"

ALL OVER AND OVER

NOVEMBER 9, 2006

Just woke up from a nap in the backseat, AKA The Van Infirmary, AKA Tim's Room. The momentum of the road zipping by under us hypnotizes and lulls us each, each at a different rate and each submitting to it at a different moment. But we all wake up together every time momentum is broken and we're pulling to a stop somewhere.

I woke up in the parking lot of a Stuckeys and stumbled in half-asleep to take a piss and buy a bottle of water. Every day I need to have one handy, but never take more than a sip until we're within half an hour of our day's destination so I'm not stuck holding my pee all day or making us stop over and over.

Coming to in Stuckeys I was stunned. The place was packed, like Saturday-night-at-the-club packed, Thursday afternoon at the convenience store. Everyone was smoking and standing around. And everyone was super dirty, caked in mud on their bodies and their clothes. I couldn't imagine what all these people were all doing all day, how they all got so dirty. I guess they can't afford a change of clothes or water to bathe? That's a poverty beyond what we ever see in the city. I made a conscious effort to try to fall back asleep as soon as we got back in the van.

For almost an hour I had sat at Eric Carter's kitchen table with him; the entire time, though present for our conversation, I was attempting to cling to the lingering details of my dream last night. I didn't want it to fade and I knew so from the moment I was woken up.

I dreamt vividly that me and Amy were looking for an apartment. We found a very big house that we could afford. I mean it was inside an apartment building, but when you opened the front door it opened up into a giant mansion. We were excited and decided to take it, even though there were two strange drawbacks. One: there was an unfolding circus in the middle of the living room. It would fold back up and put itself away at night, but opened again every morning with striking geometry and clowns and horses and Ferris wheels and contests. It was all sorts of rusty browns and icy blues, like maybe a Paul Klee painting or some kind of early 20th century modernist coping with The Great War. It would unfold and open up with its own unique physics independent from those normal laws that governed the rest of the house.

The other strange thing, number two: my old girlfriend, N____, was crashing on the couch with a friend for a while and Amy and I had to agree that if we moved into the place, the giant place with the circus, we would let the two girls stay with us for as long as they needed to.

The first night we moved in, I was sitting in the living room watching the circus fold itself back up, immersed in its inner workings. Though it folded up not just its physical forms, but also all of the spaces within its boundaries, it was far more mechanical than poetic. The entire expanse of the circus folded over and over on to itself until it fit neatly under our hard wood floor. Tucking itself in under there, it whispered, "Good night." All of the people that worked at the circus got folded up into the floor, but the people that were visiting the circus for the night stepped out. I stood with all of them, waving goodbye, waiting for the circus to finish packing itself up before I would let them all out and lock the door behind them. It occurred to me that this would be a new nightly ritual and I wasn't sure if it would end up being something that I would enjoy having to do.

As I was standing in the small crowd, about to show them to the door, N_____ and her friend came in. It was late and they were drunk and I imagined crashing on a couch in a room in which you had to wait for a circus to fold itself up each night before you could get to bed was probably a pretty good excuse to go out every night. Her timing, returning as soon as the circus was away, was perfect. She and her friend giggled and glanced across the crowd, demurely acknowledging the crowd as a whole before giggling to each other.

She looked a little older than I ever knew her to get. She was dressed up kind of fancy-yuppyish, like a hairdresser that works somewhere where she makes a lot of money. I stared at her. She looked beautiful. She saw me then and smiled and walked slowly over to me and put her hands around my neck and ran her fingers up into my hair and slowly kissed me. I was aware of having no idea where that mouth might have been that night and getting half grossed out and half turned on by the idea. I got swept away in it. After kissing a while she put her hand against my chest then hugged me tight. I opened my eyes after breathing deep and being caught up in only her for what might've been a long time.

All of the circus patrons were still all standing around me and were now all looking at us confused by our lack of discretion. She put up a little bit of a fight as I slipped out of her arms to show the circus patrons to the door. Holding it open, standing behind it, I nodded goodbye to each person. An older prudish woman gave me a disapproving harrumph. A middle-aged rotund and balding man that looked like the lowest common denominator caricature of a Tourist from Ohio gave me a wink and a big smile. Pulling his shoulders up to his ears and giving me a punch on the arm, he said, "You go get 'em tiger!" I grabbed him by the shoulders and spun him, pushed him out the door and closed it behind him.

N____'s friend introduced herself and offered me her hand and I took it in mine but hardly acknowledged her, never really even noticing what she looked like behind raised eyebrows and the flashing mannerisms of surprise and imposition. She excused herself immediately and went and curled up on a couch leaving me and N_____ alone.

N____ came over and cooed and I held her at arm's length. She asked what was I doing there? And where had I been? I showed her my wedding ring. She got all playful hurt, Black Widow pouting, and said that she couldn't believe that I'd done that. I told her me and my wife were living there now and she got really happy and said that she couldn't wait to meet Amy in the morning. She was sure they'd become fast friends.

We spent all of the next days hanging out together, just the two of us, staying in our pajamas all day, behaving like happy children. She was incredibly stupid, unable to feel any emotion with the slightest complexity of shading, let alone express such an emotion. Her mannerisms and behaviors were broad strokes, cartoonish Kabuki stage acting: Eroticism, Playful Kitten, Hurt, Letting You In On A Secret, etc. Over and over she'd work me up by rubbing her tits against my chest or getting her butt within sniffing distance before always pulling away at the moment of contact and returning to the same game—"Shame on you! You have a wife now!" I knew the entire arc of the game. I knew that she was 100% unable to exist outside the parameters of this game. I knew that she was more dumb than anyone else I may ever meet and that her power over me was also, in a way, a matter of me surrendering to politeness, like *OK, if this is as much as you can understand about how to exist in the world, then I submit. It would be rude to impose my own more nuanced worldviews on you.* And I loved the game and I loved her.

One afternoon, having spent some hours wandering the circus together, we went to the kitchen. I was making her a sandwich. In many ways our hours together were like those of a child with a babysitter, both knowing that the child is ultimately in control of everything. She sat at the table quietly. I stood at the counter, laughing as I made the sandwiches, my back to her. I still had laughter-momentum and continued with whatever childish jokes that I'd had her giggling with. But when it got to be her turn to contribute to the role-playing, she remained silent. I turned. She sat sullen at the table. I also got quiet and finished the sandwich and cut it in half. I walked one half over to her and sat down next to her.

She took a bite but kept her head down, pouting. I took a bite and smiled at her chewing slowly, but she wouldn't look up at me.

"Hey," I said. But she wouldn't look up. She was crying. I reached over to her and she pulled away. With tears running down her cheeks, her face hot and red, she sighed and rolled her eyes. She started to say something, but she had a mouthful of peanut butter and couldn't get the words out. I laughed a little and she laughed through her tears and exaggerated the effort of her chewing. After a minute of working away at the peanut butter, having had time to reconsider what she was going to say, she just smiled and shrugged, wiped the tears from her eyes with the backs of her wrists.

The alarm went off.

Crossing Louisiana swamps and bogs, trees up to their necks in still water. These guys all keep talking about all kinds of stuff to which my only possible response would be, "I quit." So I'm keeping quiet.

Show last night was one of those perfect-ammunition-to-point-out-how-useless-touring-is-type shows. This was at least the fifth, if not the sixth time Make Believe has played Houston and 20 or 30 people were paid. Promoter Ryan says he's happy to lose money on us. Bartender Ryan tells us his shots were written up in the Houston Chronicle last month. Must be the biggest and toughest looking guy I know that drinks such girly Kool-Aid shots.

Eric told us he admired our perseverance returning to Houston and playing to no one. We sat up late with him, 3:00 a.m., drinking and talking bands and booking and music biz.

Sam and I did an interview earlier with a couple teenagers for their new zine. They seemed insecure that we wouldn't take them seriously, so they kept asking faux-deep questions in such general terms that they could've been addressed to anyone, "what are your thoughts on the music industry" etc. Sam and I laughed a bit when we were done. But I guess a few drinks later with insightful company—Eric—we're all as interested in music biz and gossip as anyone else.

Eric and his wife are loveable eccentrics. After years living in the Bay Area, they moved to Houston just a couple years ago, maybe to be close to her family or something. They were able to buy a house, which they never could've done in the Bay Area, and his office is in a little nook of the house. It's a ranch house, '70s-style, lots of wood and lava lamps and God's eyes and antique things and 100,000,000 records. Eric knows everything about every band that's ever existed and he's psyched to get into it about any of them. They both chain-smoke clove cigarettes. He looks a bit like David Carradine in *Nashville*. She's a couple years older than him and short and cute and surly in an endearing way. I get the impression she might impulsively gobble up some ecstasy if it were offered and I respect any grown-up that can do that. Eric micro-manages a few of our more popular label-mates and a big roster of career weirdos. He's been booking Of Montreal forever, long before they became his cash cow. "Cash Cow" might be the nicest thing that I could say about that band.

When we woke up he already had bagels, bananas, muffins, coffee, yogurt, and juice out on the table. He has a spare room with two bunk beds for bands to crash and he rattled off eight to ten bands staying over there in the next two weeks. Must get awfully lonely being the only older cool guy in Houston.

We were on the road by 10:00 a.m. to head to Pensacola. Two days ago we woke up in New Mexico and tonight we're in Florida. I tried to fall back asleep and return to that dream of N_____, but instead ended up lying around half-asleep with the clarity unique to that in-between state. My mind drifted without setting any boundaries for itself and instead of the simple pleasures of that dream, I ended up obsessing over what it meant.

N_____ is not someone I miss or ever think about when I'm at home. She has zero to do with my real life. When traveling, however, she returns to me vividly in dreams and daydreams. These days have been such long drives that we're all disoriented. I'm feeling cooped up and feverish and restless. I believe she returns to me as the ideal sex object. I miss Amy so much in such a present way. But in a more desperate and paradoxically abstract way I'm just missing connection at all, being around anyone else besides my three lovable muchachos that I spend 24 hours a day with, weeks at a time.

So N_____ returns and I never really even knew her when I knew her. Even then I was doing this to her, objectifying her. She returns to satisfy the caveman part of me that needs only touching. There's some neurons firing without direction or release and so they manifest as this sad cartoon character. And smiling through tears, what could be more humanizing, right? So she was sad because I don't know why. I'm married and her power over me is now meaningless or she's had a self-conscious flash and is grinding away at the boundaries of her sad-cartoon identity? I don't know. But what it means, I do know, is that she's been humanized in me. Not to say she hasn't been before, but it fades. I forget about her for a year or two, she's meaningless until some immediate circumstances provoke my subconscious to manifest its ideal sexualized non-human woman, and she returns until she's smiling while crying and the antidote has worked. It's my psycho-emotional immune system working shit out.

Crossing Louisiana always thrills me, long bridges dozens of miles straight ahead with only Bayou on either side. I drove until Baton Rouge, where we stopped for lunch at a very weird health food store set up in a pre-fab shed. I ate a delicious squash and quinoa special and then milled about outside. Two people fought in the small building behind the store — a daycare. I didn't hear any banging, but the screams and yelps were violent, pained-sounding.

Stunts Jackass-style on The Learning Channel. Fox News reports, "the shit has hit the fan" after Democrats take both houses.

First show in a few days to a filled room with excited people. Nice change of pace for sure and a pleasant surprise. Last time I played Pensacola, 1997, no one showed up except a few kids and then a white power skinhead crew showed up and disrupted the show by pushing everyone around. Very strange.

We've since been back twice I can think of on days off. First time Need New Body and Owls decided to all sleep on the beach, a few of us had some mushrooms. By the time we'd gotten to town, everywhere to eat was closed except Hooters. We stood outside, eleven of us, deliberating for a long time before finally our stomachs insisted *fuck it* and we went in. After standing around bashful—*aw-shucks*—for a minute, we all split again and stood around outside some more, before finally going back in, the hostess of course not pleased to see us at this point. A party of eleven bearded and tattooed scumbags is bad enough, but a party of eleven judgmental scumbags: fuck that.

We were seated, overlooking the Gulf, which was beautiful. Our waitress was the perfect analogy for our meals, all the superficial signifiers meant to obscure the absence of substance. And I don't mean *No Substance* like she lacked subjectivity. I just mean that she wasn't attractive according to Hooters' own prescribed standard of attractive. I can still picture her years later, so plain with stringy bleached hair and short shorts and a flat chest even. None of us talked much. Maybe the most awkward hour the eleven of us would ever spend together. The vegetarian options were iceberg lettuce with ranch and curly cheese-fries.

Sleeping on the beach was great until it came time to sleep. Then rolling over in the sand, pulling your blanket over you just to get a face full of sand, not as romantic as it seemed to all of us at first. We were woken by a beach patrol police woman walking down the beach and yelling at us each directly to leave until I heard her say, "Jamey Robinson! Is that you?" And it turns out Jamey's next door neighbor growing up that he hadn't seen in 20 years was a Pensacola beach-patrol police woman. She let us stay as long as we all agreed to stay awake.

Another night at the beach with Need New Body was on the shore of North Carolina where they park that giant battleship and filmed *Dawson's Creek*. Three times we played there in a loft on the third floor above a lawyer's office. After cutting my hair outside the show the first time through, I decided to make a tradition of it each time we'd return. One JOA line-up laughed and said I looked like *The Jungle Book* on the street — topless and barefoot in cut-offs cutting my own hair.

Owls and Need New Body went to the beach one night there. We all got blazing high and witnessed the glow-in-the-dark sprinklings of the ocean—bioluminescence—and couldn't believe it. Lightning bugs, sure, but I never even knew it existed in the ocean until seeing it. We'd each go in up to our waists and let the waves hit us and then watch the thousands of minuscule Christmas lights glow on our chest hairs, dunk our arms and wave them around. We sat on the beach that night, so high, and the beautiful North Carolina shore and North Carolina anywhere always makes me so pleased. We all jammed together on acoustic guitars and hand drums. I remember being struck by how free and easy these mysterious new friends of mine were, but how it was all a little bit embarrassing to be a part of, such a hippie-drenched connotative moment, a jam on the beach. I knew I liked all of these guys so much and they all seemed so able to fall into it so easily. Who would I be to judge? That may have been the night I learned how to jam again as an adult.

With his crazed positive eyes and big brown beard, the bartender at Sluggos tonight reminded us all of Jeff from Need New Body, super-cool and friendly. We hit it off right away. He was more of a punk-type dude, *This Bike is a Pipe Bomb* or whatever, so I was surprised when he told me at the end of the night that he'd seen me play solo in Chapel Hill years ago and loved it.

Sluggos is a cool shit-hole. All vegan junk food menu, I had the vegan club sandwich and loved it. It's in the ghetto, got Pabst and little else, all ages, vocal PA, everything falling apart. I'd been there once before on another night off. Good Life and us got hotel rooms together, couldn't find anything decent and ended up together in the flea-baggiest pit we'd stayed in in years. Che was doing sound for Good Life and grew up in Mobile, learned to do sound working for the woman that owns Sluggos. Kasher and I went over there with him late; the Black Keys were loading out as we walked in. That's the closest I've ever come to knowing what they sound like. Che was greeted with hugs and kisses all around. Kasher and I sat in a booth and compared ideas we had for screenplays. I ate a vegan chili dog and sat for a long time with an old man that the club paid to sweep the sidewalk. He told me about living across the street from there his whole life and still making love to his wife after all these years and how it was strange to suddenly have all these white kids hanging out on the sidewalk smoking. But it was OK with him because they paid him to sweep up the butts.

We thought that we crossed another time zone, lost an hour today. But we didn't and the drive was long enough that by the time we arrived we were all disappointed to have not lost the hour, another hour to sit around Sluggos. Even leaving as early as we do each day, we still always end up driving a couple hours in the dark. Those are the hours that get you. If you get somewhere to see the sun go down, any drive is fine. But to still be driving each day and not get anywhere until after dark, it begins to feel like our days are four hours long and the other 20 hours are all one long night of insomnia fits.

After loading in, Sam, Nate and I went to the hotel to check in. We arrived an hour earlier than we thought and they told us that the show would start an hour later than we thought. We did nothing for 45 minutes and by the time we got back to the club, the time that they told us the show would start, Ecstatic Sunshine was already done and loading off. So even arriving hours early we still somehow end up hurried.

The show was fine. We played well and people were super-excited. I finally have one nostril back to full capacity, so it's a lot easier to sing than it has been. The stage was small and I had about a two-foot by two-foot area that I could stand in, so I felt a little limited, but otherwise enjoyed it. Some meathead jocks kept yelling "Captain Jazz!" and "Owen!"

and "American Football!" and that was super clever and interesting. The crowd got pretty offended when, kidding around, I called them all "posers." It never occurred to me that grown-ups could actually take offense at that, but their collective reaction wasn't in jest; it was true stabbed-in-the-back hurt.

When Nate's hi-hat tambourine broke, we stood around for a couple minutes before he said that he just wanted to call it. I said, "Thanks, goodnight" and people flipped out. It was really sad to hear people sincerely plead, "But good bands *never* come here," and "Please, we *never* get to see good bands." Yikes.

Driving through Texas across the sci-fi swamp-scape of Louisiana, through Biloxi, Mississippi and Alabama, I never feel like I know what to expect or how I'm going to relate to people. But nothing could've prepared me for the Owen super-fan I met, a young man that joined the Marines to learn "Business Skills" because he wanted to start a record label. He said that he doesn't anticipate being sent to Iraq, but if he is, it isn't as big of a deal as people make of it. And he'll be out in three years and then have the "Business Skills" it takes to start an independent record label. Of all the long ways around something that I've ever heard of, I think this might be unparalleled. He was very disappointed that I couldn't tell him the tunings for a couple different Owen songs. After thinking that I was just being difficult and didn't want to give away the magic secret, he finally walked away disappointed.

Bobby was so bummed that we didn't go to a kegger with some 18-year-olds that he went straight to bed. Others warned us, "stay clear of those dorks and their keggers, they're . . . *Boring!*" Which I certainly didn't doubt, and which we other three agreed would probably be the case, but with his insatiable quest for new experiences, even missing this disappointed Bobby a little bit.

ALL OVER AND OVER

I told the audience tonight that I had one copy of a Japanese import limited-edition pressing of an Owen song called "Tartar Sauce" performed in a Druid chanting style and pressed as backwards lock-grooves on 360-gram vinyl. This record was the vinyl equivalent to a normal record as the ribs that flip over the Flintstones car at the beginning of the show are to a normal slab of ribs. And because it's lock-grooves, it's like when the Flintstones run somewhere and the background loops, the subtext implication being one of existential dread and total impotence, running and running and running and going nowhere.

People lost me a bit, so I told them that the intro to the Flintstones is actually a place in my house and I know that they've all been thinking of it as a *Time*, but that's the confusion. It's actually a *Space*. In fact it's a place in my house, "The Beginning of The Flintstones." That's the name of a corner of a room in my house, *"The Beginning of The Flintstones."*

Break open the place please—
Sorry, I don't have time to.
Diamond streetlights / Strobing security

Ashcroft's TIPS program—These Idiots Snitch. Neh. Dang.
The Russians when I was a good kid and a good guy—
It takes a lot of guts for a lot of team players to make a parking lot work.

Ghetto gas station tonight, asking the manager why the Diesel pump wasn't open, I noticed that my fly was down and started fussing with it while he's answering me and realized that the zipper had broken. My pants manifest strange white guy in ghetto gas station peak oil insecurity.

God is everything except what all these God-namers say. Bible belt, Bible belt. I think I can make out the little dipper over the wall across the street.

Malachi. Shaken awake from afternoon half-naps, I'm always thinking of Malachi. Having blossomed into the agreed upon laboratory prayer, I'm the laboratory goblin in the snow globe.

*

NOVEMBER 10, 2006

At the Pensacola Pawn shop to buy Nate a new hi-hat stand, the man—working there maybe or maybe just standing around—keeps grabbing a hi-hat stand and saying in a thick southern accent, "This here is a $170 snare."

I thought I'd imagined it and only had to say, "Oh yeah?" before he responded, white spittle at the corners of his mouth, "Oh yeah, this snare here would go for at least $170."

How strange to live with Pentecostals as a real force, in close proximity: the woman that rings you up at the grocery store.

"Organic Gardens" advertises "Hydroponics Sale."

At Subway the sandwiches have the texture and look of sandwiches but taste like air. Is it my cold? Too many years smoking?

Sam offers chill pills all around. The first 40 miles of our drive north up an Alabama State Highway.

Car dealerships, car dealerships, car dealerships.

Pensacola Pentecostal Church of Hurricanes-we-deserved-for-our-sins.

Fun City, Waffle House, Baptist Church, car dealership, Florida Greek restaurant. Six-lane highway through the could-be-anywhere section of town: go-karts and motels, the palm trees newly planted around the newly built hotel, their tops cropped short into army-brat flat-tops. Houses are boarded up. Everything is sheds along the road, all the buildings aluminum. Confederate flags, bail bonds, trailer parks, a flag of a crab, "Low Carbs" sign at the gas station, a sushi bar connected to the casino. A lot of the signs are down and left to read only as dirt outlines; car dealership, "Driveways for Sale." A man on a moped crosses the railroad tracks. "Music, Jewelry, Guns, and Much, Much More," even a grenade at the pawn shop. The trucks don't rust in the arid Southwest, that's the difference. Hydraulic machine shop, trucks up on blocks, homes to buy and bring and build. Small engines store next to the empty mall, smokestacks pop up along the tree line, not deep at all into the woods. The factory alone is not abandoned at the heart of the town.

A fart that we all thought we'd choke on ended up being The Outside when we opened the windows. "Someone else outside farted *really* bad," we joked; sour broccoli, chemical stench. And trees down in bunches, gas stations boarded up. Pine Oak St. has a sign bigger than the street sign that says, "Dead End." The clouds are inflated puffs bumping around through bright blue, low and happy just to be above the houses. Sometimes the sky will have different depths to it, and I'll get lost in between my shifting focuses and I can't believe that this is the world that I am a part of. What ratio of water and light could make such bulges and swirls bloom? The cords attaching each to The Beyond recede, like feather flames licking and sprawled. Church after church after church around here keeping people kept. A man sleeps in a boiled peanuts truck on the side of the road. "Outlaw Choppers" billboard. Cotton fields red and white knee-high static fields.

Another "Dead End" sign points towards the road to the cemetery.

A school bus rusted out and abandoned.

A gate is so overgrown that it could never be opened.

What stories are being told to each other around here?

A tall waterslide in the woods.

Another factory, this one with a long skeletal mechanical arm bent at the elbow, crosses the sky. The sky is a stew of warm gore in shades of only blue and white, the guts of the cosmos spread out across the giant autopsy table of Northern Florida, Southern Alabama autumn afternoon. The trees seem only branches themselves, balding with bright tufts of green like shaggy eyebrows. Burned out shed. Burned out acre. Each tree seems a unique and friendly beast. Each driveway has half a dozen mailboxes at the end of it. This is the hurricane evacuation route the street signs say.

A dirt road to the post office.

ALL OVER AND OVER

What driving must've meant to my father as a young man, Central Illinois farm-boy, Catholic handsome and ready to burst into Fight or Fuck as the opportunity presented itself.

A coordinated plot of fences stretches for half a mile. Its fresh white coat of paint is so quaint that it's menacing.

A giant, old, knuckled tree. An abandoned City Hall boarded up.

Dirt roads with no names cut through tall evergreen processionals. Streets I can't help but imagine myself being dragged down to my doom, kicking and no one to hear me scream. Or never, ever otherwise going down at all.

"Green's Monuments" in Bluff Springs Headstone Sale. Burned out yard. Burned out acre. New aluminum buildings next to bent-up tin roof abandoned buildings everywhere. The old building is twisted inside out. The "Downtown Festival of Lights" sign wasn't on. They must have built the town around this old tree. Yards with mattresses and car batteries and piles and piles of what? Everything's blown out. All the paint is peeling, all the red bricks green with algae. The pharmacy at the gas station at The Panhandle Café. A hardware store's Gazebo Sale. A power station among the houses. How long must these trash heaps have been left here for them to become indivisible rusted entities, no longer modular? Lawnmowers lined up next to bicycles and hubcaps. Railroad tracks and backyards with sheds that back up against them. Church after church after church. A flea market set up at the abandoned gas station. Family Dollar, Dollar General. A single shack out in the skeletal-treed swamp. Abandoned gas station and another.

Alabama.

The clouds have twisted into majestic cotton elk horns. A building's been left fallen. A sign hand-painted "Produce" over a rusted-out metal machine shed full of scattered mechanical parts. That's a verb—*Produce*—like a command, or it's a noun?

There sure were a lot of big specialty dolls at that gas station flea market. Truck on the front lawn, house in the back. Siamese truck fronts like crippled gargoyles guard a large plot of rusted, mangled garbage: ex-houses, ex-RVs, ex-campers, ex-snowmobiles, ex-four-wheelers. There was once a big fire here. Some small trees have begun to grow, but most of the burned-out remains haven't been removed yet. The clouds so low they themselves seem like an umbrella. Some of the trees are tagged with wristbands, blue, orange. Tinfoil covers the windows of a house.

Isn't this fucked up enough that there's nothing else to do if you're from here?
I don't know exactly what I mean.
I mean: Isn't this place so fucked up that if you come from here, what could you do?

A transmission tower in the field behind the one-room church. Dazzling popcorn popping cotton fields surround us. Now the road goes lower than both sides of the road and we see the edges of the cotton fields zip by from below, like crab-armies pinching against each other in a blizzard, the shells and soft. The clouds have opened up. A single snake's head with an open jaw is left. Been behind the Miller Hi-Life truck for half an hour, two-lane highway. Cotton must be difficult to get to. Angela's Family Restaurant is for sale and that's by the side of the highway even.

And now on I-65, 100 miles to Montgomery. I was up all night nervous and annoyed about this *Orchard Vale* benefit. Who makes such a fuss about getting people to donate prizes for a trailer's screening? So embarrassing. And now anywhere I go at home people are going to ask me about it. I mean, I guess Braden did that. Usama has done it, Jim Finn. People do it. But still, I feel like such a braggart or something, making this big fuss like the Brady family putting on a play in their backyard.

Last one asleep, first one awake, as always. I became mesmerized by a woman on TV that I'd never seen before—

Jessica Alba. I was watching this show on mute while everyone else was still asleep. I missed the beginning, but it must've been *The Fantastic Four* because one guy turned into The Thing and another guy got plastic-y and another one flaming and then Jessica Alba turned invisible. It's brilliant!

Abandoned gas station—

It's brilliant! The most stunning and perfectly desirable woman on earth has to take off all her clothes to activate her secret power of invisibility. Not sure about the exact mechanics of the conceptual design, but I know it's a heavy tease full of connotations for the sub-psyche.

Bobby woke up and laughed at me for watching it, told me that the goddess's name is Jessica Alba. I feel crazy. A magnetism inside me aches for her, like a Charlie Horse along my ribs or nausea. But that's normal right? Everyone knows that. That's how it is.

Broke down in Alabama once ten years ago. The tow-truck driver had one hand and a hook and even with five of us, we were freaked out by him. Sam, being our number six, didn't wake up until the van was already up in the air in the garage. When he opened up the door and called out, "What's going on?" the mechanic and the tow-truck driver got mad at us for not telling them that he was asleep up there. But we were all too afraid to say anything.

I called Jade Tree from a payphone to tell them the situation. Darren called back in a fake Alabama accent calling us faggots and threatening to come and kill us. Of course we all flipped out. He was calling the payphone after all, claiming to be watching us, so why wouldn't we believe him? When we checked into a motel and locked the door we called Jade Tree to tell them where we were. When the phone rang and it was the same voice on the other end threatening to come kill us Big City Faggots, we all ran around the room crying and screaming and trying to keep each other cool. I stood next to the door with a baseball bat expecting to beat a man to death as he tried to break in. When Darren told us it was him, after making us sweat and write out our wills for hours, well, we learned a lot about Darren that day. He'd always been the quiet one. He was still fat and self-conscious about it back then. It's been all downhill with him since that one afternoon.

My only other time in Alabama, besides just driving through, was picking up my old girlfriend N____ who'd been staying at her grandparents' down here. An awkward silent lunch thinking *Good lord these people have no idea who this crazy bitch really is.* And then thinking that I guess I didn't either.

Stranded those couple days in Alabama, the six of us in one room at Super 8, we never found anything else to eat besides a Hardee's. When we first walked in there, the people working asked us if we were the boys from Chicago. Not many vegetarian options at the Alabama Hardee's. But eating lunch with N____'s grandparents that day I was longing for the Hardee's option. At least Hardee didn't take my diet personally.

Fox News this morning had a global recap of how pleased all the Iranian Mullahs and Iraqi Al Queda people were about our mid-term elections. *A Victory For The Terrorists!* Homeland hotel room culture is getting way too scary for me.

*

ALL OVER AND OVER

NOVEMBER 11, 2006

Read some more Zizek in the van, about halfway through the book now. About 45 minutes into it each day it'll hit me that I hadn't retained anything of the last few pages. It's a little too complex to read in the van.

Read a little simple spirit-affirming Ram Dass and took a nap. Woke up in the parking lot of a mall in Montgomery, Alabama, Bobby stopping at a Panera for coffee. After the second time today that Nate gets up and walks away when I sit down at a table, I told Bobby that I'm not going to Europe if he doesn't snap out of this in the next couple days. Bobby said that he can't blame me at all and he feels the same way. It was the first time that I've admitted to any of them that I've known all along that this would be my last tour and he said he feels the same way and doesn't blame me at all. I explained that I had been assuming that we'd finish up what's already been booked, maybe even record another record, but I'm done with shows. But now with Nate like this, it's not even worth it to me to see through what we've already committed to.

I drove the last 150 miles to Atlanta. The bright purple sunset behind us, bright enough to blind me in the mirrors, expanded the shadows ahead of us. Everyone slept. I drove in silence, thinking through all the possible conversations and scenarios, how to get out of this band as soon as possible.

We pulled up to the club at 7:30. The other three bands were all loading in. Nate told us all to be careful loading in on the slope here because his amp fell over last time and we were all shocked to hear him speak. We loaded in quickly and I sorted out directions to the hotel and left to go get Amy. The whole drive across town, as thrilled as I was to get her, I was more overwhelmed with a stomachache about Nate and being stuck in the van another minute with him and his holier-than-thou Psychic Warfare.

The Doubletree Buckhead is behind some other hotels in a fancy tourist part of town. I had to drive past it and back a couple times before seeing the knee-high shoebox-sized sign. There was nowhere to park the van, just a short garage, so for a few bucks the attendant told me that I could double-park for 20 minutes. The woman at the counter looked me up and down when I told her that my wife had already checked in. She called up to Amy's room and said, "Hello, yes there is a . . . (long pause and smirk) . . . *gentleman* . . . (pause and smirk and cock of the head) . . . here to see you."

She told me the room number and I headed up. Seeing Amy for the first time in over two weeks was intense enough that it wasn't even altogether joyous. As soon as I saw her I felt dizzy. We hugged and fell over on to the bed. I immediately began missing her, miserable about her having to go home in a couple days and me having to continue traveling another week without her. I'd been counting down the days until this moment since we left Chicago. But it only occurred to me that afternoon to look beyond her departure Sunday night and see the rest of the itinerary.

After too brief of time together at the hotel, we had to head back. The show was already starting and we were long past due for the parking ticket that the valet promised me after 20 minutes.

Driving back across town Amy told me about her email arguments with her uncle all week and the momentum going into our *Orchard Vale* fundraiser. I listened and was happy to be listening, but didn't say much. I was so happy to be back around her, all I could do was plot how to ditch the tour and get out of town with her. It's the first time that I've felt right in weeks. I've gotten used to it. I've hit my stride. And in response to Nate's complaint—a week ago now—about my constant negativity, I've been making a conscious effort to maintain a positive outlook.

That's what seems strangest to me about his bottoming out and hating me so hard now. This tour I'm lighter on my feet and more content than I've been in eight years probably, at least six. Knowing that this is my last tour and not eating ephedrine and not being distracted by coping with the paranoid apocalyptic phantoms that it evokes, the constant visions of the earth opening up and swallowing us anywhere we may be or the spontaneous transformation at any moment of the entire population into rabid dogs all snapping at each other's throats—these are the constant and perpetual visions I've been shaking off and slinking through for years now, every moment, every day traveling. I *must* be easier to be around now. And *this* is the tour that he decides he can't deal with me? He'd have been justified at any other time, but he never seemed phased before. Suddenly, I get easy-going and he flips out about not being able to deal with my mood swings and negativity? As if being around someone 24 hours a day for weeks at a time you can expect their mood to remain constant? But even more than that, everything that he's accused me of is *exactly* how he's behaving.

A few days ago, almost a week now, when I first acknowledged that I recognized something was up and asked him to verbalize it, Sam and Bobby both told me not to worry about it, deal with what he said, but they weren't going to take sides. For days I've been thinking that I must be crazy, I must be provoking him in some small ways that I'm not aware of. But I guess that's the goal of such Psychic Warfare—to make the other person self-conscious and second-guess their every mannerism.

I was relieved that when we got to the club; Sam and Bobby both separately greeted Amy by telling her that Nate was flipping out and I've done all I could do to deal with it and they don't understand his problem. Phew. It really isn't me.

This is all we do know: he is slamming doors, slamming down anything he picks up, accelerating and braking fast when driving, cutting the wheel as if trying to flip us at every turn, grimacing whenever addressed.

Maybe without me around tonight those guys have brought it up. Maybe it'll make a difference. I called around 2:30 a.m.

to offer them the half a pizza that me and Amy wouldn't be eating, but the front desk said that they hadn't checked in yet. I can only assume that they stayed at the dance club. Everyone does seem to loosen up whenever I'm not around.

That last JOA tour, after the New York show when I headed out to Jersey to stay with Tunney at his suburban funeral home and everyone else went to Ann's, when we met up the next day everyone was beat and hung over having stayed out until 5:00 a.m. doing karaoke. By all accounts Mike had turned into the Party Animal coach *and* mascot, psyching everyone up over and over. It's not in any *aw-shucks* prudish manner and I don't think it's necessarily self-satisfied to note, but his behavior is generally 100% opposite mine. And I mean to draw no direct cause and effect, but I have to notice that when I get out of the way, the parties ensue. Of course that's far better for me—not having to be around for any party. But it does make me feel a little bad, like are they all dying to party every night and I'm silently squelching it? I've certainly never gotten that impression. Or is it that they all celebrate a little time away from me? I can't care about that either as I too celebrate my stolen moments alone.

All I hope is that maybe they cheered Nate up tonight or maybe they got him to open up a little bit without me around. Either way, if at some point he suddenly starts to just be my buddy again, I know that I'm going to have to just go with it. But it seems now, from the middle of it, that his aggression has been sustained and deep enough to be irreparable at least without more work than I'm about to put into it. It really does *not* seem OK to me to impose this kind of thing on anyone you live in such close quarters with. You cannot think it'll be just fine as soon as you're ready for it to be fine. I'd like to be bigger than that and not hold a grudge, but it's going to be tough to not just snarl at him whenever he snaps out of it and wants to pretend that nothing's happened.

He's gone to jail for this band. He plays two instruments at once and works up a sweat in his gym outfit. I play no instruments, just howl in this band and I've largely been keeping my cool while we play. None of that is my fault. I don't feel guilty for any of it.

The tour has been total shit in every manner: insane drives, low turnouts, no money. That too is not my fault unless he resents me for bringing him into this years ago, which of course may be the case. I may be the focal point of his rage at an institution. Makes sense I guess. But so does me not feeling guilty about that.

Living takes on different shades with age. People die and keep dying and continue to be dead.
Dad's eulogy—what was "the gift that the dead give the living" that I referred to? I could use it now, but it's not returning.
That marine the other night that kept asking me over and over what tunings different American Football and Owen songs were in; it was so funny how he just kept naming song after song after song.

Me and Amy got to the club a few minutes before the first band was to begin and went into the bar. The woman bartending was friendly enough to spot us two drinks even though I hadn't gotten tickets yet. I asked if I could upgrade to a better liquor with an extra ticket or an extra dollar and she said, "No." I asked where A_____ was and she said it was his night off, which never occurred to me could be within the realm of possibilities. A_____ was the young, fashionably sloppy hip-kid that runs the place and always took good care of us and encouraged us to hang out. He looked like a slightly chubbier, nerdier Johnny Knoxville or maybe just had the same kind of smart-ass charisma. On the Wall of Fame mural with the Sex Pistols, Ramones, Fugazi, Public Enemy, etc. he slipped in a funny life-sized photo of himself from behind, sticking out his butt and looking over his shoulder at the camera. Somehow he's the kind of guy that can hang a picture of himself like that in his own club and still manage to be likable. I'd miss him for the night.

ALL OVER AND OVER

We'd played there half a dozen times in the last three years. Its opening was a relief to us after years of never having good Atlanta shows. One JOA show with Braid and one with Will Oldham were both good. Otherwise, it was years of playing to no one until this place opened.

People seemed to like coming here enough that if they were on the fence, they'd teeter towards going—all ages with a separate bar with good DJs. We'd often end up next door at the big dance club connected to the place, enjoying ourselves in a kind of *I'd-never-end-up-here-if-it-were-up-to-me* kind of way. They had an ongoing Pirates-versus-Ninjas theme party that we ended up in the middle of. Everyone had to dress as one or the other without telling anyone which side they'd be on. The spontaneously formed allegiances stunned everyone.

Robin usually showed up too, but hadn't. Sam said that the doorman gave him a message from her for us, but he couldn't remember what it was. She never did show up and I was a little disappointed that she wouldn't meet Amy. Robin was as fancy of a lady as we knew, and we always enjoyed seeing her and hearing about her bi-annual trips to strange places. We've stayed with her at her townhouse and drank white wine by the fireplace all lazily wrestling her giant, friendly dog. The night was turning out not to be our standard Atlanta night that I'd imagined Amy would be dropping in on.

J_____ did come by soon after me and Amy sat down. We talked through the entirety of the first two bands and though I do always enjoy seeing him, and very much appreciate that he comes out to find me every time, he really is such a weird dude. It's very infrequent that I want to interject in a conversation to tell someone what I've been up to. I'm so conscious of getting people to talk about themselves because I know that I'm busy enough with enough different things that that alone can come across as self-important or self-absorbed to people that I don't know well or see often

ALL OVER AND OVER

so I prefer to listen. But J____ goes on such an incredible monologue about how *Great* he's doing and how *Awesome* his life is, it's hard to not want to just eventually break his momentum for a second. And man he gets impatient when someone else tries to tell him something about him- or herself. For a guy whose industry-fame rides on nudging people to not take themselves too seriously, he sure does take himself pretty seriously. We gossiped about all the weird old timers all over the place as I do with all the other weird old timers that I run into all over the place.

I'm only 32, but these are the guys I know everywhere: the old guys that stand in the back at shows and rattle off all the bands that whatever band is playing is ripping off without knowing it, trying to figure out the influences lineage handed down to this next re-invention.

I excused myself and went next door to the Internet Café to use the men's room. Drank an espresso to sober up and wake up. In the past, before bringing a laptop with us, we'd always sit here for the night and catch up on emails, but now I just popped in and out.

The Plot to Blow Up the Eiffel Tower was playing when I returned. They're a San Diego band, dependent on being handsome and fashionable, but only half of them came across that way. They alternated between spazzy and heavy, *politics are radical when we're making out* and *dancing is radical* kind of stuff. Nice enough dudes that I felt a kinship with as fellow travelers, but as a band they lacked the depth that they hoped to imply. A weak manifesto perhaps? A weak manifesto certainly does detract from music just being as it is.

The band room was slim and the passage to load on to stage was tight. Because of these very real architectural barriers we were slow to get set up. I tried to distinguish between our past shows here, but couldn't. I know one time I ended up hanging upside down from the rafters above the stage while singing, my legs chapping and burning under my knees, digging my feet deep into the ceiling between some pipes to try to hang on until a long enough break to let myself drop without missing a line. Thinking of it now I'm glad that I didn't break my neck. I was safe maybe thanks to that barrier Higgs talked about after flipping totally upside down and falling off the stage at North Six and landing on his head and shaking it off. Maybe I'm scared of having lost that protective shield and Fear is what causes one to lose it. Faith alone sustains it. Either way, I don't need to do that shit anymore.

The crowd was enthusiastic and I was a little drunker than I have been, a little too conscious of Amy the entire time, knowing how lame it all seems to her. She told me that she opened the Jade Tree checks that I'd been waiting for for months and could not believe that it was equal to a two-week paycheck of hers. Ah well, it obviously couldn't have been all about the money all this time, even if the inability to financially sustain it may have everything to do with having to forget about it.

After our set Amy was shaken. Halfway through the show she had taken a wrong turn out of the lady's room and ended up lost in the maze of the dance club next door.

Before grabbing a cab to head back to the hotel, Amy and I had to duck in the van to grab a few things. Right next to us, between us and the car next to us, a guy came clumsy backwards and bumped into us and kept going without noticing. I looked up from what I was fussing with and saw another guy following him with a giant Exacto knife, the size of one of those bouncer's flashlights, but bright steel with a huge blade sticking out. I pushed Amy into the van and jumped in after her, closing the door behind me right as the guy passed us. For five minutes or more he chased the other guy around the parking lot daring him to take a swing at him. As they circled the cars in a long slow chase, people kept trying to get the guy with the knife to cool down, but he'd turn towards each of them for a second until they'd each back down. Me and Amy sat. I tried telling Bobby and Sam inside the club to get some club security outside. Once they had drifted far across the parking lot, Amy and I ran for it and turned the corner and got a cab back to the Double Tree.

We showered together and ordered a pizza and ate it in bed watching *The Matrix* on TV.

We had only slept a couple hours wrapped up cuddling when I woke up in a panic from a bad dream. I dreamt that Amy told me she has "just been doing *everything but*" with a few dudes since I've been gone. I flipped out and walked around and found her again and asked her if I imagined that or if she really said it and she's like, "no big deal, just *everything but.*" And that's when I woke up with a start. She was happy to be wakened because she too was peaking in a nightmare. Ye Olde Dream-Inside-a-Dream: In her dream we were asleep together at The Double Tree. She woke up in the dream and turned over towards me. I didn't budge so she shook me to realize that I'd slipped out and replaced myself in bed with a dummy, like a jailbreak in an old movie. As the globe that I'd used for my dummy-head in her dream rolled off the side of the bed and crashed to the floor, I woke her up screaming from my bad dream.

I guess traveling must really not be good for a marriage. Our first night together in over two weeks and we have simultaneous nightmares about our insecurities with each other.

Went to the Whole Foods back near the club before leaving town. It's familiar enough to us that Sam said he feels like he's at home when we get there. They've adopted a rip-off counter of Eats: the place across the parking lot with cheap veggie soul-food options, which itself might be a variation to adapt to the influence of Soul Veg down there. Exquisite Tofu Pot Pie.

We ran into The Plot to Blow Up The Eiffel Tower guys and exchanged niceties. One of them had disappeared last night and the others were waiting for him to resurface. He went out prowling, which wasn't weird for him, but it was weird that he hadn't called yet. They said they played Milestone in Charlotte the day before Atlanta to eight people.

I'd also dreamt that I got home and got a job at an art gallery. I was pretty psyched about the idea, so I walked over to Borders and bought my first issue of Art Forum in years. Amy thought it was pretty funny to arrive to the van and find me flipping through Art Forum looking at paintings, Sam running up and down a flight of stairs, Nate juggling in the parking lot and Bobby stopping a couple walking by so he could pet their dog. He just kept petting it and petting it and petting it. None of us in a hurry to go anywhere, each of us amused himself in the grocery store parking lot on a busy Saturday afternoon. She joked that she couldn't imagine why we weren't enjoying the tour and I looked at my three associates and each of them did in fact appear absolutely fucking bonkers.

As we pulled out of town Bobby was upbeat and chatty, trying to rope us all into getting along. He told me that it took him two hours to get paid last night and they all just wandered the dance club people-watching, waiting for the money. He told Nate to stop being a dick. When I asked him how the conversation went, he said there really wasn't any conversation. He just told him to stop being a dick and hoped that it might work.

Bobby's noble attempt at getting us all to open up a bit fizzled out after Nate flew into a spontaneous rage about this guy in another band the night before that was "so arrogant and overbearing" that he "wanted to kill him with his bare hands." Yikes.

Sam started telling a long story about crashing a motorcycle when he was twelve and it went on and on and on and on and on but it became really funny because of that. It had a sniff of the quality of being made up as he told it, but maybe he just has to dig through a few more layers of sediment to retrieve memories than most people have to.

After a while we all fell into our silent zone that we fall into. Amy was restless and kept telling me that she wanted to talk and I said, "Ok, . . . about what?" She concentrated. "Hmm. I don't know." After a pause, brow furrowed and lips scrunched, she asked, "Do you think your mom would like Ethiopian food?"

It was a short drive, just four hours or so, so we were able to get to the hotel early and chill. We drove past the club first and were all pretty bummed to see "The World Famous Milestone" and Charlotte in general. I've always loved North Carolina. It's never seemed like The South to me, but just a big, state-sized, wooded San Francisco.

I'd spent ten days in Chapel Hill years ago in a cabin in the woods just outside of town. My old lady Rachel's friend Julie owned it. I was putting together *The Gap*, taking walks through the woods, reading a Guy Debord bio, re-watching the two different edits of *Killing of a Chinese Bookie* over and over making meticulous notes about their structural differences, listening to *Hunky Dory* over and over, eating every meal at Weaver Street, visiting Julie at her studio and getting taken through all the studios of all her friends, surprised to find so much abstract metalwork to be the common language in just pre-9/11 Chapel Hill. There was a great used book and record store around a bend, just behind what must be the main street where it splits. It looked like a little one-room schoolhouse. From there you could walk along a trail through the woods next to railroad tracks and end up at the food co-op. I'd sit and nibble on a hot-bar lunch in the yard with the Zelda Fitzgerald biography for hours each day.

Everywhere I've ever been, I've never been anywhere else for so long at one time: four or five days at a time sometimes in New York when I was a lot younger, 20 or 22; a whole week in Tokyo in 2000; four or five days at a time once or twice a year in Lawton with Amy's family. But I'd never before or since had ten whole days somewhere, and since then I've always felt more at home in Chapel Hill than anywhere else. And Asheville and all the hippies, I love the whole state.

Once Todd and I played as a duo in Asheville. A girl we met at the show offered to let us crash with her, so we followed her out to a farmhouse. We'd watched *Texas Chainsaw Massacre* stoned out of our minds only the night before, so we were a little freaked being out in the country at all.

Once we got to her place, I had to run back to the car to get something, but a big mean dog wouldn't let us out of the house. She was upstairs and we heard a lot of stomping and voices. Her boyfriend seemed none-too-pleased that she'd brought us back. But we'd never meet him because we split. We ran for the car and peeled out. Lost through pitch-black country roads at 3:00 a.m., crazy paranoid and country-folk-phobic, a pickup truck's bright lights blinded us all at once from close behind and tailed us through tight turns. We had no idea where we were or where we were going. Finally we were pinned sideways across an intersection, nowhere to go, and the pickup parked, blinding us from the side just a few feet away so we couldn't turn around. The girl who had invited us back to her farm approached and screamed, "What the fuck?" We told her that we didn't want any trouble with any country-folk. We just wanted to go and we were sorry to have bugged her. She insisted on looking through our car. She thought us city-folks had robbed them blind and ran.

She remained pissed and told us to fuck off before and after pointing us back towards town. I tried to explain that being from Chicago it was just that whole *no-one-to-hear-you-scream-thing* that I couldn't deal with.

And another time in Asheville—Salvia at the Head Shop!
*

ALL OVER AND OVER

NOVEMBER 12, 2006

Priceline is funny. We're in Baltimore to play a loft party and the cheapest hotel is the Wyndham downtown, two towers each 30 stories tall.

Just dropped Amy at the airport on our way into town and I feel sick maybe, lump in my throat, sitting in the backseat, so embarrassed that I really am about to cry in front of my associates.

Woke up early and drove through dense and wet gray-world all day, 9:00 a.m. to 6:00 p.m., traffic jams all the way from Richmond to Baltimore. Great little health food store with a hot bar in Richmond, sitting with Amy, our only time alone together, I felt anxious. The long drive to BWI felt like a procession to the guillotine.

DC, even just driving through, is always creepy; the Masonic Temples and monuments, the density of power—all spells cast, backed by corporate force.

Pulling into Charlotte yesterday, our prospects seemed grim. It was raining. We got to the club. It was in the middle of the ghetto. But when we headed over to the hotel we then realized that the whole city seemed to be a ghetto. The hotel was downtown and everything was closed. Short of ordering room service, which was way too expensive to do, there was nothing around anywhere to eat.

I checked my email for the first time in a few days and had a correspondence between J_____ and G_____ forwarded to me, in which G_____ referred to our upcoming European tour as "a financial disaster." He made it seem like we'd make zero money except for merch.

We all met in the lobby to head over to the show and I brought this up to everyone, excited to maybe have a way out of doing the tour without having to feel like it was my fault. They all sort of downplayed it, blaming it on a language barrier or G_____ had higher standards than us, etc. Bobby emailed him a reply of a simple A or B to choose between and he shouldn't be able to remain ambiguous responding to that.

    We headed over to the World Famous Milestone to load in.

*

ALL OVER AND OVER

NOVEMBER 13, 2006

Is it Sam's birthday?

We felt distressed loading into Milestones. It was a shit-hole beyond any sort of shit-hole that one ever really sees in the real world. Holes kicked in the walls, the walls themselves all varieties of wood nailed sloppily over each other. Band names graffitied over every inch—Bad Brains huge over here and Black Fag bars over there, Bauhaus on the ceiling in the back—perhaps more band names than anywhere else on earth. The couches were ripped up and gross, each table wobbled with a broken leg.

Which reminds me—the handsome guy behind the desk at The Double Tree was on crutches. Later when we saw him out from behind the desk, we saw that one of his legs was deformed in a severe and strange way, bent backwards halfway between his knee and ankle and sticking straight out behind him, even shrunken a little, as if modest.

Milestones had a bar set up waist-high across the front of the stage. It was maybe the sixth to tenth place that I've ever played at with a bar like that. Maybe it's just the region where rock clubs think that's a good or necessary idea—Tallahassee, South Carolina, Alabama—but it immediately registers to me as an omen: a dozen people, tops, will turn out for the show and the people working there will be spooky at best.

Once loaded in, me and Amy needed to eat. I asked the promoter, who was actually a young, well-kempt and articulate guy, friends with Owen and Kasher. So I asked him about vegetarian food and his response, at 8:00 p.m. on a Saturday, was "There's a Taco Bell on the other side of town." When he saw that I wasn't having that, he walked me over to a guy whose ex-girlfriend was once vegetarian and asked him and that guy replied, "There's a Taco Bell on the other side of town."

The rain was coming down hard. The parking lot was a mud pit. This was of course even more foreboding for the turnout, but I was secretly pleased. At a practical level, it kept everyone in the neighborhood around the club inside, which seemed to our advantage. But beyond that, I was secretly excited for Amy to witness tour at its absolute worst and most futile and ridiculous, and for my associates to know that she was seeing it. Every bad tour-development works to my advantage when it comes to quitting, making it a little easier for them to understand my decision. And although I can't *provoke* any bad turn of events, I am always secretly pleased when things get to be their worst.

Amy found the restaurant listing in the free weekly and asked the promoter to give us directions to the neighborhood that had a lot of these addresses in common. I got the atlas from the van and knew from looking at the map with him that he had no idea where we were. Sam jumped in with me and Amy and we headed off through blustery rain, following the guy's directions as far as we could, stopping to confer with the map again and again, passing the hotel, circling downtown, re-crossing our path, cutting back and jumping over our own jet-stream before finally finding a Thai restaurant. We sat and ate and took our time, just as content to have been driving around lost than to have had to sit at Milestones. We talked about how tour sucks and how we wouldn't be getting away with it at all if we had to pay for van rental and how Bobby, by owning the van, has totally enabled us. We answered Amy's questions about slang that she didn't know but always played along with in very specific terms. She had funny epiphanies for each phrase, "Oh, you like *that*?" and, "So I shouldn't call my brother that to my mom anymore."

I made them both laugh telling them stories of my dad trying to explain to me as a ten-year-old what it means for "legs to go all the way up" and what a "milking pussy" is. They laughed about the drunken dinners, my dad bringing

203

a friend home and both of them obnoxious while my mom cooks and asks them to calm down and they'd put on Chuck Berry and dance with me and Mike, throwing us through their legs and flinging us back and up above their heads, spinning us around, trying to explain the term "douche bag" in a slow and deliberate manner that an eight-year-old could follow, and my mom, all the while, the good sport with clenched teeth.

Getting back to the show, our minds were blown; the parking lot was packed. What we assumed to be a wasted Saturday night might not turn out to be so bad after all. Inside the bar was packed, half the people looking like a Make Believe audience and the other half looking like a Rob Zombie movie about to lock the door behind them and turn to us all at once. Lots of methed-out looking types, longhairs, bald-heads, leather jackets, camouflage, lots of T-shirts about guns and having a gun and being ready to kill without qualms at the drop of a hat; glazed, angry eyes. But then these other Joan of Arc geeks, skinny kids in cardigans. The first band started grinding away, two guitars and a drummer, super-awesome, like U.S. Maple playing Black Flag or The Coughs if they sounded more like drills and less stompy; The Coughs with a more complex assembly line cacophony. Super-awesome surprise for the weird Southern show that this had turned out to be.

Bobby was freaking out. "The graffiti is real!" And I thought, *yeah, so?* Until I realized what he meant: Bad Brains had painted Bad Brains, Black Flag had painted those bars and Bauhaus—Bauhaus even! The promoter told us that the club had been open since 1969 and suddenly the "World-Famous" part of the moniker took on new meaning and even the name Milestone, which we'd laughed at before as if it were taunting us, now seemed like an initiation.

Amy hung on my arm the whole time. When I had to run through the rain to do my breathing exercises and make myself burp in the van, she insisted on joining me. She sat watching me, laughing at me, attempting to carry on a conversation the whole time.

Ecstatic Sunshine sounded amazing and, as always, people were truly perplexed or in awe.

The promoter wanted us to wait a little bit before we started. He'd made an Iraq documentary and now was making one about the club, so he and Amy talked about their similar trajectories. I talked to some kid that described himself as a Joanfrc.com message board regular and all his questions seemed to confirm this: "Will the new Friend/Enemy ever come out?" "What's this movie?" "Where's Victor?"

Because of our low expectations the show might've seemed better than it actually was, but it *seemed* great. The crowd was present and excited. And unlike any other rock club has ever made me feel, I felt the energy of all the bands in the walls soaring up through me. That has never occurred to me before when playing. It's always the same circuit and everyone knows each other and the bands are all like old pro-wrestlers sitting around the locker rooms together taping up their knees. But this time, I was inspired by the continuity of the tradition—this specific room.

I tied a kid to the bars at the front of the stage with the mic cable. It was funny and when it was done I was surprised to see it and surprised to have done it. Playing is always a bit of a blackout, at least when it's at its potential best. More often it's flickering black outs interspersed with moments of total self-conscious awareness.

Amy took a Xanax and passed out in the van immediately. She didn't want to drink after feeling that she'd drank too much the night before. So this was her move? She's never not surprising.

This total metal-head looking kid came up and asked me to sign a copy of almost every record we've ever made and it was a total shocker. He told me that he's only seen us once, eight years ago when he was fourteen and no one else was at the show and he doesn't even know why he went but it's stuck with him ever since and that's so cool. Makes me feel a little more responsible for the shows that no one shows up to. I signed each CD with a brief description of the space that the artwork represented and it was really cool to see them all at once like that.

The promoter, who was now our drunken buddy, was excited that the show had gone way into points and we almost doubled our guarantee. Until the issue of who was to pay Ecstatic Sunshine came up and then we all talked in a circle for fifteen minutes. We had to admit that there was a true gray zone between the specific wording of the two contracts. Eventually, with all of us in a circle around him, we came up with an equation that made sense of the extra $60 in his pocket and why the expenses would all be stated as they were if he were to pay them. So I guess we busted him and so he paid them. Still a nice enough dude though.

Amy was knocked out and I was wound up. All of our wake-up calls were in five-and-a-half hours to get her to the Baltimore airport on time.

Miserable to be up so early, I coffee'd and showered assuming that I'd drive first to make the burden of delivering my wife less of everyone else's problem. Amy couldn't wake up. Finally when I saw Sam walking down to the lobby and Nate already returning from the pool, she snapped into gear.

We found a bagel place and all ordered separately before it hit us that we'd just spent about 4000% more than if we'd just ordered a combined half-dozen bagels. Bobby tried telling the cashier that she should ring us all up together like that and she had a very astute response: why wouldn't people find each other in line and do that all the time?

The drive to Baltimore was a gray drag. I slept soundly and deeply sitting up for the first hour or two and then was content to watch Amy sleep next to me for the rest of the day. It was gray enough out to feel like you're half-asleep all day anyways, the daze of a few gray days in a row.

It's pretty driving through Richmond, a genteel southern city with a touch of the east coast Megapolis vibe. It's beautiful crossing the river towards downtown: the long trains parked in the yards and all the signs of antiquated modernity, fossilized industrial remnants of the Big Bang of the early 20th century manufacturing and distribution routes.

After sitting in traffic for hours, the roads finally opened up the last half hour to BWI. Me and Amy wrote messages to each other on our hands. When we arrived I walked her in and said goodbye and stood there choking back tears while she told me to hang in there, kissing me softly all over my face. I called the hotel for directions and we went over there. As much as I was miserable missing Amy, just twenty minutes later and she's probably not even to her gate yet, checking into the hotel, I got hung up on how cute the girl at the front desk was: Middle Eastern or Persian with dramatic features and big eyebrows and fucked-up teeth all coming together perfectly.

So funny, playing a loft party and staying at the Wyndham downtown. The hotel had the façade of being super-fancy, the lobby and the shops in the lobby and the full attention of a half-dozen attendants. But once up to the tenth floor to our room, the carpet in the hall was coming up, bulged in the middle, its slack always easy to scoot around but impossible to flatten. The bathroom in our room had only an exposed glaring neon long cylinder for light and the room was dirty; not dirty in the way my apartment might get dirty—things out of place—or a rock club is dirty—sooty—but more like how a public pool's locker room might get dirty.

We headed over to Matthew's loft to load in and eat dinner. Driving through the winding colonial streets of Baltimore it hit me how small the city really is. I've always loved it, even if I've never really liked the few places to play or the shows themselves.

First time there, I was seventeen on tour with Gauge as a "roadie"—whatever that means. Lost in the ghetto pulling into town in the afternoon, we pulled over at a gas station to check the atlas. Gub was sitting shotgun, his elbow on the rolled down window. I was behind the driver's seat. He was talking to me when I saw the tip of a gun put up to the back of his head and heard the loud pop. We all jumped and screamed. A little kid was laughing hysterically with his cap gun. Gub laughed like a manic, which he always kind of did anyways, as we pulled away.

John, the original Lungfish bass player, took us to this weird loft he was living in. That was the first time I ever saw any kind of "home studio."

It was the only bar show of the tour, playing with the band Liquor Bike. We stayed with one of those guys and he worked at the studio where Shudder to Think was recording "Pony Express Record" at the time, so he took us over to check it out. Craig was in a booth recording vocals, wearing sunglasses and a scarf over his tank top. I was such a fan, had seen them play so many times, I just walked up and stared at him through the little window, assuming for some reason, I guess, that it was a two-way mirror. He lowered his sunglasses to the tip of his nose and they had to ask me step away so he could get on with his task.

Most of our shows there over the years have been at Ottobar, which then turned into The Talking Head. Once, a couple days after September 11, Owls and Need New Body all sat in one van together parked outside of there listening to the president's speech on the radio. Another time there with Need New Body, Higgs came out and we coordinated plans for him to tattoo me the next morning. Last time we were there, last year with Michael Columbia, we all hung out with the bartender and smoked weed after she locked up the bar. When a couple more dudes showed up and she let them in and locked the door behind them, we had a collective Whitey and all sprinted for the van, hurrying back to the Scooby-Doo-style haunted mansion hotel that we'd gotten downtown. It was the last show with Michael Columbia, so when I ran into Dave on the street back in Chicago months later, it was the first time that I'd seen him since then, and he greeted me with, "What the fuck happened to you guys that night? Did you have some kind of band secret code?" and I had no idea what he was talking about until he told the story back to me.

But the shows were never really that good at that place. 40 people seems sold out and 60 might be too packed to move, but none of the amenities—i.e., a toilet—were decent. The crowds were never much more than indifferent and the money always sucked.

We were excited to play a loft party at Matthew's place, could potentially be the best show of the tour. Matthew's place was on the sixth floor of a downtown building with lots of graffiti all over it—2012, community-building messages, theater and politics—bohemian and hippy graffiti, not tags. You take a small, fucked-up elevator to get up to it and the elevator requires a trick for shutting the door right and lots of warnings about being trapped in there if the trick isn't performed correctly. Honestly, after a night of coming and going, it really seemed like a hoax or superstition to me. It didn't seem likely that stopping the door just short and then pushing it in for the last quarter of its length before it shut, was really going to make a difference. But who wants to be the one guy to not do it and get stuck and realize that there was a reason after all?

The loft was familiar and homey all at once. Some heavy drone music coming out of one room, couches everywhere, a homemade looking stage with a small PA, a pile of wood in one corner, a ping-pong table buried under whatever had been left on it long enough ago that everyone probably forgot that they'd ever even had a ping-pong table. Matthew and his girlfriend made us delicious squash ginger soup and warm bread with garlic butter and it was hearty and autumnal.

Entering Baltimore, all the weird Masonic temples, and the signs on the highway — *NASA this exit, NSA this exit* — creep me out enough that it was a little hard to shake. I was feeling cooped up and decided to go back to the hotel for a bit. Down the densely graffitied elevator, through the older dudes hanging out on the corner even in the rain, for a goose chase for cigarettes and a rainy tour of downtown Baltimore. Everywhere was kind of familiar even though I'd never have thought that I'd know my way around. There's the monument that Higgs once pointed out his uncle had climbed and refused to come down from as a teenager in the 1940s.

Once back at the hotel, I only had half an hour to relax, but it was worth it.

(The brick streets of New Brunswick in the rain bouncing red and yellow lights from the traffic.)

Walking back to the van, I talked to Amy on the phone while she still sat at her gate. Should she take this morning-after pill or maybe we possibly conceived last night and maybe that's OK? Stepping on to the crowded hotel elevator, I couldn't keep up my end of the conversation.

Back at the show, the place had begun to fill up. The first person I saw that I knew was Lexie, who used to live in Chicago and has been booking The Talking Head the last four years. She gave me a big hug and coined the nickname *Cap'n Dad* to sum up my new style, which I wasn't aware that I'd adopted. One time, five or six years ago, wasted after the bars closed, we had a great noise jam together. She screamed and howled with zero sense of self-consciousness and we all loved it. This moment has been the subject of pretty much every conversation we've ever had since.

Next I saw Roby, who's been living here for almost a year now. She's the same excitable and excited rugrat that I've always known her to be, and she gushed about Baltimore and what a great community of weirdos and all these cool things that she's been making and has seen. It was a shot in the arm to see her, as always.

Rjyan was with Bobby around the corner. He has his face shaved clean but a crazy long neck-beard grown out that connected to his sideburns at the corners of his jaw. I gave it a tug and asked him what he called it. He said when Higgs first saw it he said that he "appreciated his facial expression."

I sat with Rjyan for a couple beers listening to him vent about all these things that he thought he was just figuring out, but that I could've told him he'd figured out years ago. He has deep and aggressive ideas of performance and engagement and I always like to hear him out and see what he's getting into next.

Asa arrived and sat in a corner by himself with a coffee. I sat with him and chatted and it's always striking how humble and kind he is. He kept asking me questions about myself, but refused politely to tell me what he had been up to. Such a vast difference from everyone else I know and run into everywhere. Told me it's a good time of the year to be traveling and it must be nice seeing people and playing music and of course I couldn't disagree. He's always such a great example of process over progress and seemed so happy to tell me that everything is as it has been: working at the museum building displays, lots of Lungfish practice and new songs even if they aren't doing much else. Told me about making weird art out of cutout patterns and I can only imagine, loving his guitar playing as I do and all the depth that he gets out of simplicity and repetition, that these must be some heavy repetitive cutout patterns.

A few people had mentioned Baltimore house music, how it's distinguished by its simplicity and repetition, which is striking when considered in relation to Lungfish. Maybe the city being so old gives people an immediate connection to the past that people in a lot of American cities don't have and maybe that somehow provokes repetitive art. I tried to explain my hypothesis to Asa, but the first band started. He mentioned that he and Higgs were starting a new band with new people and I got the impression that it might be these people.

They were called Thank You and they blew me away. The place was packed with people of all ages, 50-year-olds out in full force in a way that's super-unique for a Make Believe show. Two guys played strange patterns on guitars and old keyboards while a tiny woman freaked out playing long, tricky, flipping, and stompy drum patterns with small clicky polyrhythms continuous underneath it all. There were Silver Apples moments, Steve Reich moments, Can moments, and all of it put together as sound for its own sake. No narratives or acquired dynamics, parts continued on and on until they'd peter out and cross-fade live into something else which would just start as it is and go on and on.

Higgs showed up soon after they started and we talked briefly but were mostly both absorbed in the show. He looked skinny. Said he'd been on tour for two months and was taking breaks to stay in different places for a few days at a time.

We had talked about playing before Ecstatic Sunshine but they insisted that we play last. A third of the audience left when Thank You finished, but from then on everyone stuck around for the night. By the time we played it was 12:30 and we were all kind of drunk and tired and couldn't make it perfectly through a single song. The people in the front were excited and dancing and the place remained filled. But it was still a little embarrassing, especially because it seemed like such a "scene" show, lots of people there in bands we like.

I sat with the soundman for a while when we were done. We'd met before a few times. He had lived in Chicago and we knew a lot of the same geeks. He was immediately open and insightful with a deep knowledge and subtle sense of musical context. I enjoyed sitting with him very much.

Went back to the hotel and passed out soon with some intense, labyrinthine new *Dead Alive*-type movie with James Caan on, totally blown away by it, but exhausted. The dudes hung out and drank and chatted around me and I slept through it.

Walking around the hotel this morning before anyone else woke up, a vaguely familiar-looking woman dressed head to toe in Suicide Girls gear asked at the front desk about Internet. Suicide Girls bomber jacket, sweatshirt, and sweatpants, but in case I wasn't sure — she had the laminate. Must've been a burlesque show in the same hotel. I saw the whole posse a little later and it was such a dumb circus even if particular details were distressingly sexy.

Bobby insisted on a late checkout just to leave the room by 12:15. He called at 12:20 telling us all to meet him and Matthew at "some place next to the shiny place a couple blocks past the monument." By 1:00 Nate and Sam assembled at the van, which was blocked in by a big tourist bus. We followed Bobby's vague directions and ended up finding him and Matthew at an Indian Buffet. The brothers that run the restaurant are musicians and it was their record that had been playing between bands last night. What a difference it makes to play Indian music instead of rock music between bands at shows.

Matthew told us about Dustin's house, which is a couple hundred years old. It's four stories tall, but only as wide as a door, so it basically ends up being a winding staircase with no space big enough for more than two people to stand next to each other. He told us Dustin is either profoundly superstitious or very in touch with the spirit realms because he's convinced that his basement is haunted and has never been down there again since deciding so. He's also hung a shower curtain in front of his fireplace because apparently in his specific ideology that must keep the spirits trapped in there. The membrane separating Life and Death is no obstacle, but this shower curtain offers a little security.

Got an update from G_____ informing us that we stand to make 1800 Euros plus merch. But we have to pay for our own ferries to England and back. Reading it, my mind was made up immediately to cancel. This was not the deal that I agreed to. If he had presented us with this deal at first, we all would've said no.

But no one else was feeling the same as me. They all thought that we were now obligated to do the tour, so I expected a blowout. But, planning on quitting already anyways, I guess I see no reason to go through with the tour if I'm doing so only out of guilt. Just not sure what's the right time to break the news. The longer I wait, the worse it is for everyone. But the sooner I do it, the longer I have to be living in a van with people that are hating me. I don't doubt that I'm justified, but I doubt any of my associates will see me as being so.

Still raining: day three. Even loving this strange colonial harbor town—Baltimore—as I do, I felt thick dread being there. We're all already weird with Daylight Savings Time, dark an hour earlier. But now entering the later time zone and all of us so pooped, we can't get moving until at least noon. Add continuous rain and it's an equation for guaranteed alienation.

We stopped at the Maryland House rest stop. Years ago, on tour with Jets to Brazil and Euphone, just tagging along for the sake of the drift, we got stuck in a traffic jam for hours. After a while we made it to The Maryland House and stopped there to wait it out. But it was so packed that all the restaurants had to close because they'd run out of food. All the restrooms were destroyed, disgusting. And we were all trapped, hundreds and hundreds of people, the entrances and exits all clogged. That horrible afternoon returned to me as we headed up to Jersey.

I imagined a rush hour hundreds of miles long, dense and continuous, sprawling along I-95 without a break from Baltimore to Boston. For all the time I've spent moving up and down the east coast, I still can't get comfortable there. I calm myself by noting: The Bible Belt creeps me out. The Pacific Northwest creeps me out. California, I remain claustrophobic its entire length and width. The Southwest is great even if I'm aware every moment that it's all built on illusions that environmentally speaking just cannot be sustained. Of course the Nascar Southeast is spooky. So my problem is obviously me, not any space that I may ever enter or leave.

ALL OVER AND OVER

New Jersey Turnpike—billboards and endless lights red ahead of us and yellow to the left—through the rain from the back seat. The world past the window seemed like a screen moving behind us to imply motion, like a bad special effect from an old movie or the beginning of *The Flintstones*. Sometimes when the door to an elevator opens a split-second early, I look at the floor and like to play a trick on myself that the building is moving and the elevator remains still. When I don't consciously choose to play this trick on myself and the effect still happens, I do not appreciate it.

When I asked Higgs last night about his European tour with Rob and Ben that he bagged at the last minute, he said, "I just couldn't get on that plane." I told him that that must've been a very satisfying indulgence to cancel plans and he said, "Oh yeah, I do it all the time. It's better to not make plans in the first place, but I'm still working on that."

He was gone by the time we played, and though it disappointed me a little bit I appreciated him coming around to say hello and didn't take it personally. I think the only times he's seen us play, we've played first and then he splits by the time the other people he knows play.

But I still feel obligated to watch these opening bands in New Jersey that we ate dinner with.

When we pulled into town we were pleasantly surprised by how pretty it was. Our last New Jersey show was last year in Long Branch. We showed up to this total biker bar to be greeted by a burly, bearded, tattooed dude, who after giving us a gruff looking-over, asked, "Which one of you is Binky's buddy?" I said I was and the dude immediately hugged me, proclaimed, "Any friend of Binky's . . ." and suddenly we felt protected. He was the sweetest guy, went overboard to take care of us in a room that seemed like it could potentially turn against us at any second.

We stayed at Binky's loft that night with Michael Columbia, listening to heavy ragas and checking out weird paintings, fucking around with all his weird drone instruments, getting high on the roof. His place was downtown Asbury Park, a pretty old-fashioned downtown that had been abandoned.

He tattooed me the next morning, a design we arrived at together. His work stunned all of us. I have a lot of friends in common with the dudes that he shares the studio with and they all hung out the whole time while he worked.

He took us to a weird diner where everyone knew each other, the place packed and everyone a character. We all left thinking that we'd just left Twin Peaks.

The time before in New Jersey was Joan of Arc/Make Believe/Love of Everything in a big, shitty space, tons of kids abusing the room in a downtown that looked like it'd already seen enough abuse.

The only other Jersey show of my life was in this kid's parents' kitchen in a mansion out in the woods in the middle of nowhere in the '90s. A show had fallen through, so Promise Ring, Joan of Arc, and The Van Pelt all played for each other, the kid and his couple friends, and Ted Leo. It was a great, fun, weird night, BBQ tofu and up all night afraid of my memories of the *Communion* book-on-tape.

Who would've known the old downtown of New Brunswick is beautiful, tight old brick streets and old shops in small, old-fashioned buildings? Of course there's Starbucks and Payless Shoes and Rite Aid in the way. And maybe it's the filter of the rain and the ability to walk around at all without bombed-out and abandoned places making up most of the landscape. Or maybe it's just a Monday night—first night of the last week of the last tour of my life—and I'm so desperate for it just to be over that self-preservation instincts have kicked in some positivity.

A young Asian couple makes out, open-mouthed, in a La-Z-Boy in the window of a crowded Starbucks. A man outside the train station cannot believe that I don't want to buy cocaine. I go into a bar/café across the street from Starbucks and The Gin Blossoms dude bartending there must not like the looks of me. He stands right in front of me, looking at me while he sings along to Boston or REO Speedwagon or whatever it is. He never acknowledges me until finally, after the second chorus, I get up to split and he calls out from behind, "You need something man?"

*

NOVEMBER 14, 2006

New Brunswick on a Monday night: among the biggest turnouts of the tour, super surprise. Too bad though that enthusiasm can sometimes manifest so clumsily.

Of course it's cool that the promoters were excited about the show. But unfortunately for us, they were *so* excited about the show that they decided it should be not only their friends' band's record release show, but also their own band's first show. They did certainly bring the people out and that's great. But not going on until 12:45 a.m. on a Monday? Everyone that's ever played in a band knows a four-band bill that starts at 10:30 on a Monday is a drag.

We pulled into town around 6:30. The New Jersey Turnpike is so sad to me, like the Simon and Garfunkel song, bums me out at such a deep level, the endless straight line of mysterious each-others. The rain made New Brunswick beautiful. Looking for the club we got turned around through downtown's tiny brick streets. And though we didn't go far, it took a long time, all the streets choked with rush hour and rain, which, actually, is evidence of the predominant cause of my Megapolis anxiety: all the arteries lead only into each other, there's no open anywhere. What if the evacuation that'll eventually have to happen everywhere at some point has to happen here today? I remind myself so often these days of how this probably won't be the week of collapsing infrastructures and spontaneous pandemonium and resource riots. That'll take at least a couple days to go down. And having the advantage of always being on the lookout for it, I'll recognize it for what it is at its earliest signs, when it just starts to get going and that'll give me a head start racing home to Amy.

When I'm anywhere inside of it—The Megapolis—it's impossible for me to think of *anything* except all of it blowing apart. So it requires a conscious awareness, my mind demands a conscious re-ordering to exist within it.

ALL OVER AND OVER

It was Kali to me before I knew the name. But just as *It Is* demands *It Isn't*, I need to flip it back over. Seeing only the *isn't* it someday will be, I need to re-focus on the *is* as it exists each day, each peaceful evening of leisure after the streets get choked at dusk and the rush and pulse of the afternoons end and everyone working together against each other keeps the whole thing buoyed.

Was that a Chili Peppers logo neck tattoo?

Bink, leaving to catch the last train back to Asbury Park, texts at 3:30 a.m. "God Bless this train and Cheryl the stripper that sat with me sniffing coke and teaching the inner-workings of Christian-Science and massage therapy. Praise!"

New Jersey with all its *new* everything must be the place most ripe for enlightenment, the perfect intersection of The Spiritual and The Physical. By being stripped so completely of any conspicuous spiritual dimension, New Jersey actually imposes spiritual awareness—begging everyone to seek out, what is this unnamable vital quality that's lacking? Everything is Surface and some intangible sense of hardworking normalcy—The Common Joe—is sanctified. And if perfect harmony is in fact living within all the simultaneous realms simultaneously, then New Jersey must be the space to provoke this ability. It forces the individual to internalize and create some sense of The Sacred within him- or herself by offering nothing but physicality at its most artificial. Immanence: finding holiness in the common. It makes perfect sense!

A longhaired stray cat across the flat backdrop of the hotel's fence, cutting across a perfect horizon line, stops and plays with a sock.
Amy tells me I was just named #144 on *Newcity*'s list of 150 Famous Chicagoans according to Google.
I just saw our music video that we shot in L.A. and it totally

sucks and is embarrassing and isn't anything like what we said we wanted to do.

I dreamt vividly of my dad again last night. What makes someone that was so absent in my life when alive so present when dead? Maybe I let my guard down when I sleep and that allows him to keep approaching me to let me in on how he knows that we should've both worked harder, could've been better for each other? That seems just as likely as his holographic appearance being born from my own mind's cobwebbed corners.

Three Latina maids on the steps in back of the motel; reading their mannerisms, one's obviously telling the other two about something intense. They nod.

Whenever Jerry Springer and his foaming, backwoods, inter-family gladiators come on, who can see anything but 1) Dystopian future-world coming into fruition or 2) All this just has to all blow away soon?

I also dreamt last night a kind of teenage-espionage dream. I was a kid in high school and I found all sorts of material evidence that my biology teacher, a long-standing well-respected member of the community, was somehow stealing from the school. In the dream I had the entire process of the scam figured out and each step left some physical evidence, all of which I acquired and pieced together. I let on that I knew what he was up to and he immediately turned me into the principal and the police, saying that I was on drugs. No one could believe that this man of high standing could be doing what I said he was doing and instead they all assumed me paranoid delusional. It was a very Kafka dream of being locked into some fate innocently, just because the accusers choose to do so.

Nate juggles in the parking lot while Sam watches Pee Wee Herman and Bobby is Pee Wee Herman and we continue not-leaving for the Art Museum in Philly. I'm ready to drive away without them. I've daydreamed of running away so continuously for weeks, but only now does it occur to me to steal the van when I do so.

The shows, as fun as they may ever be, are really my least favorite part of the day. I'm happier sitting in the van in quiet. For days I've been looking forward to getting to Philly early to go to the art museum, been talking about it with everyone, getting them all psyched up. And still we're going to miss it. One hour drive today and we still won't get there on time. I feel like I could tear each of their faces off their heads with my bare hands.
Old cemetery, help me keep my cool.

My argument for backing out on Europe is simple: if this had been the deal that he'd approached us with originally, I never would've said yes. He changed the deal, not me. And the deal now is not good enough.

Delaware Water Gap and some of these long bridges open up for a second into the America that people must've seen hundreds of years ago, just for a second.

Pulling into New Brunswick, we first went to the show. We called the promoter because he wasn't around and he told us to go over to his friend's house where he had made us dinner. He gave us directions.
The number of pizza places per capita must be the highest in the nation. We counted eighteen pizza places in the 1.5-mile drive to the kid's house.
When we arrived at the house, fifteen people were standing around in the kitchen smiling at us in silence. It was elbow-to-elbow and everyone shook hands all around and introduced themselves and it was the guys who lived there and the promoter and his brother and the two local bands and a couple of their girlfriends. It was an absurd amount of names at one time so I ended up not retaining a

single one. They served us homemade eggplant parmesan, and bruschetta and wine. It was nice. You could tell it was a college dude's bachelor pad, but they were trying really hard to be kind of formal for our sake and it was kind of cute.

Bobby and I sat with plates in our laps in the living room. Seven or eight kids sat there silently and watched us eat for a long time until one of them asked, "Are you guys pretty bummed that Rainer Maria broke up?" We both just stared at him blankly. After a minute, neither of us responding to his question, we continued to eat. The kid harrumphed and got all, "I dunno. I just thought." Finally, I told him that I was happy for my friends to be doing what they want to do.

We all sat and ate in silence for another minute until the same kid, obviously disappointed by us, registered his complaint by saying, "You guys must be pretty tired, huh? I mean you guys seem pretty tired." And we again both just stared back at him with blank expressions. I mean, we want to be polite or whatever, but yeah, I'd bet we probably are pretty tired, right—driving all day every day and playing late, stuck in a bar every night?

I got so angry that this kid thought it was rude of us to be exhausted, and for people to assume that we have to meet and be everybody's buddy or else we're dicks. Anything less than exhausted friendliness and gregariousness means that you're a dick. Bobby finally responded, "Thank you," and I got up and excused myself. I tried bumming a cigarette and it turned out the only guy who could bum me one was the talking guy. I did feel a little bit annoyed with myself for being short with him and thought I could live with myself a little easier if I stepped outside and talked with the guy one-on-one for a minute.

Before stepping out someone asked me how the tour was going and I told them that I spend most of my time praying for death or at least the theft of our equipment or some other excuse to go home, just because I really wanted to make these kids understand, *Yes, I am fucking tired and you would be too and my job, why I am out here, is to play music for an hour a day and I'm good at it and it means a lot to me to do my best for that hour each day. It is not part of my job at all, as I see it, to walk into some stranger's apartment and have fifteen people that I don't know look at me expecting me to dazzle or somehow entertain them after a day of gray dormancy.*

One kid who lived there, rolling his eyes, laughed, "We just blew off the *veggie tray* in your contract. That's alright, right?" and I shrugged and mumbled, "Guess so," but wouldn't give him the satisfaction of laughing with him. Is it hard to fathom that some vegetables might be nice to nibble on when you're stuck at a bar for the zillionth night in a row after driving hundreds of miles every fucking day of your life? Does it really make me such a diva to prefer vegetables to snack on to no-vegetables to snack on?

On the porch the kid asked me how "All my friends in Chicago are": Davey, Bob Nanna, Victor. I told him that none of them live in Chicago and that I haven't spoken to any one of them in years and he was truly shocked. He said he "imagined we all got together and played football with each other every Sunday." He asked me which was my favorite track on the NoYes record and I told him that I was hanging around when they mixed it and it sounded good, but I hadn't heard it since. His mind was blown.

He told me about interviewing Mike last year and how much Mike likes Make Believe and "I could tell him, come on, just between me and him, what do I *really* think of Owen?" My walls finally went fully up. I could only respond one word at a time to the kid.

Back over at the show, loading down three flights of stairs, halfway through the load I notice that I'm the only one loading and no one else is anywhere to be found. I stand around and when Sam and Bobby finally both pop up, I walk off leaving the van open and half-unloaded, cursing.

The New Brunswick brick streets, night air and drizzle

I get back to the show and am happy to find Bink. We met

about six years ago, first time Need New Body ever came to Chicago to play. Griffin was doing sound at The Hot House and got them a show. Bink's band Lord Sterling was out with them and it was one of those four-shows-in-nine-days-type tours, crashing at people's houses for too long and trying to get on different bills at the last minute everywhere. Eleven of them stayed with me and A____ for two nights, a couple sleeping out on the porch, some in the vans. Bink traveled with a bag of weed the size of a pillow.

The first night that they all stayed over we walked over to The Street-Side and got wasted. We closed the place, spending most of the night arguing with this obnoxious kid from Pittsburgh that had jumped in the van with them and they'd since been fighting with continuously. Bink was a tattoo artist and was tight with Higgs. We hit it off quick and have always stayed in touch, even though I wouldn't recognize any of his band-mates if one of the were standing on my foot. One of them joined Monster Magnet so Lord Sterling fizzled out, which is cool for Bink because he's doing more improvised, drone-y Eastern-influenced stuff, which is more his speed these days anyways.

It was great sitting around with him for an hour or so, talking about what we've each been up to, what we're each working on and working towards. He's really the sweetest, mellowest, coolest guy—one of the people that makes traveling worth it. He loved Ecstatic Sunshine and it was great for me to see a friend get excited about something new. By the time they were done and the second local was still to set up it was already 11:30.

The place was packed. Myspace-type show: lots of people singing along to the couple songs that we have posted on Myspace.

Nate navigates Philadelphia towards the art museum, manning the map while tripping.

Mushrooms and the Philadelphia Art Museum!

Armor displayed so you can see your reflection in the glass and it looks like you're wearing it.

ALL OVER AND OVER

Children's armor.

Ornate rifles with intricate inlaid pearl.

The flat eyes of the life-sized fifteenth century Christ of Philadelphia next to the window, and the cityscape behind him; last time I was here I ran from the room in fear all at once after being hypnotized by it.

Sixth century Iranian stucco—texture from repetition.

The walls of the Indian Temple seem about to startle to life: gods the size of men.

Crystal ball, seventeenth century China: Now I get it about crystal balls.

The Tree of Jesse—deep Christianity.

Seventeenth century Dutch still life's, portraits.

Abduction of Europa—everything points towards something, which is itself looking back at and past all the pointing but for one seahorse staring at the viewer. (1726-27).

Birth of Venus 1634.

The view from the front window, down the avenue, the Christmas tree.

Video: Mircea Cantor (Deeparture).

Matisse.

Joan Miro.

Cornell boxes.

The Source of Life—Leon Frederic.

*

NOVEMBER 15, 2006

Our fundraiser for the movie is happening at home tonight, lots of anxious energy over the phone.

We cancelled Europe. I can't believe how mellow and in agreement we all were that we really had no choice. We agreed to the tour at 250 Euros per show *profit*, which meant coming home with 6,000 Euros. Then two weeks out, he tells us it will be a "financial disaster" and we'll make 1800 Euros *minus* four ferries and a few days off to pay for ourselves. By my calculations that's a rate reduction of 70% at best and probably more like 100%. Even knowing that of course we wouldn't have agreed to the tour in the first place under those conditions, it's still hard to cancel with such little notice knowing that so many people have put time and effort into it.

G_____ wrote me an email to try to make me feel guilty and the for the first time I didn't feel just disappointed, but also mad, like he was really just doing a bait-and-switch and trying to take advantage of us. At best he was naïve to make us the original offer that he couldn't live up to. And more likely, he never intended to try to live up to it. It really made me angry that he'd try to appeal to us to have respect for the work that he and other people have put into it while he himself doesn't have enough respect for us to not cut our agreement by at least two-thirds at the last minute.

Shitty position to be in, but we're all feeling a lot better now that we've all agreed that it's not worth doing. After we all sat and ate and talked it through, I felt super-lucky to be in a band with these guys. We agreed to go home and work on new stuff instead.

The skeletal belly of Manhattan: passing through silhouetted webs or branches, a building built over the tunnel highway.

And even though I told them all that I'm done touring,

they're still into writing a new record.
Wonder what this new life at home will bring. Art History program somewhere?

Thing is, I'd really *really* love to go to Europe. I hope my associates understand that. I just can't go with the best possible financial outcome being one-third of what I originally agreed to.

After the show in New Haven going so late, we all stayed up late drunk and talking. We'd Pricelined a room, but it was accidentally half an hour in the wrong direction. It being rainy and the show going so late, we decided to eat the expense and get another room nearby. For the first time in my life I purchased an onion dip and sat as hypnotized by it as I always end up being when I visit my mom and she has it. It could be like visiting my mom anywhere I go. We tried to make sense of how these kids treat us everywhere; this gray area we exist within.

We got a late start and I was irritated, impatient to get to the museum. We headed to a place in the Healthy Highways book, back downtown by where the show was, only to find that the place had closed. It was already after 12:30. I was annoyed. We should've called ahead.

Nate had eaten some mushrooms but figured they wouldn't kick in until we got to the museum and for some reason we all agreed it was OK for him to drive. Sam kept fucking with his tripping-mind, talking about how everything is just numbers. We got to the museum by 2:20, called the club and told them that we'd be an hour late so we could have an extra hour to wander the museum.

The two hours at the museum were undoubtedly the happiest time I've had in weeks with the exception of seeing Amy. Only the last 20 minutes I figured that I might as well check out the contemporary wing while I'm there and nothing really connected with me except for a video of a wolf and a deer in a gallery together. It was heavy and simple and got you thinking about all kinds of different stuff and was put together really well.

Other than that, the Picassos and Pollocks and Cornell boxes might just all be too familiar to me now, like I have some cultural tolerance built up. I felt indifferent to them after 90 minutes of older work, all with such greater historical depth to them, accrued aura.

Plenty of great bands have replaced their singers—AC/DC, Can, Iron Maiden, Van Halen.

Philly notes: weird dicks at club, the church, Jade Tree, Hiltz, Sean, Harpers, Khyber, Need New Body, vegetarian restaurants, fights on stage, Jamey, Sarah, band meeting, Need New Body reunion, show-mic-cable, after show, fight kid, Sam with girl, Jamey's house, emailing G_____.

*

NOVEMBER 16, 2006

Possibly the worst band I've ever seen is playing first at the Middle East tonight.

Amy read me the list of raffle prizes for our fundraiser and it's nuts: $100 Reckless gift certificate, $50 Lula gift certificate, $50 Asrai Garden gift certificate, dinner at Le Bouchon gift certificate, two passes to Drag City comedy night, $25 Hard Boiled gift certificate, $100 Odd Obsession gift certificate, $15 Quimby's gift certificate, free subscription to Stop Smiling, $50 Penelope's gift certificate.

That's *insane* that they talked all these places into donating so much. Obviously that's so generous of all those places and feels good in terms of community support, but –

gah—how embarrassing to ask, and to now owe people. Humiliating. Why do I find every step of this process so humiliating? I wish we could just quietly be making our self-financed thing in private. So embarrassing.

The stage at the North Star bar in Philly has been rebuilt three times, each new stage built on top of the old one. Loading up the steps through the back door, it looks like a strange Neopolitan. The soundman was a dorky Cool-Guy and very formal, made me miss Hiltz at the church.

I'd met John Hiltz on the east coast Captain Jazz tour. His basement was a legendary venue in New Jersey hardcore. I'd seen it in all the zines and couldn't believe that we were able to get a show there and Policy of 3 even played. John played in Greyhouse and Born Against, but to know him one would never in a million years imagine him to be a drummer for hardcore bands. He's always moving slow and slack-jawed and mellow and has a bit of a millionaire vibe to him even though he's actually super hardworking. He reminds me a little of Cassavetes's character in *Love Streams* and has always looked a bit like him to me. He'd be in Chicago a lot back in the mid-90s. He dated Kim and we all hung around each other some.

The house manager guy at North Star Bar can only be described as a Big Moron. He walked around shouting and being a dick and it sort of made me feel bad for him, like the poor guy must really have *zero* going for him if these little displays of power are somehow satisfying.

Jamey had come over straight from work, covered in splashes of paint. He'd pulled his back out one too many times as a mover and so his body demoted him to house painting — equally laborious, but with less shocks of stress. It felt great to see him. After sitting for a while on the stoop outside the club, talking, the manager guy started screaming, "Who's kicking the door?" and opened the door hard into us. We told him that we'd been sitting still, and squinting at us suspiciously, he nodded and said, "I don't think so."

Jamey and all the Need New Body dudes really are the easiest people I've ever known to just fall right back in with. Before touring over and over with those guys, and getting to know them all, Philly was already a more common stop for us than it is for most bands. The Jade Tree guys have lived in suburban Delaware for years. Philly was their Good Ol' Boys hardcore scene. We'd pass through to get mocked.

Jesus Christ, has there ever been a period in my entire life that I wasn't bullied?

*

ALL OVER AND OVER

NOVEMBER 17, 2006

Entering the state, coming north from the city, bare trees and golden brown brush line the long open roads, slow bends through quiet, low mountains. Always old houses and occasionally a barn or a river, a garbage processing plant, a fireworks outlet, an adult outlet, a Burger King, small towns with steeples that peak a neck and a head taller than the rest of the town, back ways with small sheds, creeks cold and brown over jagged rocks, antennas on top of mountains, a volunteer firehouse. Sunset already and we've hardly been moving three or four hours.

Just a couple days from home where we may get to stay for the whole month. Yesterday, the stomachache of guilt all day worrying that we've done the wrong thing. But "breaking even" can't mean the trip paying for itself. It has to be coming home with at least as much as if I'd stayed home and worked.

The scattered lights of industry through skeletal woods and up ahead a town climbing up a mountain. A parking lot for cranes, old houses of chewable vitamin pale orange brick and white aluminum siding.

The sky itself more alive than anything it's blanketing, diffused and buoyant bright pinks and whites.

Ann and I at 4:00 a.m. talking about how she doesn't see how society is going to progress past bloodshed and aggression and war if she's still operating on such a primal level as to let the sunsets effect her as they do. I said I felt the exact opposite.

The sunset's reflected in the wall of windows of an industrial park's outer-most building. The few houses are in clusters together, each cluster far from the others. A power line cuts across the skyline. An old hotel or monastery atop the mountaintop and now a city opens up below us, visible, for just a single quick bend around the side of this slope. A high school football field, the tracks through the center of the town, more abandoned artifacts of industries fled and the big buildings to house them, all the brown rivers' levels climbing. In the flooded soccer field across from the truck stop restaurant, hundreds of ducks play a lazy game.

In Boston the other night, immediately after our show, sneaking out for a smoke, I found the best spot in Boston. I was reminded of the first Borges story I ever read, "The Aleph."

My uncle's mom's funeral is today. I feel terrible that I am not there. My mom is crazy to tell Amy and Ryan not to go.

Barns and silos along the river through the hills. The sky now shades of gray. The fields flooded, the houses, some with lit windows. I love these hilly old towns, the Morgantown, West Virginias of the world. The textures of all the half-collapsed houses.

But this spot in Boston, the best spot in Boston, I found it right after we finished, stepping outside to smoke. In the corner of a corner restaurant, dark, a three-piece Middle Eastern band played. People sat at tables close up to the stage. From where I stood in the corner of the window looking in, the reflections of the cabs at the cab stand behind me looked equally as real as everything inside the restaurant. Cabs would pull up just exactly so that their front bumpers would touch the band. As they'd remain parked waiting for a fare, all the people at the first table closest to the stage appeared to be sitting in the backseat, occasionally being served by a waitress. Eventually each cab would pull away, running over the band and leaving behind its illusory passengers remaining seated.

Blue-black beautiful dark sky, Cracker Barrel billboard reflected on pond-surface, truck stop, a U-Haul with its hood up, Paul Bunyan Products must sell lumber, refineries in the valley, an American flag in front of each like everything else, low clouds just above the mountains.

Our own van's headlights reflected off the back of the truck ahead of us is our only proof that we too are as visible passing through the landscape as it all is to us.

Red pickup truck display, six of them parked in a half-floral pattern. Even parts of Pennsylvania are The South.

An old lodge with two windows on the second story lit and a long row of lower level windows lit too, looks like a menacing, straight-faced pumpkin head on the side of the road.

Took our time leaving Boston. It must be the biggest city that we've played the most times and still don't really have any friends in. There's Mike Brown, who we're all buddies with and like and even keep in touch with a bit, but he's been working as a roofer for the last two years and always has to be up at 5:00 a.m., so he can never really make it out.

There's also this one kid that comes out most of the time that I always hang out with, but I don't know his name; plays in Sunburned Hand of The Man. I first met him in Athens, GA, when he was still probably in high school. My brother had played there the month before and had brought my mom along on tour with him and she ended up sitting with this kid the whole night and hitting it off. So when we showed up to play a month later the kid was all excited to tell me about hanging out with my mom.

That Athens show was super-weird. Sitting at a stoplight, the only guy I knew in Athens, but didn't know how to get in touch with, K_____, crossed the street in front of us, like the secretary leaving town with the money in *Psycho*. So I jumped out and we ended up hanging out, going out to dinner and running into J_____ from Atlanta who was hanging out with this Omaha guy that used to drive Ann crazy, G_____. We all went back to K_____'s place to check out these field recordings that he'd made while traveling Southeast Asia and J_____ and G_____ just mocked us the whole time.

It was the first few weeks after 9/11 and everyone still had raw nerves, a ready-to-talk-to-anyone attitude—interesting time to be traveling. I sat outside the restaurant for a smoke and talked to a man in a daze whose mother had died in her hospital bed five minutes before the first plane hit the towers. He thought he was the luckiest man on earth that his mom lived up to that last minute and never had to see what we all, at that time, assumed things would become—and which they largely have.

The show was in a strange all-ages place a family had opened in tribute to their son who had killed himself. R.E.M. supposedly helped finance a big part of it. Michael Stipe was at the basement show The Promise Ring played in Athens, but left halfway through their set.

And so anyways, I met this kid there and he was a geeky teen and I forgot about him for some years until he resurfaced in Boston, always high, and now a member of Sunburned Hand of the Man. But neither he nor Mike Brown came out this time, so it was mostly just restlessness.

I remembered playing The Middle East when Isotope was playing downstairs and walking with Bitney to listen to some African dance class that you could hear from the street. I walked over there and stood around. A few kids that were obviously on their way to our show walked up and I put the shields up and looked at my feet and played possum.

Another time we played upstairs and The Undead played downstairs. I went down to check out that show and there were six to eight people paid. Bobby Steele and some dudes that had been in Dee Dee Ramone's band were rocking it while a couple Irish Lynch Mob skins pogo'd and a couple punks stood at the bar at the back.

Of the countless times we've played Boston, only three haven't been at The Middle East. The strangest Middle East show was Owls, Milemarker and New End Original downstairs two or three days after 9/11. It was the club's first show re-opening after Arab on Radar had infamously played there—The Middle East—on 9/11. Security guards with metal detectors and dogs were out in full force. Spooky. I stood in the back and listened to Milemarker make fun of New End Original, then stood in the back and listened to

New End Original make fun of Milemarker, then played and wondered if they'd introduced themselves to each other and were hitting it by off mocking us.

The first time that we ever played Boston it was at a church in Harvard Square with tombstones dating back to the 1600s. It was with The Promise Ring, Jejune, and The Van Pelt. I was sick and puking on the side of the building when it was time for us to go on and I remember Rama Mayo, the promoter—who I became friends with a little bit for a few years, but now can only picture David Spade—standing next to me insisting that I was faking it to try to play later on the bill. That was the second time in my life that I had to go on immediately after puking.

First time was in Lincoln, a couple days before Captain Jazz broke up. I hadn't eaten all day and so decided I should eat some of those big horse-pill vitamins with some warm Pabst for nourishment. I then stood outside dry-heaving while everyone stood around waiting for me inside. That was the night we met Ann and Andrea and Justin. All the Cursive guys had been at that show too. We all ended up going skinny-dipping together after the show, but wouldn't put together who all was present that night until it came up once twelve years later.

The next time we played Boston anywhere except the Middle East was a loft party: JOA opening for The Make Up. I remember when The Make Up showed up being stunned at their ability to spontaneously become the center of attention and be alright with it, comfortable and remembering everybody's names. We'd been out long enough that I was feeling beat up and I went out to the hall and up a flight of stairs to be alone a while. After a few minutes I heard groaning and sighing and looked over the edge to see Ian on the landing below me, by himself and unaware that anyone was seeing him. He moaned and twisted and seemed to be in a lot of pain and I stood silent watching a minute. It was exactly how I was feeling, but I didn't know that everyone else also felt like that after living in a van for weeks, in my case living on whiskey, weed, and ephedrine, up all night and wandering all day. After seeming to wear himself out, Ian bent down and touched his toes, took a deep breath and collected himself and returned to the show, returned to being the center of attention. That's Professionalism.

The electricity went out a couple times during our set that night. Some strange ladies told me that they were Ian's mom and sister and I watched the show from the side of the stage with them and never doubted it as they told me funny stories from Ian's youth. Only later when I mentioned to those guys that I'd been hanging out with Ian's family and they said that Ian doesn't have a sister and his mom lives wherever, did I realize that the ladies had been fucking with me.

And fucking Boston, I always get lost, every time. One time on a Travel Channel job with Chris, it took the two of us three hours to find the photo store two miles from our hotel, high through The Big Dig.

Another time, playing with Hella and Need New Body next door to the Middle East, Al Grossman showed up to gush to Hella about what a huge fan he was. He was about 60 with a giant shock of thick white Dylan-hair, like a flaming-haired manga character. His son, who must've turned him on to Hella, looked uncomfortable as his dad kept talking. I got the impression that Grossman had kept his sunglasses on since Dylan went electric at Newport.

Hockey fans leaving the game in Buffalo just called me "Osama."

So Al Grossman wanted to collaborate with Hella.

But I do always love to see the signs downtown "Government Center" and get The Modern Lovers song in my head.
*

All Over and Over #4

GOING HOME

ALL OVER AND OVER

NOVEMBER 18, 2006

Sunset in Cleveland, I'm just waking up. The clouds are very, very orange Georgia O'Keefe puffs over the sprawl of industrial bridges and refineries.

The show last night was indistinguishable from all the others. I guess there were some pleasant surprises in the details. Nice place, Sound-lab in Buffalo.

Indistinguishable, in flat layers like screens, the clouds move in front of and behind each other.

Sound-lab was like the Rodan of Buffalo, a city in which every single house could use a coat of paint. It's impossible to guess where anyone might work or go to if anyone actually lives in these houses, because there seems to be nothing else there. It has its Detroit or Gary-isms, giant concrete blocks, tall and long monuments of abandoned function. But it also has way more small family houses than either of those cities.

Off the BQE that giant cemetery at night expands back and back until Manhattan's skyline rises up out of it like a continuation, and from that specific angle it seems strange that the skyline doesn't always appear like tombstones to everyone.

And now Cleveland feels like home, 90's sharp bend at downtown. A city of two significantly different histories for us: Speak in Tongues—ghetto over and over, good turnout, weird place, Dan—and The Grog Shop—Jets to Brazil, breaking bottles, 9/11.

Guess Europe is going to happen after all.

But yeah, Sound-lab and its cool, older proprietor Michael, very cool. Huge turnout and everyone seemed really into it. The back door was left open and a hockey game had been going on down the street and let out right before we started.

While we played, a couple hockey-schmoes walked in the back door and past us from behind the stage to sneak in. We all kept looking around confused as people kept coming in. Nate threw a stick at one of them while in the middle of "Temping." Playing a tricky drums-and-keyboard part, without a glitch, he took aim like an archer and hit the guy in the back as he was sneaking in. The crowd loved it.

This creepy hippy Damo Suzuki-looking dude was hanging out backstage from the time we got there, drinking all of our beer. Once Sam figured out that he wasn't in one of the bands he told him that he had to leave and the guy immediately got violent and threatening. Sam asked the people working there to kick him out. They all agreed that he was a creep, but said that they didn't want any more trouble from him and they feared kicking him out might provoke him.

I've only played Buffalo twice before: JOA once in 1997 on some ridiculous, total hardcore bill and the room emptied out when we played. And then Owls the week after 9/11, played some ridiculous metal club, a hockey-obsessed sports bar, soundman with a mullet and Molson, the works.

A kid interviewed me that day. Fried paranoid on weed and speed and from being out on tour for weeks when no one in the whole country knew what was going on—Anthrax in the mail, Ground Zero smoldering on TV 24 hours a day—and I was living in a van with two junkies, playing to no one every night. The interviewer kid provoked me to bitch—about everything. I ranted like a foaming-mouthed lunatic because I was crazy, burned-out, and bummed out, high and stupid. Among the zillion things that I raged and howled about was Mike from Troubleman owing me some small amount of royalties, maybe a grand. Of course the kid later only printed the part about Troubleman and nothing else—as if I'm a foaming, ranting Troubleman-hater first and foremost, instead of honestly portraying me as the foaming, ranting hater-of-everything that I truly was. Mike has still never talked to me again, six years later. And I sure learned a lesson about interviews.

ALL OVER AND OVER

Usually when we're in these parts we play in Rochester at The Bug Jar. (Finkbeiner, Charles, rich girl's parent's house—movie theater girl, Herzog guest list.)

Last time JOA played there, about six weeks ago, just as we're finishing and I'm beginning to pack up my stuff, this kid grabs me from behind. And like anyone's instinct at being grabbed, I pulled away. A few minutes later, he walks up again and grabs me and I lean in close and tell him to stop grabbing me. He's wasted and responds by telling me our set was "Watered Down Bullshit. Why'd you guys *water it down* so much?" I responded that I appreciated his opinion, but I couldn't worry about what everybody thinks and we just had to make ourselves happy. He was really pushing himself on me re-iterating his point over and over—*Watered Down Bullshit*—and I left my stuff to pack up later. I took a walk around the block.

Rochester has always struck me as probably the U.S. city with the highest percentage per capita of handicapped people walking around—lots of one-legged people on crutches, midgets and dwarves, obese people too big to get out of wheelchairs. It's strange, unsettling.

Getting back to the Bug Jar fifteen minutes later, there was a large group assembled right outside the door. The kid that had been yelling at me was in the middle of it with a few friends on his side and another bunch of thugs was also worked up. The security guy was in the middle of everyone, screaming, trying to diffuse the tension. But when the kid that had been grabbing me spit in the security guy's face, the security guy responded by pepper-spraying him. The crowd scattered quickly, everyone screaming, and filled the intersection, stopping traffic, everyone throwing punches. The pepper-sprayed kid took off his shirt and screamed as he stomped his feet heavily, lifting his knees up to his chest with each stomp, stomping in a wide circle, puke and tears hanging in long, thick cords from his red, swollen face. I watched from across the street, leaning against the outside of the club, just a few feet away from the mayhem, but feeling pretty confidently removed from it for some reason, if only by being the only person out there that didn't know absolutely which side I was on and who to turn to and punch first.

A kid with his head cracked open wide and blood running down his face surprised me all at once in my face, yelling at me. Maybe his eyelid had gotten torn a little because his one eye, popping out wide open, never blinked. He must've been in shock, unaware of how totally drenched and caked in blood he was. He pushed me against the wall yelling, "All this is your fault. You told him, 'you're just *a fan*. I don't care what *a fan* thinks.'" I appealed to him that that's not something that I would ever say because I don't think in those terms. I wanted to explain that what I had said to the kid was the only possible manner of self-preservation that I could think of to respond to a kid that grabs me and shouts in my face like that. Sam grabbed me from behind and, pushing the kid hard back a step, he pulled me inside the club. The doorman closed the door behind me and stood watch to make sure that no one else could slip in after the reconnaissance mission to fetch me was completed.

It was so bizarre that this chaos could've been born out of a JOA show. The 90% of the audience not involved in the fight were all pushed up against the two picture windows that cornered the door, watching it all go down. No one could leave without walking through it.

Back in Ohio—the ultimate seems-like-anywhere. Could be Pennsylvania or Michigan or Indiana. Pulled into town and went straight to the Days Inn. "Days Inn Bowling Greene"— sounds like a caricature of tour.

Called my uncle first thing to tell him that I'm sorry about his mother dying and he said it's a relief that it's over. I thanked him again for performing my dad's service and Mike and Ryan's wedding and told him how bad I felt that I couldn't be at his mom's service. He said he got me and Amy's plant and the joke around the house had been, "Which part do we smoke?" I appreciated that.

ALL OVER AND OVER

He goes in for his surgery Monday morning, gets home on Thanksgiving. I told him me and Amy would visit Tuesday or Wednesday and I'm looking forward to doing so. He sounded legitimately freaked out and was making jokes to deal with it, but the jokes were all falling just a bit off-target, proof that he was at least a little out of sorts.

Five bands tonight at Howard's Club in Bowling Greene, Ohio. We go on at 12:45. Lots of kids out at the ultimate Midwest wood-with-names-carved-in-it-bar, a bar I wouldn't trust the popcorn enough to eat. So I'm down the street with the vending machines at the laundromat.

L_____ was already waiting for us in her and Bobby's room when we got to the hotel. All this getting dark early has been making the drives seem longer than they are; can't read or write in the dark. I have to remember my book-light for Europe. Maybe I'll splurge on an iPod if I can figure it out. Might save me over there.

I emailed G_____ and the German booker M_____ to tell them that we will accept their revised offer that M_____ came up with. Just need to make sure that the odd elements of our backline and the flights with such late notice are all affordable. The new version of the tour is eight days shorter, makes us more money and is routed much more efficiently. It looks great. I'm excited to do it even if it means no second and third France shows and no Spain at all. Too bad the most beautiful places to visit are the least profitable for us. But going seems so much more right to do. And maybe we'll be perceived as hard-nosed negotiators now—ha. Wonder how angry G_____ is about the compromise. Is this good news for him or embarrassing, but still good news or just embarrassing?

After canceling I certainly did feel better about the decision once a couple other professional-types all put their two cents in about the situation. The French and Luxembourg bookers wrote to tell us how sorry they were for us and how it's too bad and not our fault and totally understandable. M_____, who ended up going back and cleaning it up and fixing the whole thing, told us that he couldn't believe how G_____ had set it up. Uli wrote to say that this strange G_____, who he made clear he distrusted all along, "shit us a pile of lies."

*

ALL OVER AND OVER

NOVEMBER 18, 2006

Bowling Greene, Ohio Saturday Night Streets. The attorney's office obviously used to be a funeral home. There's a church back in the neighborhood off the main street a block, it's in charming disrepair, old enough that if it were kept up it'd look phony and quaint.

Couples are out walking, each shivering with their arms crossed or the men hunched with hands in pockets and heads down. The parking garage is lit up and empty. Half the meters have plastic bags over them and every spot is filled.

I saunter alongside some nineteen-year-olds for a moment. The young guy tells another young guy and a girl, "He told me I'd make a lot of money if I ever worked at a gay bar." The other two seemed neither amused nor sympathetic and just shrugged. This intensified the guy's anger, which I hadn't quite determined yet for sure was in fact the dominant mood. "What the fuck is that?" He said, now in a sudden rage. "I could've killed him."

Pulling up to the shit hole Battle of the Bands for Bikers that we're at tonight, I smoked a cigarette across the street. A mid-fifties white man in neat and clean sweats, kind of a big guy, looked like a high school coach, made a scene screaming at this other guy. The man being screamed at was shorter and chubbier, Latino and seemed confused. He repeated over and over, "I don't know what you're *talking* about. This is *crazy*." He appeared truly unable to comprehend what the coach kept screaming so dramatically. The coach repeated with an exaggerated sigh, as if it required more of an effort to scream than he felt like he could muster but he felt he had to do so, "You stole from me! You've been spending my money all up and down the street! You've emptied me out!" And the other guy just shrugged and insisted quietly, "I don't know what you're *talking* about." The coach screamed again and they took turns like this for a good while, a few minutes at least. It was enough time for me to wonder how two middle-aged men could make such spectacles of themselves.

Finally, the coach reached over to the other guy. I thought he was going to choke him, but instead, in one clean swoop, he reached into the man's front shirt pocket and grabbed something. "My fucking debit card is in your fucking pocket!" He waved it in the other guy's face, but that guy continued to insist, "I don't know what you're *talking* about." The coach switched his refrain to its next iteration. "You had my fucking debit card in your fucking pocket! You had my fucking debit card in your fucking pocket!" And they took turns like that for a minute.

Finally one silence lasted a little more prolonged than the other prolonged silences in between their rounds. It seemed about to be violent when the coach instead turned around and walked off. He headed to the left behind the building. After watching him walk off, the other guy hung his head and turned to walk off in the other direction. But less than thirty seconds later they bumped into each other at the next corner, approaching it perpendicularly to each other. They were both shocked for a moment before each picked up exactly where he had left off.

"You had my fucking debit card in your fucking pocket!"

"I don't know what you're *talking* about."

"You had my fucking debit card in your fucking pocket!"

But this verse was short, trading only a few fours back and forth before each man retreated back in the direction he had approached the corner from.

What the coach didn't know, as he entered the bar we were about to load into, but what I had seen clearly from across the street, was that approaching from the other corner, the smaller guy had beaten him into the bar by only a few paces. This completed their bedroom-farce to its full potential, but had me dreading going into the club.

Long gray-haired bearded bartender and soundman.

One girl in a jersey, football I guess, stood on a keg and waved a beer can in each hand smiling at all the passing cars. As we loaded in, some kids were on stage setting up, one was playing guitar and Nate laughed as we passed each other in the door between trips. "That's an American Football song." I guess the kid was attempting to speak to us in some kind of code.

They've hung a sign over the old Bowling Greene Post Office. It says, "Senior Citizen Center." There's a Thai Restaurant in Oklahoma City that obviously used to be a Burger King and there's an Indian restaurant in Hyde Park that was obviously a Subway.

Two girls leave the frat bar next door to the show. One says, "Thank God for everything right now," and the other one starts laughing so hard that it becomes no-longer-laughing and more like just-can't-catch-my-breath, hyperventilation about to black out like my marijuana-OD at nineteen.

An Asian guy with a harelip walks out of the Make Believe show on his phone. "I just saw the band Joan of Arc. It was awesome."

They've turned on all the Christmas lights up and down Main Street. All the trees and streetlights are now small galaxies. All the college kids are out as the bars close, all at their absolute worst, piggy-back rides and one, joyously even, actually screams, "How dumb can dumb get?"

Pizza is still open as it always is. Just in time to get home, my hours have flipped over. We've been out long enough now to never see daylight and not notice except for memories of Amy's sleeping schedule.

Five fucking bands. The first band was really young kids, seventeen or eighteen, and very formally asked me to watch them and the best I could answer was, "I'll try," and I couldn't even live up to that. I guess I could vaguely understand that it might've meant something to them for me to have done so, but really I couldn't even force myself to consider it.

This place has my solitaire video game that only all of the last places on earth that you ever want to end up always have. By necessity, I sit at them when I see them. I always play until I get the high score and then I always sign my full name,

Tim Kinsella, because I think it's a funny autograph to leave at all of ultimate shit-holes we ever end up at. Anywhere you'd ever want to be would never have this game.

Momentary Lapse of Reason-era Pink Floyd blasts out of the bar next door.

Through sustained conscious effort I have trained myself and it's sticking a little. Every time I see a tree I think, *a tree is not a tree*.

A beach volleyball player-looking-guy screamed, "*Jooooooooooan of Aaaaaaarc!*" in my face as he walked out. Who the fuck's life is this?

*

ALL OVER AND OVER

NOVEMBER 19, 2006

Rainy day in Bowling Greene, called for a late checkout, but still have such a short drive to Lansing today that there's going be a lot of time to kill somewhere, which is always, of course, the last-day-of-tour-predicament: counting down the hours until you're home and there's nothing else to do but count down the hours.

What would a movie about a maid at a hotel be? She'd be Latina or Eastern European. Is that what *Bottle Rocket* was about?

The reflections of all the cars on all the motel windows looks like a long row of garages.

My awareness from the Philadelphia Art Museum is what I want to try to carry with me. I hardly saw anything made later than 1850 and the earliest artifacts are exactly that: more artifacts than art, functional pieces — a helmet from 500 B.C., an arrow tip from 500 B.C., whatever.

But then even the suits of armor all had etchings and inlays of Christ. How many thousands of Christs must be in that building? And very few of those, maybe just some newer ones, don't have a far deeper understanding of their faiths in poetic and symbolic terms than religious people now could ever have. Is it only that they had a concrete sense of it as History? Their own worlds, being more similar to Christ's world architecturally and culturally, made it more immediate and it's this immediacy that creates such depth? The Industrial Revolution killed Christianity's poetic nuances? Maybe it's my own shifting perspective that gives me this impression, some basic knowledge of other religions allows me to recognize poetic and symbolic depths beyond the literal readings of the American Christianity that I was raised with.

Between Bowling Greene and Toledo: lots of barns with patchwork roofs and matte finishes, old houses far apart from each other with nothing in between except flatness and visible distance. The Islamic Center of Greater Toledo stands out among the farmhouses, newer than anything else and its surface all the same age, no depths of decrepitude, no signs of having been repaired. An old hotel has collapsed in on itself, folding up as if in retreat or entering quiet retirement. Barns, barns, barns swoop into the suburbs and then it's construction sites, skeletal beams for what might be a library or more likely a gym. The houses around a man-made lake all look identical.

Two small trailers are parked in tall brush. One of the trailers has a picnic table outside of it, which seems more settled to stay-put than the trailer itself does. A lake is nearby, and smoke stacks aren't far either. Every car we pass, if someone is sitting shotgun, they are asleep.

Dustin showed me his drawings last night, all kind of repetitive tightly-wound vaguely human forms with a sort of melting crayon Kindergarten quality that's still somehow tightly controlled. My favorite was of a man who stands still as the road moves through him.

Old Toledo, the old lumber yards and projects, brick and square and broken windows and bent-up fences and industry again and old bridges across the industry like a functional jungle-gym whose function has dissipated. And all the houses with attic windows and pointed tops and porches, the kind of porch you want to put a couch out on, but probably not the kind of neighborhood you'd want to do that in. And train yards, Everywhere-America, your train yards and auto supply centers. Shit-hole Toledo like shit-hole everywhere. The strange Lego-looking castles of industry and is it always about to rain here? Some bungalows have taken out their wreaths, some antennas and new red coats of paint, some flags, some trees near the brown river, some angular. The backside of a factory, blocks long, is collapsed, its halls revealed and walls given shape by an unnamable single event. Every color, every braided combination, every lock, the life of the pile. But what's seeing to me: Toledo sky, the metal skeletons about to pick themselves up off the ground and stand up straight like a giant strange praying mantis, going to eat its lover after it fucks, its lover in this case the entire electrical infrastructure of the city, the conduit and every socket of the old Catholic school dormitories. The trees spill out over the highway as if in retreat. A fence grows through the trunks of some. Lots of cars on driveways look like they'll never be going anywhere. The sheds in backyards, the above-ground pools occasionally, but not as often as the new porch that looks way newer than the rest of the place. And a string of green houses.

Standing at an intersection this morning, a kid called out to us from a passing car, "You guys were awesome last night!" and the baby in the arms of the man standing behind us cheered.

Tractors must be at the center of more local economies than any of us know. A bus parked in a backyard.
Circling downtown to get to Guitar Center Toledo off the Airport Highway Exit; we heard some kid might be playing a Nirvana covers set, got to get there and check it out.
And of course, at the outskirts of town we could be anywhere: Red Roof Inn, Wendy's, IHOP, Chili's, Circuit City, McDonalds, Movie Theater, Boston Market, Best Buy, Walmart, Office Max, Target, Pet Smart, Fifth Third Bank, Burger King, Verizon, Rallys, Arby's, Lube Shop, BP, Subway, Speedway, Sprint, Dairy Queen, Rite Aid, Big Lots, Family Dollar, Little Caesar's, Walmart, The Lady Devils' Softball Field, Outback Steakhouse, Walmart Parking Lot—I heard they let you sleep in your car there—Self-Storage Center, Hair We Are Hair Salon, Who's Out Walking The Dog. A little kid and a littler kid, dumb little brother or whatever, walk along the road and wait to cross the tracks. The older one puts on his headphones to amplify his sullen strut. Sam's Club, Kroger, Bob Evans. Nate has called three times for directions, Guitar Center Toledo doesn't know itself where it is—"near the Firestone, past the Penzoil, next to the Radio

Shack, by Dollar Tree past the Hobby Lobby by the Payless Shoes, near the Pizza Hut and the A&R Bloc, Tan-Pro, TJ Maxx and Fashion Bug, Jenny Craig."

Guitar Center, how? How can anyone do it? All the Metallicas and tappings and slow-hands all collapsed and combined. Office Max, Courtyard Inn, Quality Inn, Residence Inn, Extended Stay America, Knights Inn, Old Navy—everywhere recognizable by magic-hypnosis logos. A hundred yards away the barns begin again and the houses that look more like aluminum-sided mausoleums. Two more caved-in houses, these two next door to each other. The Mega-Church Mall.

A "Viva Bush" bumper sticker on an SUV. Must either be a millionaire or totally ignorant, let me guess . . . Maybe that's what I'll say to the next Republican Hillbilly that I come across, right before he shoots me in the face. "Oh how nice for you, you must be a millionaire."

The density of active and self-aware Consciousness rebounding and ricocheting, perpetually increasing its speed in the cities—that must be what people would term "progressive."

A giant junkyard in the woods, hundreds of abandoned cars

– So of course as the information that's been processed through a human brain gets more sparse, trees and fields and ponds and horses, of course the mind would turn back in on itself in such a space. It could hardly help but do so.

Power lines, power grids, tree-webs woven in between branches.

Michigan: crazy state of heartbreak. Crazy remaining state of heartbreak remains. Crazy perfect hurt. Strange Nothing-Place, but body. Vacancy everywhere. Venison sausage, venison jerky, venison salami. How quiet people can be to each other.

A father has laid out his floor tiles in the pattern of his only daughter's birth date, and still nothing to say between them. Has she grown up to look too much like the mother that left him years ago? He'd drink buttermilk with pepper on long drives.

Skinny and twitchy and spaces and all their space-concoctions.

I'm in love with the idea of me-standing-still always and everywhere. Just being still, as the road passes through me, occasionally stopping at different densities, each of which thinks of itself as a Place, and I climb around: this is familiar, this isn't, this is new and good, this is new and not good. And I fill up all my bins, throwing things each into its bin as quickly as each thing hits me.

But Michigan, at home in the past and always blowing snow, the roads are always slick and it's still always sad and beautiful.

I love a hotel bar. Sunday at sunset, football on TV and the sound of it always makes me feel like a kid. So much of how everything is run for the benefit of the top 5% at the expense of the bottom 95% — I don't get how we all let them get away with it. But football I've been fully socialized to accept. I suspect it has a sadness to me that most people don't respond to. Maybe I don't actually get it and the sadness I feel any Sunday that I'm somewhere in public and overhear a football game is actually a sort of itch of a missing limb. I regret—not regret, but miss in a simple, romantic manner—what football was to me as a kid and I know that it can never be again.

The experts—retired linemen and hard-consonant retired coaches, handsome ex-quarterbacks—all disgust me—their know-it-all manner of talking as if there were somehow some consequence to their opinions. Their gruff, performative masculine vanity, it's everything I hate about anything, which is of course not hate for things as they are as much as a love for the potential of how things *could* be.

But of course a perfect world couldn't work. Only an imperfect world could ever be perfect. These simple flippity-mantras I remember every day only resonate in an immediate, real way with me when they do, and it's not up to me to control if and when they do. But I can keep these truisms present, to be prepared to accept this world and myself in it when it hits me to do so.

And Sunday football games, I guess maybe outside-autumn-anything shocks me into it.

Amy's dad has taped every Oklahoma football game since the dawn of the VCR and watches them all over and over. I guess we each choose our own hypnosis.

Two men move couches in the hotel lobby. There's a mirror in the corner against them and they appear to spin in circles like figure skaters.

No word yet from the Europeans to let us know if our details are possible to coordinate on such short notice. (Touchdown Arizona.) I'm as happy or unhappy to go or not now that it's all up to them. I feel good how it's all turned out, knowing now that it's on our terms or not at all.

Sam got an email from J_____ yesterday. It's as long of an email as one ever really sees, all about our old friend's re-emergence and J_____'s efforts to help him. After six months in jail, then homeless and sleeping on the El, then straight back into rehab, I'm happy to hear that he's apparently back on his feet again. But of course I'm skeptical that it means anything more than that he's OK for a minute again. It's always all, "This time it's different" and every time it's hard not to hope at least a little bit that it could be.

But Sam didn't respond quite as positively as I did. I suggested tracking him down—never letting him in my house, never carrying anything I value around him—but seeing him. J_____ wrote to suggest that Sam and him reunite, all in hints of course, and Sam got pissed in a way that I never really see him get. I guess he must've felt more let down than I ever did. Even at his most functional, our man has always appeared incoherent and out-of-control to everyone else. Sure I've always felt kind of bad for him. But I've never expected anything from him except to fuck up everything that he will ever have access to fucking up. So I've never been too let down.

Sam wrote J_____ back in a terse tone telling him that it's absurd for him to contact people on our man's behalf. He told him that if our man is really so much better now and he really feels so bad now that he understands everything that he's fucked up for himself and so many other people, he should be ready to reach out on his own. Sam is pissed that any of us should be expected to reach out and I can't blame him even if I'm mostly just indifferent.

In Michigan, all exhausted, twelve hours until our own beds. Same hotel Sam knocked himself out dribbling into his own face on the 24-hour basketball court.
*

ALL OVER AND OVER

NOVEMBER 20, 2006

Michigan rest stop: Someone wrote above the *COMPLETE* brand toilet paper logo, "The Blood of Jesus is . . ."

Pulling into Lansing yesterday and getting to the hotel, Sam insisted that we'd stayed there before, but it didn't seem any more familiar to me than any other hotel.

We had a couple hours to rest and all knew that we had no reason to get to Mac's early, so we all went our separate ways. Nate went to the pool and when we all convened later he confirmed that we had in fact stayed there before. Since the only other time we played Mac's was in a blizzard and we had D_____ along with us and went to stay at his parents, we figured out it must've been when we played the Temple Club with Cursive.

D_____'s parents' house was a great reprieve from the blizzard. They were rich and conservative and we had an awkward big breakfast with the whole family, all of them dressed alike as if posing for a family portrait that might happen at any second. None of us really even knew D_____ that well, so when his dad started picking on him about being the only one in generations to not go to the same college, it was heavy and weird. He later told us that his sister had just graduated from there and George W. Bush was the keynote speaker at her graduation.

When we stayed at this hotel before we all sat in the 24-hour hot tub together, drunk around 3:00 a.m. It was connected to a big pool and a sauna and an athletic center with a full basketball court. Nate and Sam went to play basketball as me and Bobby stayed in the hot tub, lying back with our arms out of the water on the tile lip.

After a few minutes we heard loud banging and turned to watch a game that our associates had invented, which involved throwing the basketball at the floor as hard as possible to try to hit the ceiling. By the time they figured out how much force doing so would actually require, and the bang of the ball on the floor got loud enough for us to hear it and turn to watch, there was only one more ball thrown. Sam got a running start and hurled the ball impossibly hard against the ground only to have it bounce back equally hard right back into his face. He was lucky to have not broken his nose and was in a bit of a daze as we all ran back to our room, Bobby and I dripping a wet trail down the hall.

Mac's was still the same shit hole that we'd remembered it as. Without a blizzard outside it seemed slightly more hospitable, but someone had been working on a spray paint mural at the back of the stage all day and the fumes were thick.

We'd been laughing since New Brunswick about how many otherwise perfectly-fine band photos must've been ruined by the bad mural at that club. But places somehow think it's a good idea to let terrible artists ruin their rooms.

We were trapped there for a while last time—bored bored bored. I ended up standing and staring at the Haymarket Riot poster, stunned by Kevin's long hair. After pondering it in a daze for five minutes, I ran to find Sam to pull him over and show him, and found him standing across the bar staring exactly as I had been at the same poster. Strange the ways you end up keeping up with old friends.

They bought us some Papa John's pizzas and at least those fill you up after two pieces and don't taste good enough to threaten the damage that good pizza can make you do to yourself.

I sat with Dustin and looked through some cool *Avante Garde* magazines from the late-60s that he'd bought earlier. Mac's had my stupid video-solitaire game that they only have anywhere you'd never want to be. I couldn't break sixth place here thanks to some dick named Joe.

LaSalle loaded in and it was nice to see them and remind each other of Cursive and how awesome that tour was with a thousand kids everywhere and hospitality galore. They said they hadn't really played at all since that tour and it was pretty obvious that they weren't too inspired, all talking about their jobs they don't really like, etc. The drummer's wife was conspicuously missing, but no one could blame her after Sam had decided that he was in love with her and was unrelenting the whole time we toured together. It's a real testament to the dude's character that he doesn't just assume all of us are dicks.

Dustin and Matt stayed with us at our hotel. We had two beers and the bottom finger of a bottle of Makers to split between five of us, like being at a party in junior high. Dustin is like a sweet kindergartener with his totally un-self-conscious senses of wonder and generosity. Matt, by comparison, is terse and fast-talking, but just as nice—a higher-energy total positivity. Once again I feel like I have new summer-camp friends that will always be friends.

Getting out of Mac's was tough. A couple big dudes in big jackets jumped up on stage as soon as we were done, before we could even break anything down. They were shooting a commercial for the place but didn't know what exactly they wanted to do or how they wanted to do it. All they knew is that they wanted to get going and get it done quick. It was funny to watch. They ended up agreeing to do an air jump-shot together—like air guitar, there was no ball—but they were in full winter gear, baggy pants falling down as they jumped, on a dark stage with all of our equipment still on it.

Loaded out alone and annoyed after waiting half an hour for a hand.

Last morning of nowhere-to-find to eat. Ended up at the gross diner set up jerry-rigged in a shed next to a farmer's market. Counted the money on the road and were all pleased to come home with $1200 each.

*

ALL OVER AND OVER

APPENDIX: MAPS

APPENDIX

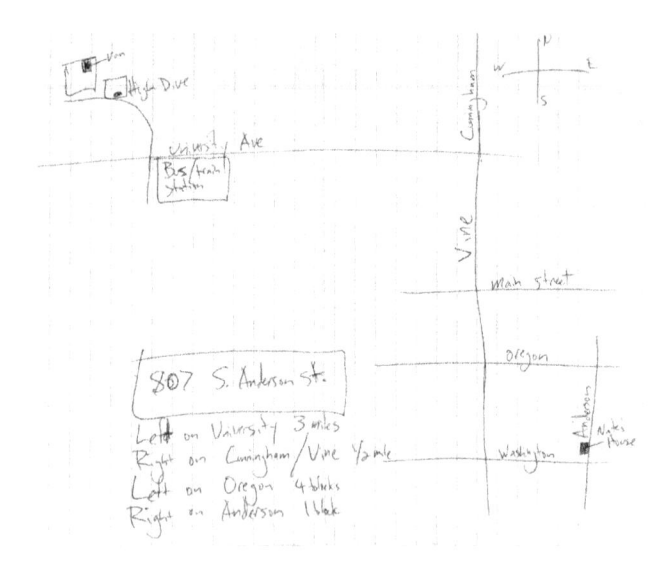

807 S. Anderson St.

Left on University 3 miles
Right on Cunningham/Vine ½ mile
Left on Oregon 4 blocks
Right on Anderson 1 block

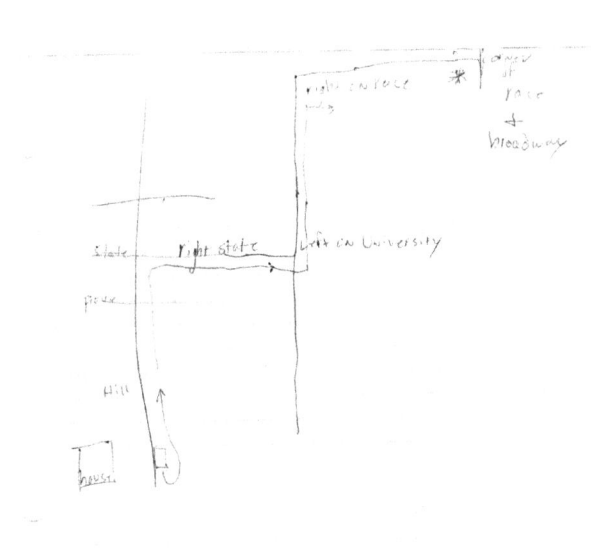

MAPS

APPENDIX

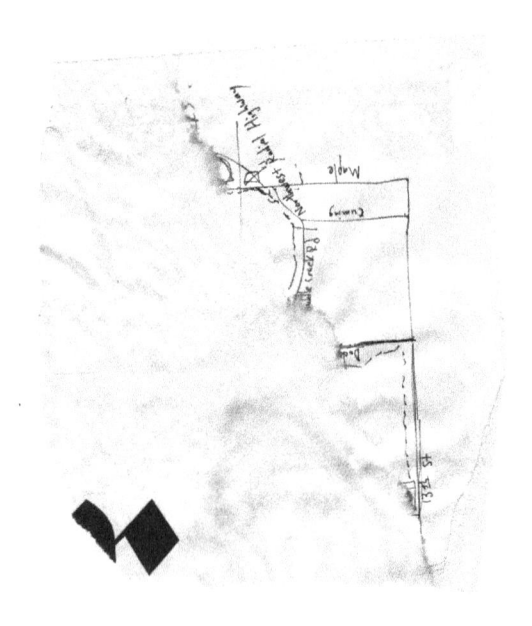

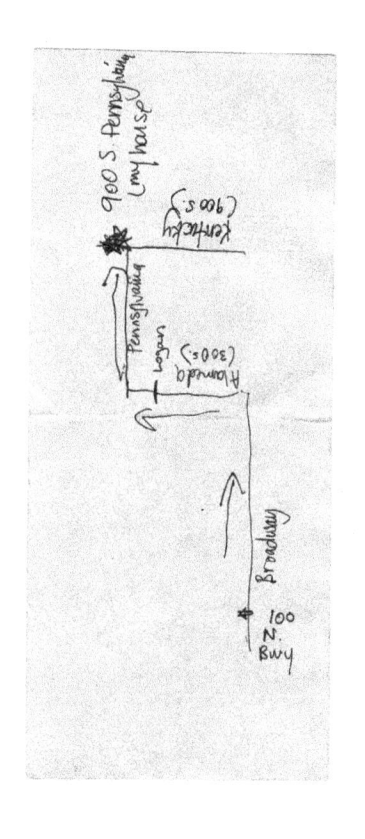

MAPS

APPENDIX

From the Library

Date:
To:

690

light
Hacke Blvd
light

W. Entry Rd

④

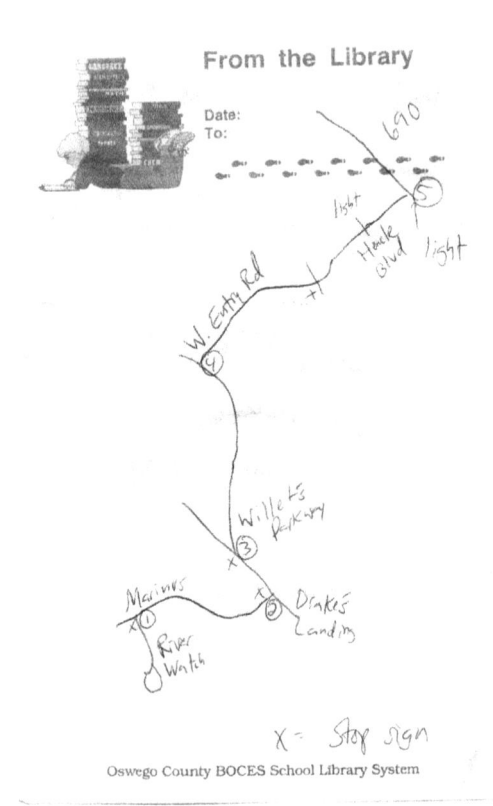

Willets Parkway

Mainvs ① ③
River Watch ② Drakes Landing

X = Stop sign

Oswego County BOCES School Library System

268

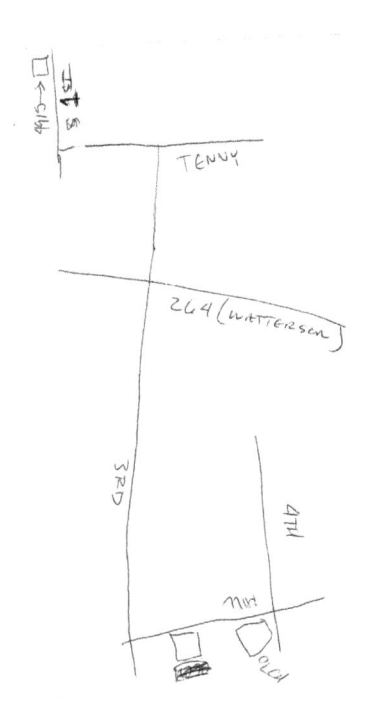

MAPS

APPENDIX

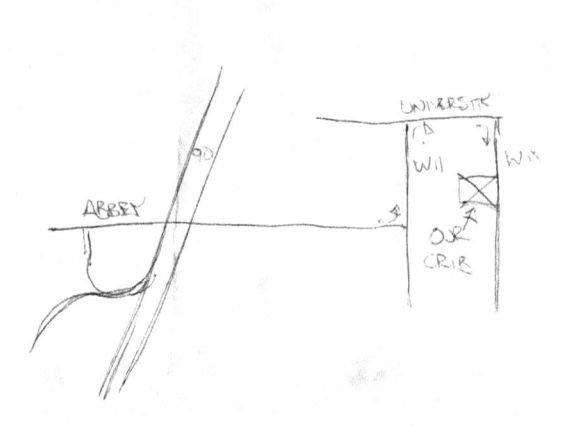

MAPS

APPENDIX

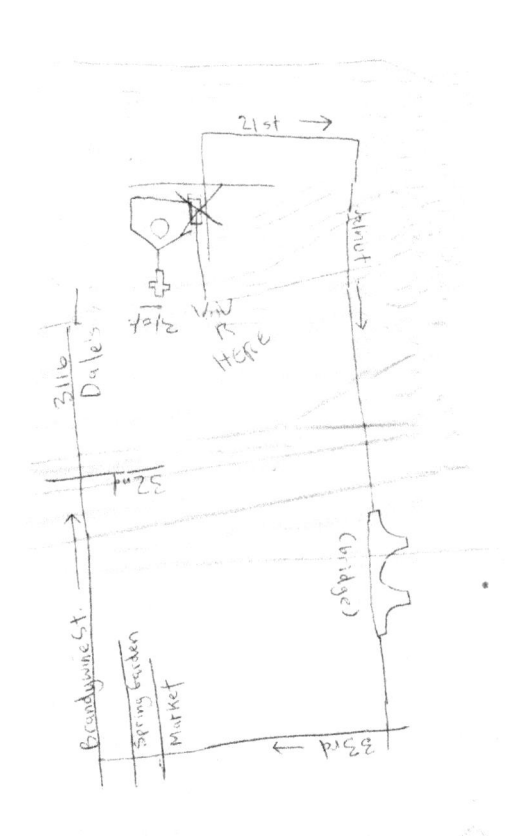

MAPS

APPENDIX

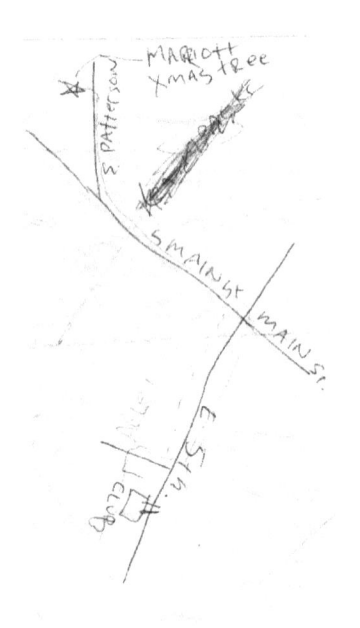

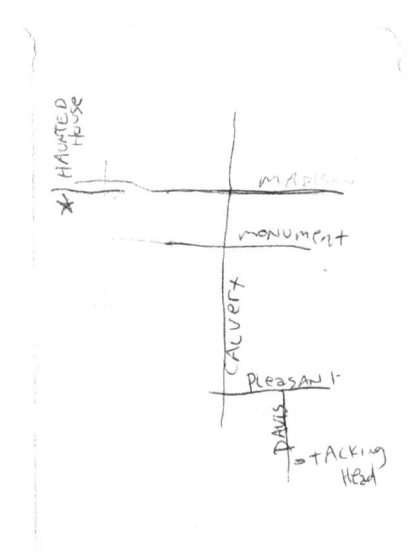

MAPS

APPENDIX

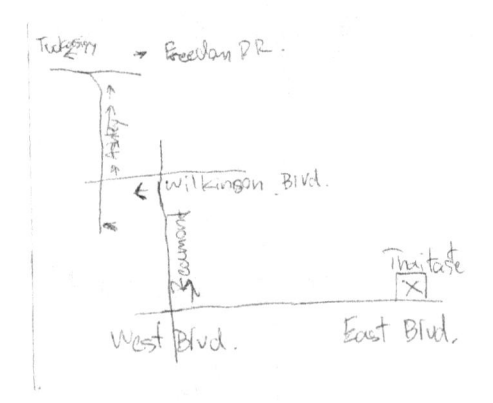

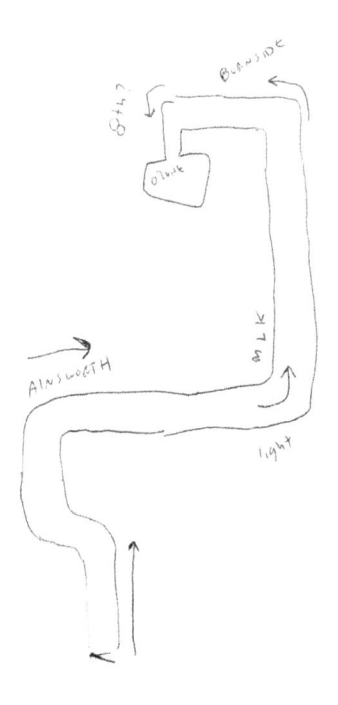

MAPS

APPENDIX

Pooh always gave honey jars as gifts, because he couldn't imagine getting a nicer thing.

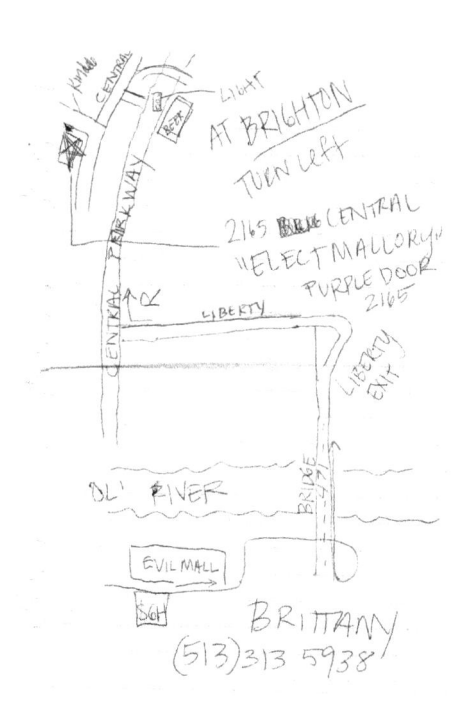

MAPS

APPENDIX

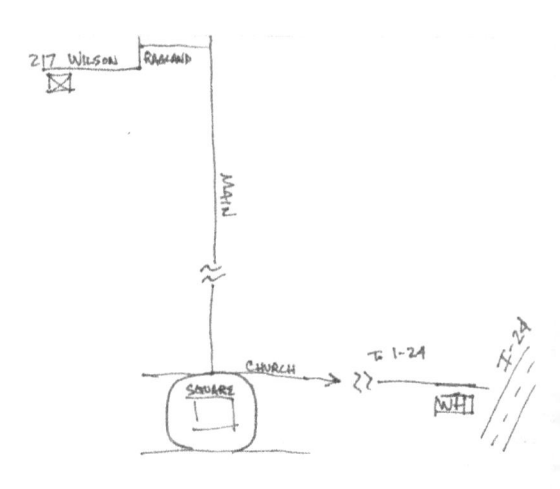

217 WILSON — RAGLAND

MAIN

CHURCH → To I-24
SQUARE   I-24
                          W.H.

DOO DOO

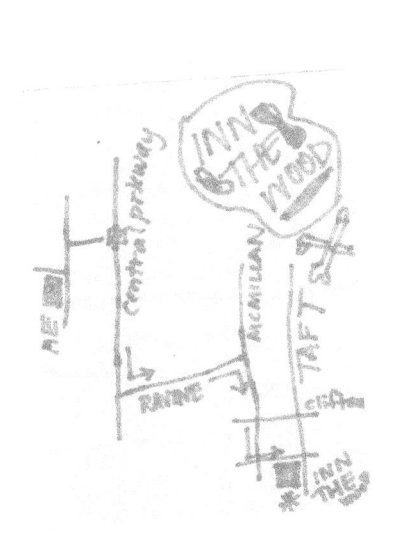

MAPS

APPENDIX

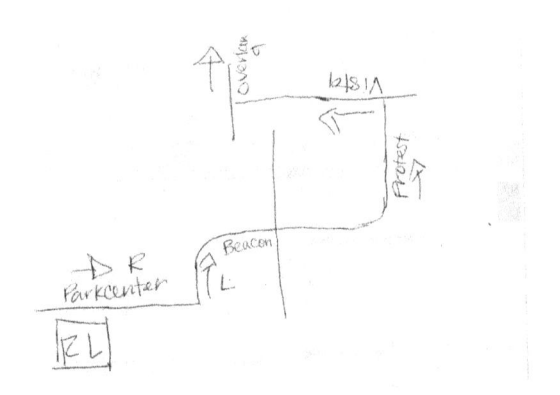

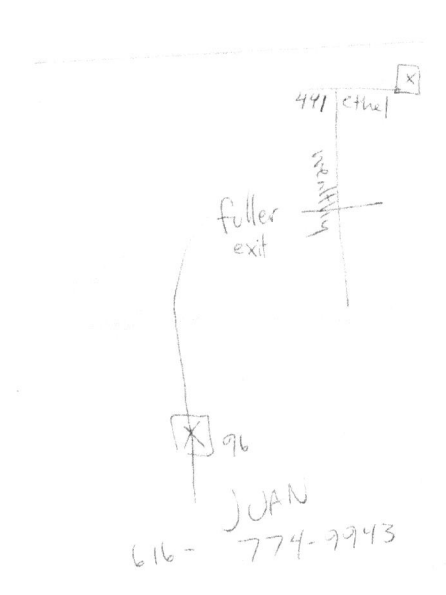

MAPS

441 ethel

fuller exit

96

JUAN
616-774-9943

APPENDIX

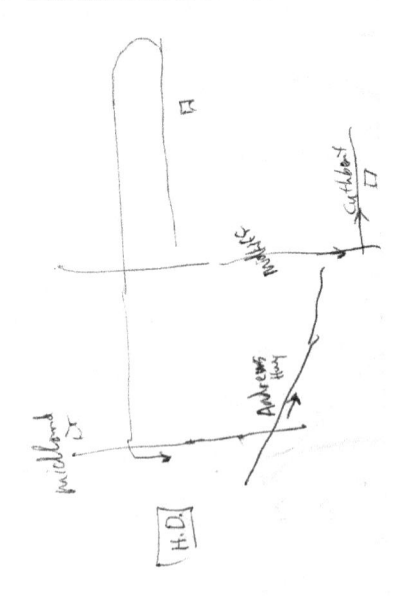

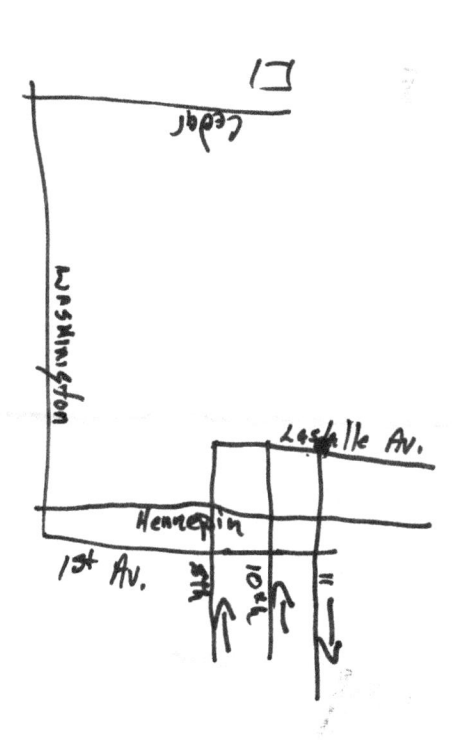

MAPS

APPENDIX

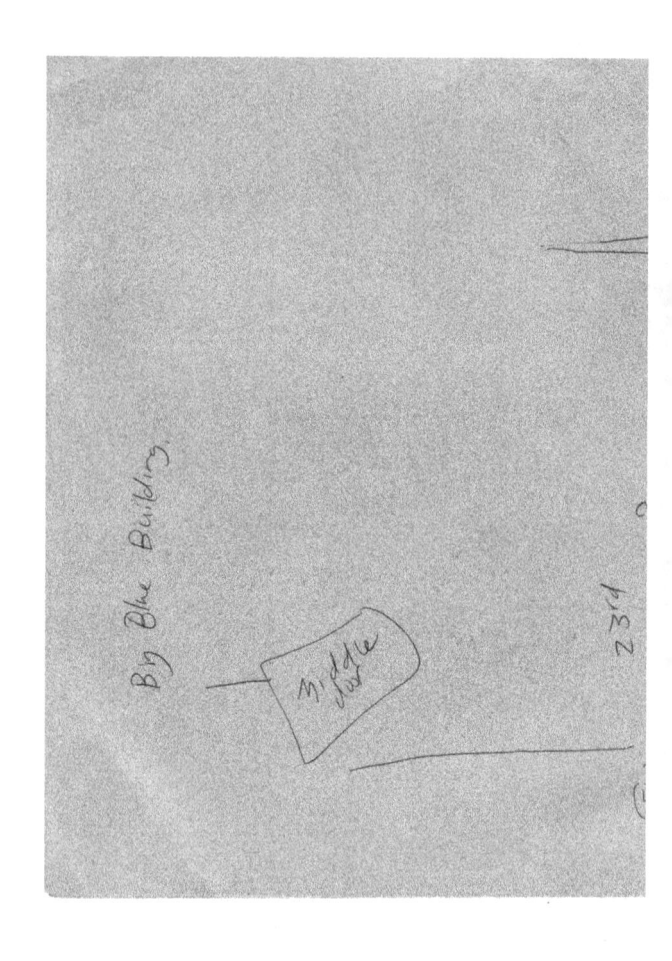

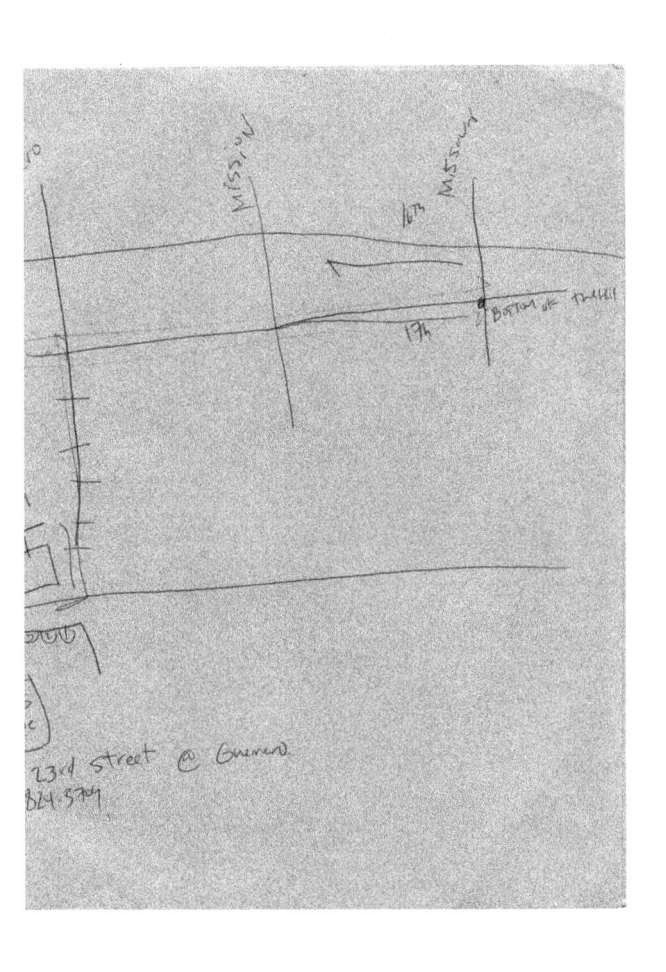

MAPS

APPENDIX

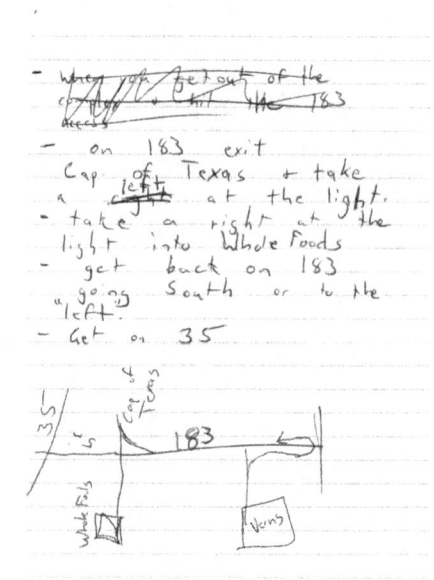

- ~~When you get out of the~~ ~~exit 183~~
- on 183 exit Cap of Texas + take a left at the light.
- take a right at the light into Whole Foods
- get back on 183 going South or to the "left".
- Get on 35

MAPS

APPENDIX

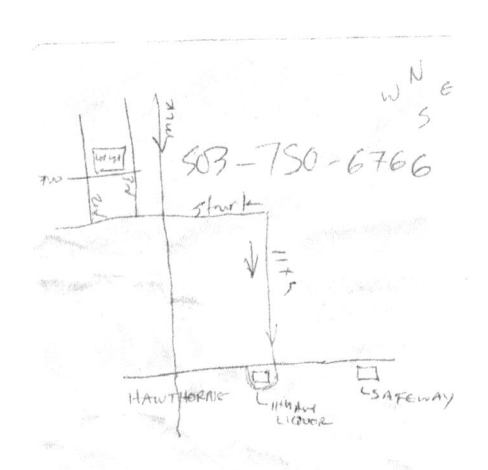

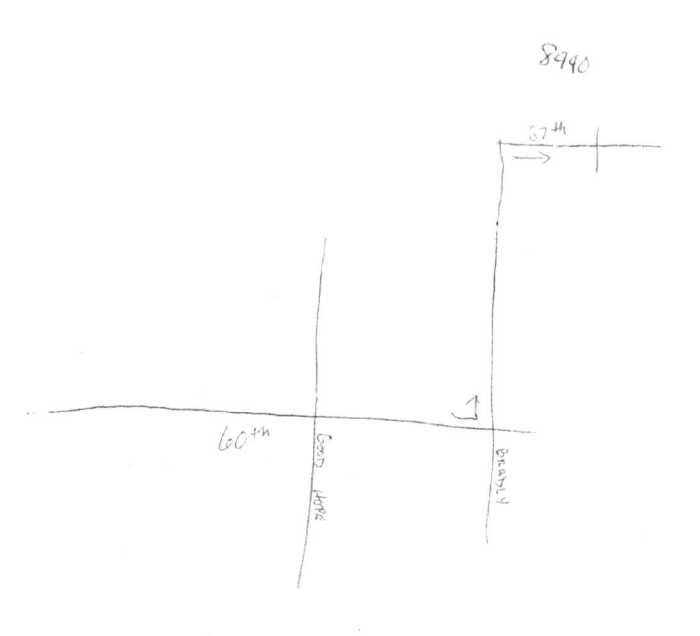

MAPS

8940

57th →

60th Good Hope Brady

APPENDIX

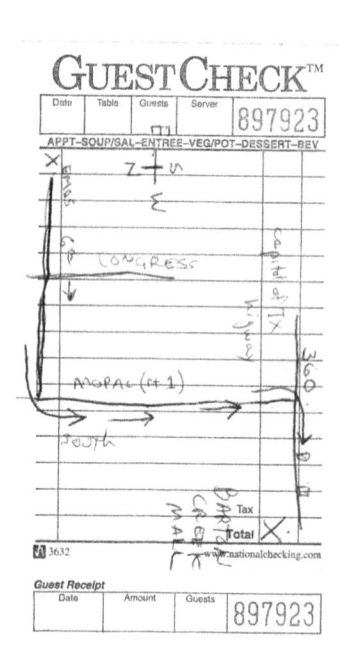

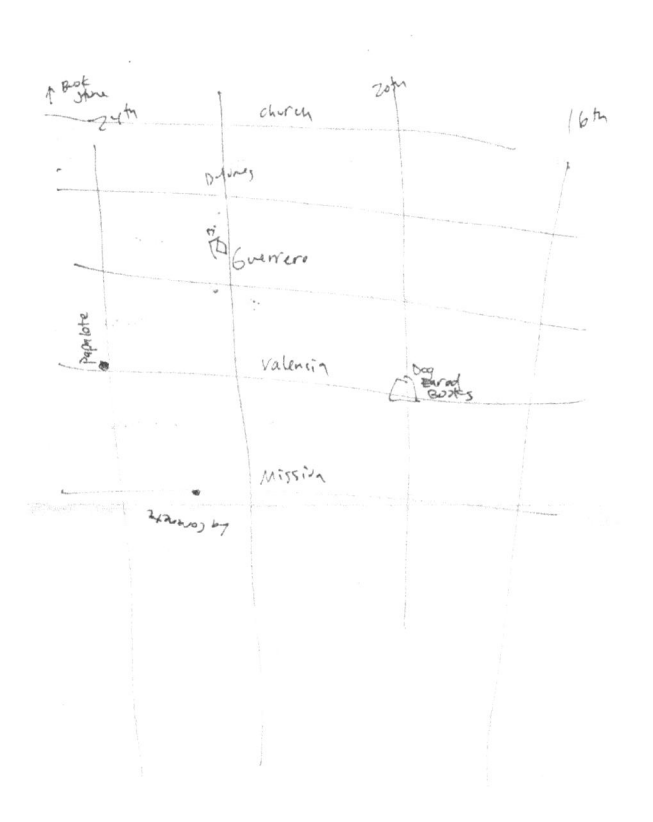

MAPS

APPENDIX

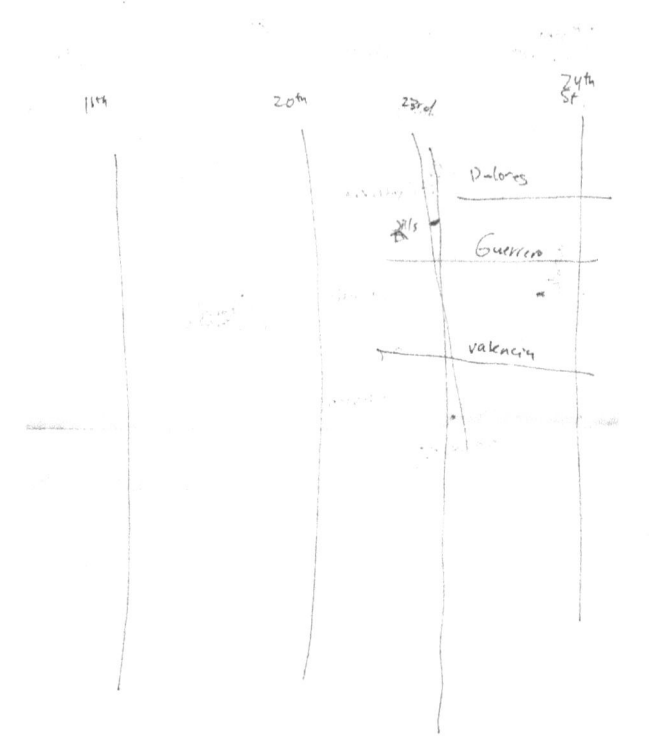

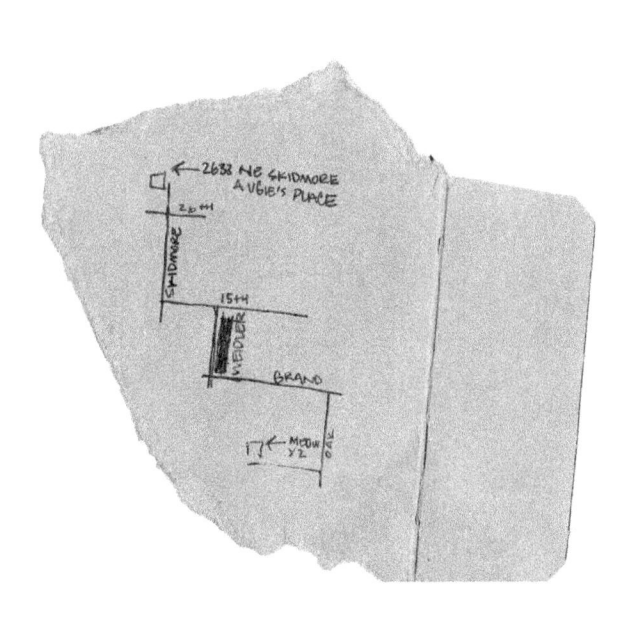

MAPS

APPENDIX

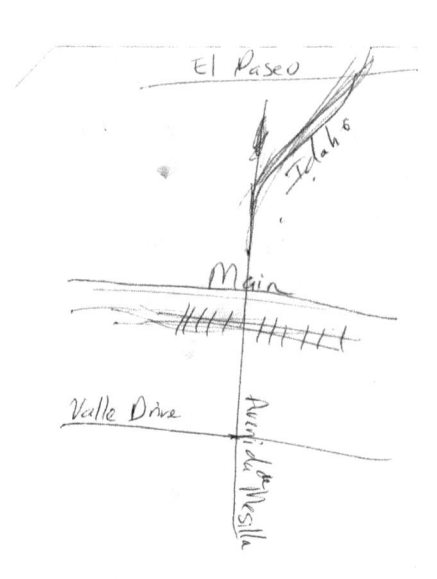

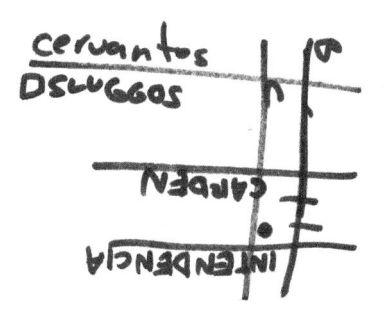

MAPS

Cervantes
DSUGGOS
GARDEN
INTENDENCIA

APPENDIX

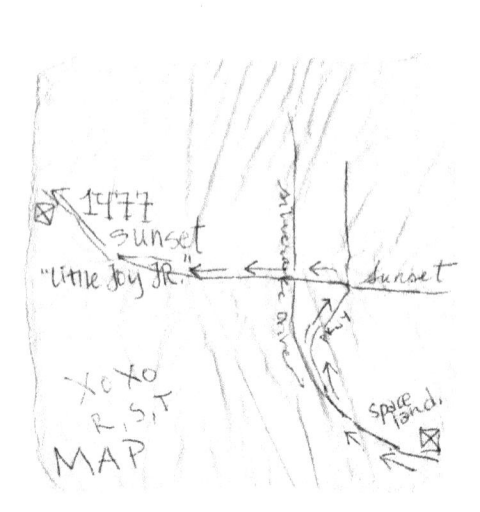

MAPS

APPENDIX

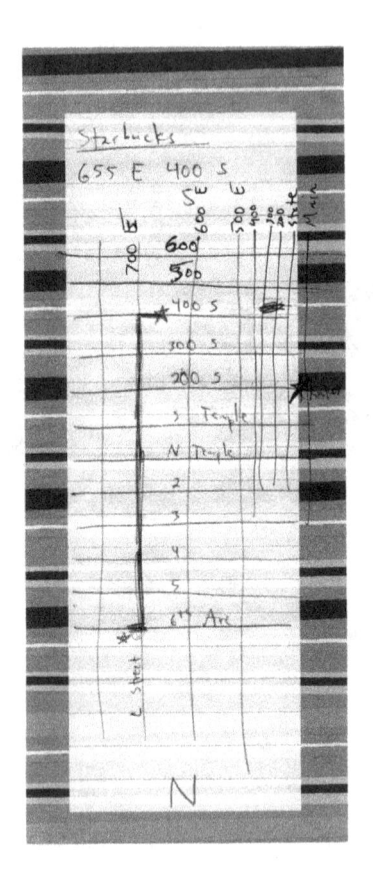

MAPS

About the Author

Tim Kinsella (born 1974) Libra / Chicago / Joan of Arc band

*fe*atherp*oof* BOOKS

**Publishing strange and beautiful fiction and nonfiction
and post-, trans-, and inter-genre tragicomedy.**

- *fp*29 HISTORY IN ONE ACT: A NOVEL OF 9/11 *by William M. Arkin*
- *fp*28 TINY *by Mairead Case*
- *fp*27 WEEPING GANG BLISS VOID YAB-YUM *by Devendra Banhart*
- *fp*26 ON THE BACK OF OUR IMAGES, VOL. I *by Luc Dardenne*
- *fp*25 THE SPUD *by Brielle Brilliant*
- *fp*24 MAMMOTHER *by Zachary Schomburg*
- *fp*23 FROM THE INSIDE *by John Henry Timmis IV*
- *fp*21 I'M FINE, BUT YOU APPEAR TO BE SINKING *by Leyna Krow*
- *fp*20 THE INBORN ABSOLUTE *by Robert Ryan*
- *fp*19 MAKE X *by various artists*
- *fp*18 THE TENNESSEE HIGHWAY DEATH CHANT *by Keegan Jennings Goodman*
- *fp*17 SUNSHINE ON AN OPEN TOMB *by Tim Kinsella*
- *fp*16 ERRATIC FIRE, ERRATIC PASSION *by Jeff Parker & Pasha Malla*
- *fp*15 SEE YOU IN THE MORNING *by Mairead Case*
- *fp*13 THE MINUS TIMES COLLECTED *edited by Hunter Kennedy*
- *fp*12 THE KARAOKE SINGER'S GUIDE TO SELF-DEFENSE *by Tim Kinsella*
- *fp*11 THE UNIVERSE IN MINIATURE IN MINIATURE *by Patrick Somerville*
- *fp*10 DADDY'S *by Lindsay Hunter*
- *fp*09 THE AWFUL POSSIBILITIES *by Christian TeBordo*
- *fp*08 SCORCH ATLAS *by Blake Butler*
- *fp*07 AM/PM *by Amelia Gray*

and some other ones, too?

Available at bookstores everywhere, and direct from Chicago, Illinois at

www.featherproof.com